DUTY, HON

A Salute to Veterans
of All U.S. Wars and Military Service

by the
Society of Southwestern Authors

Editor: Jim Woods
Associate Editors: Carol Costa
Penny Porter

Duty, Honor and Valor
A Salute to Veterans of All U.S. Wars and Military Service

Published by Wheatmark™
610 East Delano Street, Suite 104, Tucson, Arizona 85705 U.S.A.
www.wheatmark.com

International Standard Book Number: 1-58736-680-0
Library of Congress Control Number: 2006930843

DUTY, HONOR AND VALOR

*A Salute to Veterans
of All U.S. Wars and Military Service*

Foreword

WHEN I WAS A child, this prior to the events of Pearl Harbor, a man in our neighborhood passed away; it was my first experience with human death of any kind. At his living-room memorial service, which all friends and neighbors attended, I remember, but didn't necessarily understand, the emphasis placed on the fact, or assumption, that his ongoing illness was the result of having been gassed in the Great War, this before numbers were required to separate one war from another. I still remember him, Mister Blanchard, for that bit of his history, partly because I was to come into contact with another World War I veteran who also was gassed. He was my uncle, Eurie Ramsey, and I came to know him well after World War II had made history, but as I say, his injury was of the same sort, occurring in the same conflict, as that of Mister Blanchard. My uncle not only was treated and survived, but lived to normal old age. What determines the difference—one man dies at a relatively early age; another experiences a long life—but both were attacked in the same manner, at the same time, if not on the same battlefield, but it could have been. **Both were veterans.**

Military experiences, and no doubt especially war experiences, are as varied and differently remembered as the millions of patriotic men and women who have so proudly worn our country's uniform. It might be thought proper or necessary to separate those memories and experiences into two categories—those recalled by participants in the wars and those served between wars—but war or peacetime, all who wore the uniform have given their time, and offered up, or were prepared to offer up, their lives to their country. This does not denigrate the ultimate sacrifice of those many who died on the battlefields or succumbed from wounds and trauma years afterward in military and private hospitals, or at home. Any participant in any war can relate accounts of isolated survivors who would have been counted among the casualties had he been one step to the left or right, or a minute earlier or late. Those fortunate survivors obviously still fought the fight. Should they be thought of less highly than the men who died alongside them? No, and neither should those men, and women in uniform who, for whatever reason, did not partake in actual combat. **They too are veterans.**

These stories, accounts and memories are from participants in several wars, past and current, and also come from those who served between wars. Oddly enough, a couple of our war veterans' stories are from those who served on the losing side when our country was politically fragmented and our citizens ideologically opposed. Some of the accounts presented in this collection will break your heart. Some will make you smile. All will make you remember. Many of the authors, and all the subjects, have served our country proudly and well. To all of them, and to all others who served and are not chronicled in this cross-section and sampling of stories and poems, this book is dedicated. **We salute *all* the veterans.**

Jim Woods, Editor

CONTENTS

Was the Army's Secret Service *Too* Secret?

A FEW WEEKS AFTER PEARL Harbor, one of the U. S. Army's top generals phoned FBI chief, J. Edgar Hoover, saying, "Edgar, we're scheduling a Top Secret meeting with top officers of our Allies. We want you to send some plain-clothes agents to take care of security."

Hoover's reply: "General, why don't you use your own plain-clothes agents?"

The general: "My God! Do we have them?"

Hoover: "Since 1917, General!"

That, in a nutshell, explains a major problem for the Army's expert spy catchers from the very beginning—not only to catch enemy agents bent on espionage, sabotage, etc., but also battle our own Army, as only a few in 1941 knew of its own plain-clothes CIC (Counter Intelligence Corps).

In 1941, to be accepted into this secret organization a soldier had to finish basic training, be at least 25 years old with an IQ of 120 or higher, and have a working knowledge of at least one foreign language, with experience in some form of investigations. Among some 1000 agents on duty January 1, 1942, the great majority were former lawyers, judges, FBI agents, police and private detectives, credit investigators, newspaper reporters and college professors—in other words, mature, experienced adults, with backgrounds checked for loyalty, honesty and discretion.

Each new agent swore not to tell even closest relatives the existence of CIC and his connection to it. Forbidden to tell a spouse or parent caused many agents to suffer from a malady doctors couldn't diagnose, but which I've labeled *SP: Secrecy Psychosis*, CIC's occupational disease.

For me, it started in the summer of 1941 while eating dust in 13-weeks basic training in Camp Wheeler, Georgia. While washing down our throats with peach sodas, my buddy confided he was asked by the PIO (Post Intelligence Officer) to join a secret intelligence outfit.

"What does it do?" I asked.

"I don't know exactly. All he said was it's called CIP, Corps of Intelligence Police. Its members sometimes wear civvies, and . . ."

I didn't hear the rest. Civilian clothes! Thinking of fatigues, Georgia dust, infantry pack and my '03 rifle, I told my friend not to be bashful about applying. Two days later, the PIO received my application and ordered me to his office at once. I arrived under the personal escort of my worried company commander.

The PIO quizzed me intensely. But, did my qualifications for CIP interest him? NO! He wanted to know how I had learned the name of the secret organization, and if any word of its existence had leaked to others. Such secrecy impressed me. The fact the PIO said nothing of the functions of the CIP was more intriguing. He forwarded my application, perhaps thinking to safeguard the secret by taking me into it. I don't know. My one thought was, *this beats the infantry.*

Three weeks after Pearl Harbor, I was jerked out of pre-OCS (Officer Candidate School) and transferred into the secret CIP that, on January 1, 1942, became CIC (Counter Intelligence Corps)–to confuse the enemy, no doubt. But the name change confused our army even more. The secrecy was guarded so well, even from the army, that my service record for two years carried the innocuous statement that I was a sergeant at Fourth Service Command HQ. No mention was made of CIC on the record. Spies accessing these records would not uncover the secret that way!

In January, 1942, I did not swelter in Georgia heat carrying rifle and pack. I was in Chicago in the first CIC training school and should have been content but somehow wasn't. I was now carrying a heavy weight—*the secret.* The weight went up as instructors repeated that not even relatives, best friends, Sunday school teacher or creditors must learn of CIC.

Former FBI, Secret Service and other super snoopers—tops in the country—taught all manner of tricks to guard the U.S. from enemy agents. A pleasant subject in the course was trailing a rabbit (spy suspect) around wintry Chicago streets in enjoyable temperatures 15 degrees below zero—and me from the south! There also were classes in judo, physical training and a daily stint on the school's roof, clad only in shorts. And there were many other classes.

Most provoking was when we marched up and down city streets in civilian clothes so our officers could practice drilling. Grinning civilians yelled, "More draftees!" On the 10th day of this, I grinned back no more, I glared! My SP was setting in.

On completing school, I returned with my group to Atlanta to track spies with southern accents. Before being sent to my first assignment, it again was emphasized, "Do not reveal the CIC or that you are even in the army. If asked, you're a civilian working for the War Department."

Some of us set up new district offices; some went to established ones. I was to open a new district. Most operated behind a smoke screen of Such-and-Such Insurance Company. I scorned these measures, as some curious noses could ask embarrassing questions. I solved the problem of cover by examining FBI's setup. None of their offices were designated insurance agencies, bakeries or toy factories; each had Federal Bureau of Investigation on the door. I noted that known agents entered and departed, looking exactly like FBI agents—doing a good business, too. So I broke with custom and left the space on my office door blank. No one ever opened it to ask about insurance, if they opened it, they asked, "What the hell do you do?"

Next step in developing SP came as friends and acquaintances wondered aloud when or if the army would get me. I wore glasses when passing army camps, to prevent GIs booing as they had been booed a week before. On furlough, after 16 months service, my mother kept eyeing my civvies and worrying about my being out of uniform. I almost told her the truth but my secrecy oath was too strong. She must have believed she harbored an AWOL. She has yet to see me in uniform. That she takes my word I served in the army for 54 months is an outstanding example of mother-love.

After a few months under the secrecy demanded by HQ, unspoken thoughts of those around began to affect me. Am I really in the army? To test the reality of the situation, once I did not mail in the required daily report of activities. A warm, short and effective phone call from my colonel boss' office renewed my interest in reporting daily.

My respect for maintaining secrecy was jolted severely the day a munitions plant in my district phoned to report a hot sabotage case. Could I come out instantly to take charge of the investigation? "That's why I'm here," I said—and did.

That is, I got as far as the plant gate where an MP stopped me cold. There had been sabotage and he wasn't admitting anyone, as per orders.

"But look, here are my credentials to investigate that very case."

"They can be faked," he said.

I flashed my gold badge with War Department, Military Intelligence on it, which we showed those who couldn't read. No go. After further arguments, a call to the Commanding General got me in. But you see what I mean about this secrecy stuff? I was learning its limitations. I soon discovered CIC agents overseas were able to do something about it.

This is it day finally came—CIC agents were needed abroad. Volunteer? Is that a joke, son? When I applied for CIP-CIC in peacetime, we *all* volunteered for duty *anywhere*. As my only foreign language then was Spanish, overseas must mean Central or South America. Before I knew it, there I was in Australia, speaking passably good Australian.

In the Southwest Pacific Theater my SP began to disappear. HQ instructed us to acquaint the army and civilians around us of CIC's existence and mission. We gladly complied though it was a little late in the game to be fully satisfactory. For instance, during the battle for Manila while the struggle for the old walled section raged fiercely, I was blocks away at a *Veectoree* party, conscientiously advising a Filipina about CIC, how loyal Filipinos could help with evidence on spies and collaborators.

A young GI stood nearby with his mouth open at this revelation. After a few minutes he strode over, pushed me firmly and not gently into a seat whispering, "Listen, bud. If you are in intelligence, better stop spreading the news or I'll report you for loose-talk, see?" He strolled away before I could ask how things were back home when he left.

No Filipino over six years old by war's end failed to know more about CIC than most Americans, as we had probably jailed at least one relative or acquaintance on collaboration or spying charges. We operated in the open with signs over offices reading CIC or Counter Intelligence Corps. And even broadcast a CIC radio program! In that atmosphere of honest advertising, I thought my SP was cured.

WHEN THE WAR ENDED and I returned home, the first civilian I met asked, "What did you do in the army?"

"I was in the CIC," I answered proudly.

"Hell-o, what's that?"

I had a relapse.

By Duval A. Edwards,
Special Agent, CIC, U.S. Army

Naval Maneuvers

HE DROVE AN OFFICIALLY marked U.S. Navy gray station wagon right up to the lumber storage yard at the cabinet shop in North Hollywood where I worked as a sawyer apprentice. His shoulders and hat bore the unmistakable and impressive insignia of the U.S. Navy; his starched white uniform awash in braid and ribbons. He was tall and ramrod straight and moved effortlessly like a dancer . . . or a prizefighter. I thought him to be an Admiral. He introduced himself as Chief Petty Officer something or another. I've forgotten his name, flustered as I was at his interruption of my work, and my life.

"James Woods?"

He knows me! How does he know me? I don't know him. I don't want to know him. "Yes, I'm Jim Woods."

"Congratulations. We finally have the opening for you. You'll report to Union Station in Los Angeles four days from now for transportation to San Diego. By the time you complete recruit training, your class will be starting."

"I beg your pardon?"

"You are James Woods, James M. Woods? Are you not?"

"Yes, but . . ."

He consulted a clipboard. "Let's see, you signed up . . . He specified a date that was seven months prior. You remember don't you? You enlisted in the Navy."

Oh that. "Yes, I remember, but that was a long time ago. But I don't think I'm—"

"Look Jim," he addressed me informally now, "of course you can back out if you want to chance it; in such cases we hand over those names to the Army and they usually get drafted pretty quickly."

A threat. It was working; I was weakening, but he continued. "Didn't you receive our letter of the . . ." He consulted the clipboard again, and voiced another date.

Damn! He's efficient! "I did, but I didn't really understand it."

"I have a copy here. I'll explain it. Here, where it says that you have been accepted as an E-T-S-R–"

"Oh, that's how you say it I thought it said *etsir.* What does it mean?"

"Well, for one thing, it means you're pretty smart. Your G-C-T and math scores were the highest we've seen in a while. The U.S. Navy was quite impressed. We decided to put you into electronics training."

I remembered those tests. Math always had come easy for me. The general knowledge test was a piece of cake too. At the recruiting office, I had taken, and aced, some basic tests. The recruiter made a telephone call, then asked if I would mind taking these additional tests, and explained that normally they were not given to recruits until they actually were in boot camp. I could be flattered. I was game.

Still referring to the onionskin copy of the letter I may have still had, somewhere, he continued, "E-T means Electronics Technician. S-R means Seaman Recruit. You are designated E-T-S-R, and that means that after basic training, you will be assigned to electronics school. Now, electronics school is almost a year long, and at the time of your enlistment, three classes were in various stages of progress at Treasure Island, and the next several classes were full. We didn't want you to complete basic and have you placed into some other billet when we need you in electronics."

"Billet? Treasure Island?"

"Billet is Navy for 'specialty.' Treasure Island is in San Francisco Bay. The electronics school that you'll attend is there. We have another school in the East, but recruits out of San Diego generally go to T.I. We held up your actual entry into the Navy until such time as we could be certain that a class would be forming at the time you would be completing basic training."

"So, I have to go now or miss that class?"

"Right. You report this week on Saturday. Basic training takes thirteen weeks; two weeks leave after that and another couple of weeks for processing and travel, and the class is ready to start. Still want to back out?"

"I should give notice here."

"I'll take care of that for you. Who's your boss?"

"Ray, Raymond Teller. He's in the front office right now. I was just in to see him so I know he's there, the tall guy with blond hair."

"I'll see him now. You be at the train station at eight o'clock on Saturday. Go to the information booth. One of our staff will be there with your orders. He'll tell you what you have to do. By the way, travel light. You can take an extra set of skivvies and socks, and maybe a toothbrush and a razor."

"What's a skivvy?" No answer. *Well, how do you like that! I'm in the Navy! I'm going to San Diego, then to San Francisco. Join the Navy and see the world! It really does work that way.*

Chief Petty Officer Whoosis came out the back door of the shop and I hadn't moved, still contemplating the fates. "Okay Jim, Mister Teller has the word. He wants to see you. Now make sure you're at the train station on Saturday."

"Don't worry. I'll be there."

THE SAILOR FROM THE recruiting office was easy to find. At the information booth, a man in Navy uniform was surrounded by a babbling throng of guys about my age. He wasn't too friendly. Not like Chief Petty Officer Whoosis. He read off names and when the names answered, the owner was parceled aside and ordered to remain in place and remain quiet. He read my name and I started to join the crowd to the side when he ordered, "Not you, Woods. Stay here where I can find you."

Special treatment. It was noticed by several guys who gave me the visual once-over. *Who's the pipsqueak,* I could almost hear them asking. Roll call completed, fourteen men (actually, all boys) moved to a designated spot of floor tile. The uniform and I remained together. "Okay, Woods, take these men to the train." He identified the car number for me. "Keep them together. Here are their orders. Yours are on top."

Fifteen large manila envelopes were handed me. I accepted them, one palm up, the other down ready to clamp the unwieldy stack, and my hand twisted. My down-hand slipped one direction, my up-hand the opposite way, and the fifteen sets of orders shuffled to the marble floor. I hastily scooped them up and the uniform snatched them away from me. He put them back into whatever sequence that suited him and handed the stack to me once again. "Take good care of these, sailor. These men are in your charge."

"Okay, What do I do with them when we get to San Diego?"

"Don't say 'okay.' Say 'aye aye sir.' You're Navy now . . . and someone will meet you. Turn your men and their orders over to him. Cast off."

My men? Cast off? Am I ready for this? "Why me?"

"Because you're an E-T-S-R, that's why. These men are not rated. You are. That puts you in charge!"

Okay—Aye-aye Sir. Thanks for explaining it so I understand it. "Should we go now?"

"Didn't I say take them to the train? Do you think the Goddam train will wait for you? Move out!"

I walked over to the crowd, glanced once more to the uniform, who glared and turned his back on me. "Okay guys. Move out," I commanded, and started walking toward the platform, barely cocking my head to look behind me. Fourteen quiet new Navy recruits were in somber procession behind me. At the train, just because I could, *I* called roll, allowing the respondent to board only after he identified himself.

Halfway through the stack of names, Cecil Hurst queried, not very pleasantly, "How come you got this job?"

I remember Cecil after all these years because he was eight inches taller than me and outweighed me by a hundred pounds, and he didn't fit my view of a Cecil. He and I wound up in the same boot company, but not all of my men were part of the same company. I never understood why our Southern California contingent was broken up. It's just the Navy way.

"I got it because I'm an E-T-S-R, that's why."

"What the hell is a E-T-S-R?"

"You'll find out soon enough. Get on board and find a seat." *I hope that I find out what the hell an E-T-S-R is.*

Fourteen guys found seven seats together. I was the only one without a travel companion for the three-hour ride to San Diego, the only one without someone to talk with. I had time for some thinking.

ANOTHER TRAIN BOUND FOR another new place and all new experiences. The last train was less than a year ago, from Kentucky. Left there on the same day I graduated from high school. Had to go to Golden California. Had to; that was as far away as I could get from Paducah. Discovered that California was not the end of the Earth, and in retrospect, not all that golden. Once in Los Angeles, I made my way across the city, and eventually to my aunt's house in the San Fernando Valley. She and her family—husband and a daughter a year younger than me, and my grandfather—welcomed me into their home. The son, a year older than me, was in the Air Force. I got his old room.

Three months later, I turned eighteen, however, the magic age of eighteen in a state where the age of majority was at the time, twenty-one, was really not very magical at all.

I could not enter into a contract to finance a car purchase, even though I could get a driver's license even younger than that. Neither could I sign a rental contract for an apartment. In both instances, apartment and car, I was informed that I required a co-signer, someone of legal age. I was trapped, I thought, at my aunt's house. I certainly had no reason for feeling trapped. I was treated well; as one of the family in fact, and then my cousin came home on leave from the Air Force.

I didn't mind moving out to the couch for the two weeks he was home. After all, it was his room where I was staying. It was after he pointed out that the Air Force was a good place to grow up, and grow older, old enough to be recognized as an adult, that I started thinking about the Air Force for my own situation. Add to that the bonus of learning a high tech trade, anything to do with airplanes. I was sold on the idea. Cousin Roy even escorted me down to the enlistment offices, introduced me to the recruiting officer who remembered Roy, and waited for me while I went through the interrogations.

The Air Force asked routine questions about my health and I blithely admitted to having had a bout with juvenile asthma. "Sorry, Mister Woods" the Air Force said, "why don't you try another branch of the service."

Outside, my cousin berated me, "You dumb hick, why did you tell them that?"

"Because they wanted to know."

"One thing you have to learn, in the Air Force or any other branch: Don't volunteer for anything and that means don't volunteer any information. Don't lie, but answer only direct questions. You're such a hillbilly that the Army probably won't even take you."

I wasn't going to give the Army the chance to take me. I wanted the Air Force. I wanted all that fly-boy glamour. *The Navy has planes too*, I considered, *but if not planes, then all those big ships*. There was glamour enough to go around. After Roy went back to the Air Force, I went to the Navy recruiting office, down the hall from the Air Force recruiter in the same post office building.

Following my mentor's advice, I kept my answers to specific questions, agreed to take their standard tests, and later, the special ones without really understanding the importance of them. I left the recruiting office with assurances that the U.S. Navy would notify me in due time.

It was more than a few days, and then it was that ETSR letter that I didn't fully understand either, and another assurance that the U.S. Navy would contact me soon. They didn't, until the Chief showed up on the job half a year later, and by then I had conveniently forgotten the entire U.S. Navy episode. But now I was in that Navy. I had quit my good job, given my car to my younger cousin, and I was in charge of fourteen other recruits headed for boot camp in San Diego.

BOOT CAMP WASN'T ALL that bad, in spite of all I had heard. Some guys had trouble with the discipline and the sometimes-harsh routine, but I was eating three times a day and all I wanted when I did eat—both new experiences for me until joining my aunt's household just a few months ago, and such bounty was still a novel experience. My ETSR status continued to work, even with the old sailors like our First Class Petty Officer company commander who knew that I was just a boot like all the rest. I was selected to carry the company flag during marching drill—a distinct honor. Big Cecil, though, led the group on the march, and carried a symbolic cutlass—a badge of his position that eclipsed, I thought, my flag-bearer status. But Cecil was big and his commands could be seen and heard by those in the rear ranks.

Boots are busy people; staying occupied is necessary to keep our minds off home. A couple of guys did give-in to homesickness. I envied them a little bit—my own memories were not strong enough to cause me any grief about missing home. Home was Kentucky, and I had already given that up. I guess I was looking for home and the Navy was looking like a mighty good one.

Actually, boot camp now is more a blur than a memory. I learned a couple of lessons. When we first went to swim class, somehow I realized that everybody in the Navy should know how to swim. Think about it; the Navy operates in a water world. I could tread water enough to keep from drowning in calm water, and I could dog paddle around a bit, but I couldn't swim. I made sure that the swimming instructors were aware of that limitation to their star ETSR.

Thereafter, at physical education three times a week, the rest of the company worked out on the grinder, an asphalt parking lot where they did push-ups, sit-ups, and weight training—this during June and July in southern California heat. During that same hour, I was getting almost private instruction on how to swim, in the indoor cool pool. Three times a week for ten weeks I went swimming in the pool and my company sweated in the San Diego sun. I learned that the Navy doesn't toss out incompetents; they keep working with you till you get it right. I worked to not get the swimming right.

The other lesson didn't turn out so well. During the entire thirteen weeks of boot camp, we had a single all-day session in small-arms familiarization. The shooting range was a remote locale; the weapon was the M1 Garand. One thing I could do without instruction from the Navy was shoot. Most every Kentucky boy could shoot. The firing line accommodated eight shooters at a time, each position with its own coach. I was in the second eight, but the first squad had a devil of a time qualifying. No one could hit the target anywhere, much less put one into the black. I was chomping at the bit to show what I could do with their rifle.

When my time came, still early in the morning, I listened respectfully to my coach, and then proceeded to put my first shot in the bulls-eye. That got his attention. He called ceasefire and walked down to the butts and inspected my target. Naturally his action that held up the entire line caught the attention of the seven other coaches. He came back and asked if I could do that again. I accepted the cartridge from him without a word, went prone, loaded the round, and squeezed off another bulls-eye. Now all eight coaches surrounded me and voted, more or less, on what to do with me. The consensus was that I had to demonstrate my prowess, or my luck, with a third shot. I did, with the same result. I was ready to be rewarded.

Instead, I was told to take a seat in the bleachers; they needn't waste any more time on me. All day I sat in the sun-drenched bleachers. It was just as hot on the firing line for those who couldn't shoot, but who at least were getting to try. It would have been pure recreation for me to shoot the rifle all afternoon, but I simply watched. I resolved to not show off again in this man's Navy.

BOOT CAMP WAS MORE memorable for finishing it than experiencing it. To start boot leave, the two weeks before taking up my first assignment at Treasure Island, California, for electronics school, the Navy returned me to my point of enlistment, Los Angeles. No train this time, but my first-ever flight. I could get accustomed to the luxury of flying, but the cost was beyond my sailor's means. From L.A., I returned home to Kentucky via Greyhound bus. Met some great folk in Texas. Having slept sitting up in my dress blues, I was somewhat rumpled, so I went into a cleaners in Dallas just to get my neckerchief pressed. Before I departed I had been stripped down and sat in a booth in my skivvies—I learned that was what we call underwear in this man's Navy—while my entire uniform was refreshed. The proprietor wouldn't take my money for his services.

Dallas was a noontime layover and a bus change, so my next stop in town was for lunch. I found a little barbeque spot that looked promising. The service was from a center island—pick up your order and find a seat around the perimeter of the room; sit in a desk with the built-in writing arm table, like I had in high school. The man behind the island counter refused my money for a beer and a sandwich because I was in uniform. Very hungry, I woofed it down, but was not satiated, and wanted another round of both sandwich and the beer. I was embarrassed to go to the same server who had been so generous, so I went to the opposite side of the island and gave my order to a different man who served that side. Repeat. He wouldn't take my money either. "Our privilege to serve our men in uniform," he explained. I departed Texas with fine feelings for the fine Texas folk.

TREASURE ISLAND NAVAL BASE is a treasure in my memories. First, it was forty-two weeks of extensive technical school that I thoroughly enjoyed, but exotic San Francisco just across the Bay was a near heaven for a sailor ashore. Across the Bay, to the east, was Oakland, almost as good as San Francisco for this old Kentucky boy. I really was seeing the world.

On base, my thin service jacket was paying off again. The record was there of my escorting the original recruits to boot camp, and my class and test records apparently still impressed someone in authority. I was made a barracks section leader over others who were equal and superior to my meager, now Seaman Apprentice, rating. With the school personnel so numerous, we were assigned to six sections, meaning that we had the duty only one day and night out of six for cleaning the barracks and standing watch. I was to find later that standing watch in an academic environment is a far cry from standing watch in the real Navy. If our section did not have the duty, a condition that existed for us five days out of six, we were at liberty to hit San Francisco nightly, or as often as we could afford.

I discovered drinking while at Treasure Island. It seemed natural enough to frequent the bars along Market Street in San Francisco. That's what sailors do. Along with drink, there were women in the bars—another pastime for sailors ashore. This is certainly not to say that alcohol was the primary influence and remembrance of either San Francisco or the Navy in general. Sailors appreciate San Francisco for the same reasons that all visitors do—Fisherman's Wharf, the Golden Gate Bridge, the Bay Bridge, Union Square, Chinatown and the cable cars. And who could ever forget bicycling through Flieshacker Zoo and along the coastal hills?

While I was stationed at Treasure Island, my family moved from Kentucky to Bakersfield, California. It was not their intent just to get close to me, but it worked out that way, and I made weekend trips to visit them. I had no transportation for a long time though, so I was dependent on the kindness of strangers to get me to Bakersfield and back to base. It was no problem riding off base with anyone on base that had a car. I'd be dropped off at the highway south, and in uniform, seldom had to wait long for a ride. We were permitted to keep civilian clothes on base for our off-base liberty, but I found that a young hitchhiker in civvies did a lot of walking while a man in Navy blues had little trouble in catching a ride.

Upon graduation from ET (Electronics Technician) school, six out of my class, myself included, were assigned to stations on Guam in the Mariana Islands. Several classmates were assigned to specific destroyers and minesweepers; a couple went to submarine school; one man went to Midway. Guam had the reputation for being a poor duty station, but obviously, I was to find, only by those who had not experienced it. Guam is a tropical paradise.

At Ship Repair Facility on Agana Harbor, I was assigned responsibility for harbor-frequency radios and loran navigation systems aboard Navy and commercial vessels. We serviced the commercial ships of worldwide registry, whatever their make of electronic gear, but for the Navy ships, there was a certain transmitter and receiver set that became my career mark. I set up a shop with replacement units that permitted a quick change-out of on-board equipment that required repairs or that was scheduled for overhaul. In a very efficient operation that I devised and supervised, and for which I was officially commended, I earned my Petty Officer rating. In ET school I had moved to Seaman from Seaman Apprentice, and on Guam I went to Electronics Technician, Third Class.

The work was intense at times, but Guam was not all work. Scars of World War II were recent and evident throughout the island. On my free time, I explored the countryside, one time discovering a cave that still held relics of Japanese occupation — tools and a Wisconsin generator. Proud of my discovery, I bragged to the wrong people, and the Navy bulldozed the cave in the interest of personnel safety. The Navy was unconcerned for the crystal-clear pool in the cave that was home to some fascinating translucent, blind fish.

At times I swam in Agana Bay, snorkeling, as I looked over fallen planes and other relics of the war, resting on the sandy bottom. Once I swam with four sharks that failed to recognize me as an edible intruder

I accomplished one of my life goals, turning 21, on Guam, where local civilian law was strict about drinking age. On base though, anyone could buy a beer at the Enlisted Man's Club. Before that vital anniversary of my birth I could not get served in any civilian establishment after showing my I-D card. On the evening of my birthday that verified my legitimacy, I went into town and ordered a beer, and the barkeep never asked for my card. Perhaps in reaching legal age, I looked it. Never again was I asked for my identification anywhere when I ordered for a drink. Bartenders just know.

My first-ever traffic ticket came on Guam. I had been called to the other end of the island, to the Air Force base, on a fire-truck radio repair. I was driving a Navy pickup truck that I had signed out from the motor pool. As I sped through the town of Agana, I was stopped by local police and escorted immediately to civilian court. The judge was a wizened ancient who sat high above me and heard the charges. At conclusion of the policeman's testimony, without hearing from me at all, he pounded his gavel and announced, "Sixty dollars or sixty days."

"Your Honor," I finally found voice, "I have only thirty dollars."

Pounding his gavel once again, he intoned, "Thirty dollars or thirty days!" Justice, Guamanian style.

Navy justice had yet to be administered. Acknowledgement of double jeopardy does not enter into the Navy's justice system. I would be brought up before Captain's Mast (non-judicial punishment) for speeding in a Navy vehicle—except that after reporting the incident to my Chief, the good man intercepted the paperwork from the Commander's desk, and I was not charged.

FROM GUAM I WAS assigned to the naval station on Adak in the Aleutian Islands chain—from a tropical paradise to an iceberg where the base buildings were interconnected by tunnels. We could get from the barracks to the chow hall to the enlisted club without ever venturing out into the harsh, freezing temperatures. However, all personnel were assigned good foul-weather clothing, personal jackets and parkas, and boots when required, because our work did take us into the weather.

The base had an airstrip of course, and the tower electronics were mine for maintenance and upkeep. At the distant end of the runway was a guidance beacon, two of them actually, which, by design, could be controlled from the tower. Routine called for one beacon to be operative while the other rested. At the start of each day, tower personnel were required to dial up the switchover from one beacon to the other. The system never worked, but the dial switch was part of the telephone system, not part of my equipment responsibility. The beacons were mine though. Daily, I'd get the report of failure of the beacons to switch, and have to kit up for a snowshoe trek out to the beginning of the runway to manually switch them. I got to know an eagle—and he recognized me as well—that patrolled the open airstrip for small breakfast critters. At times the magnificent bird swooped low to look me over, but decided I was not his meal.

We had fun in the snow too. The high point on the island is only about 4000 feet, but it had a ski lodge. Actually, it was little more than a cabin in which recreational gear was stored. A six-by-six truck served as a ski bus, making daily trips, morning, noon and evening, taking and retrieving skiers who were off of official duty. I was not a skier, but I had a friend who claimed to be. I had met him, a Yakima Indian, while on Guam and we both had been later assigned to Adak. On Guam he, Michael Nicodemus Somday, taught me to play cribbage; on Adak he proposed to turn me into a skier. Being from Washington State, he bragged of his own prowess on the narrow boards. I finally agreed to give it a try.

We took the truck-bus up, the only method of getting to and from the chalet, then strapped on skis and headed out. It was so much fun that we were late getting back to the cabin at the end of the day. The truck-bus had departed without us, and the equipment manager left us a note to leave our skis on the porch. It was sundown and getting dark, and colder. We started hiking. Coming upon a derelict Quonset leftover from WWII days, we ripped off a 4 x 8 sheet of weathered corrugated roofing. The ridges in its construction made it difficult, but we managed to upturn one end into a semblance of a sled runner.

We would point the sled, that we couldn't steer, through obstructions and ride it until we had to exit, which occurred numerous times as we came to a rock or a ledge or a frozen creek. Whoever was the front rider at the time would tumble off to the right, signaling the one behind to throw himself off to the left, terrain permitting, so that we didn't crash into one another. We collected some bruises, and one time literally flew over a rise and into a creek, getting soaked and frozen before escaping. We reached bottom and the barracks compound well after dark, well after the chow hall had closed, but did we have fun!

I was promoted to Electronics Technician Second Class, while at Adak, in time for my transfer to—finally—a ship, the *U.S.S Harry E. Hubbard, DD 748.*

Following leave back in the States, I reported to Whidby Island Naval Base, Washington, for transfer to The Philippines where I'd catch up with my boat. We flew for seventeen hours in the stripped-down military version of a Super Constellation, sitting on wooden bench seats along the bulkhead, trying to rest our heads in the web netting at our back. There's nothing plush about Navy air transport. It was a long, hard ride, laying over one night in Hawaii, and stopping for an hour en route at Midway.

I was just in time for the *Hubbard* to embark on a world cruise, along with three other destroyers, to Hong Kong, Okinawa, Japan, then on to two stops in Australia, Darwin and Brisbane, then to Samoa, and finally home to Long Beach, California. Again I was impressed with joining the Navy and seeing the world!

My earlier travel to Guam had been aboard a huge personnel transport that included numerous civilians as well as military taking up their new duty stations. We crossed the International Dateline and those of us who had not done so before were duly initiated. Because there were women and children aboard, the initiation rites were somewhat tame. However, aboard the fighting ship *Hubbard*, well before the days of mixed crews, crossing the equator was anything but playful. The crew was divided fifty-fifty who had and had not crossed, and those of us who had not were at the mercy of those who had—and they showed no mercy.

Some of the stunts were merely degrading, but the day started with our running a punishing gauntlet. The sailmakers had sewn dozens of canvas tubes that were three inches in diameter more or less, and perhaps four feet long. The bags were stuffed tightly with cotton waste from the engine room, then trailed via lines in the ships wake, gathering hardness and salt for two days. The gauntlet started near the fantail and we raced all the way forward, more than 300 feet, through a haze of these canvas whips being swung with great and harsh energy, all in the sprit of camaraderie, of course. If we faltered we were fair game for repeated blows until we regained out feet and struggled on. There were some fistfights, and even a broken arm, and half a dozen initiates locked themselves below and refused to accept the rites of passage. Big mistake! The following day when they peeked from their protective cover, they faced a crew that now was almost one hundred percent *Shellback,* and their cowardice was not looked upon pleasantly.

We lost a man at sea, not related to the previously described Shellback hi-jinks, and it could be said that it was his own fault, but few felt like being so harsh. We were in a severe storm, the fantail and forecastle alternately awash in heavy seas, and the roll equally strong. Of course, everyone was ordered to stay off the weather deck as we rode it out. This man chose to experience the storm from the fantail, and at one fateful instance when the screws pitched out of the seas, he was no longer with us. It was reported immediately, so apparently he had a buddy with him to witness his questionable courage.

Now all aboard were mustered to the rails, shoulder-to-shoulder on our own ship as well the other three destroyers and the carrier in our goodwill task force. We didn't recover him, or even see him again, and he could have been just a wave away, for a few minutes, at least. We lashed ourselves to the rail until darkness, when we had to give up our search. The galley crew was excused from eyes on the water in order to make and serve sandwiches to those of us who had no such distraction.

The following morning, the chaplain on the carrier held a symbolic burial at sea, all of our ships connected together for the service by radio and loudspeaker. I think a burial at sea may be the saddest of ceremonies, but without the body of our comrade to return to the sea for that eventual day when the sea gives up her dead, this incident was even more heart-rending. This was a peacetime cruise and we were on our way to Australia to honor that country's war dead.

ABOARD THE *HUBBARD,* I passed the exam for my ET1 rating, worlds away from my original ETSR designation, but the promotion would not be effective until mid May, just about the time I was due to complete my tour of duty. In a burst of military efficiency, I was mustered out two days early, one day before my new rating would have become effective. That was a slight glitch that caused me only minor concern. I wouldn't take a million dollars for my

Navy experience, but at the time, I'd given a million, figuratively of course, to not stay in blue for another day.

I WAS A PART of the all in our history who gave some, but obviously, not of the some that gave all. I fought no wars and collected only administrative citations—service ribbons for participation, not accomplishment. Although I was not seeking medals I was ready to defend my country, but I was a peacetime sailor; someone must man the ships and bases between wars. Motion pictures are filmed and books are written about the nobler action of the wartime military, but for most of us, military service is a period of routine monotony, continual training and quiet readiness.

At that, though, I take pride in my service to my county and in my Honorable Discharge. All in all, I know it to have been a life changing—for the better—experience. The education I received and the skills I developed formed the basis of my professional adult life thereafter. My Navy stint was a personally useful growing-up interval from that fateful day when the recruiting Chief found me, an academically smart, but worldly innocent, kid at work in the lumberyard.

By Jim Woods, ET2, U.S Navy
U.S.S. Harry E. Hubbard, DD 748

What Are Chaplains For?

Korea, 1952

"HELLO, ANACONDA CONTROL. HAMMER Able One and Two. Two chicks inbound. Ten angels. Anything for us? Over."

Roger, Hammer. F-O reports activity on a bridge over the Imjin and on the road east of the river heading south. Bridge Coordinate is Charlie Tare 1433. Repeat Charlie Tare 1433. Make a photo run if no activity is spotted. Copy?"

"Roger, copy."

"Anaconda standing by."

I WAS ANACONDA CONTROL, a twenty-one year old corporal in the army, on detached service to I-Corps Artillery Headquarters. The Korean police action, in its third year, stationed me to a tent above the 38th Parallel, south of the double bend of the Imjin River. My G2 assignment kept me at my desk for hours on end, scheduling area flights by coordinating incoming intelligence with a wall-sized map. Make no mistake, the Korean sorties added up. From June, 1950 to July, 1953 United Nations aircraft flew more than 1,040,708 close support, counter-air, interdiction, cargo and miscellaneous sorties in support of United Nations military operations. During my stint, I directed flights of two planes, primarily photo and reconnaissance, up to twelve a day, for a total of maybe 3200 missions.

Occasionally, I miked close air support for strikes on enemy targets just in front of the battle lines, coordinating fighters, fighter-bombers or, in rare cases, heavy bomber aircraft. But the Korean War was not what I'd expected.

Back home before I enlisted, I wanted an adventure filled with plenty of heart-stopping moments. In fact, by 1952, twenty to thirty-thousand U. S. conscripts headed to Korea every month, to provide a continuous supply of fresh adrenalin, but in my drafty tent, tedious hours rolled by slowly and the days, like the food, were tasteless. Add to that, a sleep area that harbored rats and an icy cold winter that froze the bones. Every gray day resembled the one before and the one after, even to rats scratching at night in search of crumbs. I spent my free time torn between yearning to see action and wanting to ship home. A point system determined the length of enlistment. Thirty-six points rotated a soldier back to the U. S. My job rated three points per month in contrast to the four points earned by those who saw the action and lived the adventure.

I envied those soldiers who lived on the edge, men battling up and down the Korean countryside while I surveyed a large map from a creaky office chair. Before the war, I'd flown a small plane over the cornfields of Nebraska so I'd experienced the thrill of soaring through the skies. Now I yearned to be overhead in a P-51 or an F4U. The pilots above played cat and mouse with the enemy for high stakes, while I played chess for popcorn below.

Into my overseas schedule walked Father Brady, the chaplain stationed at the nearby MASH (Mobile Army Surgical Hospital) unit, my own *Father Mulcahy.* Over a few drinks one night, he listened to me rant about my three-point designation and my intention to gain four-point status by requesting reassignment to the battle zone. The padre didn't say much about my plan and he returned to MASH the next day without mentioning my idea for transfer. Soon after, he showed up at camp and ambled into my tent.

"Thought you'd like to get out of here for a spell." His Irish brogue lilted through another gray day. "I'll get you cleared. If you're interested, you can ride down to MASH with me."

"Yes, sir. Ready to get out of here, anytime, any way."

Ten miles down the rutted road, we pulled up at the hospital tent, marked with the symbolic Red Cross. "Will you walk with me?" the priest asked. "I'll do my rounds and then we'll see if the food down here is any better than Artillery's mess."

"Yes, sir." I hopped out of the jeep and joined the chaplain as he stepped inside the large MASH tent.

Inside, wounded men, bound tight with bandages lay mostly quiet. Father Brady moved calmly among the cots that filled the enclosure. I stayed a few feet behind, trying not to intrude on the words the priest offered to the GIs who waited for any comfort the priest could offer. His soft brogue carried over to me, nevertheless.

"How's it going, private? Any time you want to talk about giving your leg to the war effort, I'm here."

"Not yet, Father. Not yet." One tear, then another, slipped down the soldier's cheek and I turned away.

"In your own time, son. Just know I'm here when you need me." Father Brady moved on.

Through MASH receiving, pre-op, post-op and the holding areas, I saw the results of combat. Men who'd lost their spirit and didn't talk, unable to voice the truths of their situation. Damaged internal organs. Diminished eyesight. Ravaged limbs. I watched Father Brady hold the hands of wounded heroes and bless a soldier's last breath. He prayed for those alive, those passed on, and for everyone caught up in this particular fight so far from home.

Later, we drove back to my unit and I resumed my long hours of directing the warriors of the sky, fighting the cause in the way I was trained. I'd taken one of the most important walks in my life, one rife with the risks connected to the four point heroes on the front edge of battle. I understood more about the reality of what was then called a police action. I realized it was properly a war, not an adventure.

The chaplain never mentioned my visit to MASH. When the war was over, American deaths in Korea numbered over 50,000 with more than 100,000 wounded. Because of a thoughtful priest, who recognized a naïve young man, I arrived home intact, one of the lucky ones.

Now, fifty years later, I hold a photo of that padre, culled from my stash of Korean pictures. I realize the significant role and many variations of the job that chaplains play in any war effort. The funny thing is, I can't remember his first name. He's just Father Brady, but he may be the reason I'm here this day; a wife, four kids, three grandchildren and a rich, fulfilling life later.

One thing I know for sure. I wish I could say to him, with full understanding of all the years I've traveled since, Thank you, Father Brady.

By Connie Spittler,
a story as remembered by her husband, Bob,
Robert J.V. Spittler, Corporal, I-Corps, U.S. Army

Until the Taps

Until the taps came wafting crisply 'cross the muddy mound
in proud salute to welcome Heaven's guest,
we knew it only as a lonely, melancholy sound
and thought it nothing but a call to rest,
but that which sounded melancholy in the morning air
was neither warrior's dirge nor final call;
it whispered past the hallowed ground and mourners gathered there
to herald his arrival in the Hall.

The Brothers gathered 'round him from Tun Tavern in the East,
from Inchon and the Chosin Reservoir;
they marched in from the Bulge before the bugle call had ceased;
they came from Moctezuma's bloody shore,
from Vietnam, Cambodia, and from the Desert Storm,
then formed along a golden boulevard,
snapped smartly to attention in their dress-blue uniforms,
and saluted the Marine Corps Honor Guard.

The Honor Guard from Pearl came marching down the stair as one,
and as the final note was being blown,
Sergeant Brisco snapped a sharp salute to Christ the Son
and marched away. Marines don't go alone.

By Harvey Stanbrough, MSgt, USMC (Ret)
2nd Light AntiAircraft Missile Battalion, Yuma, Arizona for former
US Marine Corps Sergeant Edwin J. Brisco,
1922–1994, I.M.

The Ludenschide Connection

Bill Porter, an American prisoner of war in Germany, braced himself against the icy winds—and German guards with guns. A shadow of his former high school football physique, the twenty-year-old infantryman knew he was in real trouble not only from starvation, chronic dysentery and a festering leg wound, but from an increasing familiar pain, the agony of corneal ulcers that had threatened to blind him each time he caught a cold or got run down during his childhood years. Now, without medication, Bill was losing his sight, and the morning came when he collapsed in the line-up of prisoners being forced to rebuild a bombed-out railroad track. He was trucked to a hospital in Ludenschide.

The temporary hospital for care of German war casualties had been set up in the town's three-story elementary school. Although Bill was a prisoner, his leg was treated and he was placed in the eye injury ward on the third floor. There he shared a space with the only other American prisoner, a pilot whose eyes had been burned when he bailed out over Germany, robbing him of sight.

Since Bill could see out of one eye, he quickly became the blind pilot's companion and guide. He fed him—the pilot's hands and wrists had been burned as well—and took him for walks up and down the halls of the building. But empty hours haunted both young men.

"If only we had something to read, a newspaper, magazine, anything," Bill said to his friend one day. "I could read to you . . . just so's it's in English."

"I have a book," the pilot responded in the warm, midwestern drawl Bill had come to know so well. "Take a look in my jacket pocket." He paused for a moment. "It's . . . it's my Bible."

From that moment on, day in and day out, through his un-bandaged seeing eye, Bill read The Old Testament aloud. Then he read The New Testament and favorite passages until the entire Bible had been read and reread many times. They didn't realize it then, but through the words from the greatest Book ever written, a bond was growing between them as they found comfort and the strength they needed to survive.

ONE MORNING AS THEY walked down the hall, they heard the unmistakable drone of approaching American bombers. It wasn't until they stopped for a moment to talk with a nurse that Bill detected the whine of misdirected bombs overhead. With no time to search for shelter, he grabbed his friend, threw him to the floor, and shoved him under a baby-grand piano. The hospital received a direct hit . . . an explosion that burst Bill's eardrums.

Bill had no idea how long it was before he regained consciousness or felt the pain from multiple head injuries and an eight-inch shaft of steel through his face. At first, he couldn't hear the shouts of German soldiers outside the ruptured building, or the cries of victims. As a matter of fact, he couldn't hear anything except his own heart hammering in his chest. But, he smelled smoke and knew he had to get out. With his one free arm he struggled to extricate himself from confining plaster, planks and debris. Then, with a final upward push he broke through the fallen roof—and caught a glimpse of hell.

The dead lay everywhere: the nurse he had been talking to only moments before, doctors, the wounded, the sick. Everyone was dead—except himself. And his friend? *Where was he?* Could the old piano have withstood the crushing weight of roofing beams, falling bricks and cement? That's when the thought struck him. If his friend had survived, he would not only be blind, he'd be buried alive. Bill's ears screamed. His head hurt. What was his friend's name anyway? He couldn't remember. Was he losing his mind? What difference did it make? He had to crawl back down and find him. Now! *Please God*, he prayed. *Let him be alive.*

The searing pain from the steel in his face dimmed amid thoughts of what he might find. He groped under the piano. He felt a man's leg move. "Are you okay, buddy?" he asked. An answer came when two hands grasped his own.

Somehow during the next ten minutes, Bill maneuvered them both down flights of shattered stairwells. Outside, the street was milling with a confusion of police, medics, ambulances and fire engines. He found an empty bench, and the two huddled together for warmth in the bitter cold, all the while Bill dodging the Germans spitting at the Americans who had lived while their own had perished. Still others grabbed the glinting steel protruding from his face and tried to pull it out. Perhaps they were only trying to help? What did it matter? Unable to fight them off any longer, he put his head between his knees and covered himself with his arms.

"Bill," the pilot's teeth chattered, "do you think you can get back inside and get us a blanket—and my Bible?"

"Sure," Bill said. "I'll try. Just don't go anywhere," he added jokingly. "I'll be back. I promise."

The climb back up the stairs took longer than Bill thought it would, but his friend's treasured Bible and dog tags were on the bed where he'd left them. He grabbed a blanket, and with everything clutched in his arms hurried back down the broken stairs and out to the bench. His buddy was gone.

Where was he? His voice a plea, he shouted at passersby. "Has anyone seen a guy with bandages over his eyes!" He held up two fingers and pointed to his own patch. No one responded. No one spoke English. *God! Keep him safe*, he prayed. *The guy can't see!*

Alone now, and in excruciating pain, Bill crouched behind the bench and covered his head with the blanket. Hours of sirens, shouts and running footsteps passed before a young Ludenschide doctor peered under the blanketed figure. He took Bill to his office in a nearby building. There, after giving him a shot of Schnapps, the doctor sliced into his cheek and jaw to relieve the suction and removed the steel and other pieces of metal embedded in his head. Finally, he re-bandaged the eye. Still a prisoner of war, Bill was packed into a boxcar and later forced to walk to Fallingbastel, a hundred and fifty miles away, where he was interred in another prison camp until the war ended.

When he returned to the United States he wrote to the War Department and asked them to search for his friend. He placed the letter in a box along with the pilot's dog tags—and the well-read Bible. Then he printed his return address—Sigma Nu Fraternity, Lehigh University, Bethlehem, Pennsylvania.

NIGHTMARES, PANIC AT SUDDEN sounds, and mood swings would plague Bill for the rest of his life, as they do most victims of Post Traumatic Stress Disorder. But even as a young father and then a grandfather, he always found joy in reminiscing about the good things in life—before the war—and after.

He never talked about his time as a prisoner. He preferred instead to tell stories about his years as a rancher, one hundred miles from town, where he felt closer to God and his family. He especially liked to tell his children and grandchildren stories about when he was in college fifty-three years past—especially the day an unfamiliar car pulled up in front of Sigma Nu.

From the second-floor landing of the fraternity, he remembered glancing out the window at the blue Chevy—and the driver who climbed out from behind the wheel. It was lunchtime. He knew he should hurry on down to the living room where the rest of the brothers were waiting for the lunch gong, but there was something about the stranger walking up the sidewalk to the front door that stopped him. The bell chimed. Bill's roommate, Jack Venner, got up to answer. "Hello! Can I help you?" he asked.

From where he stood, Bill felt sudden moisture dampen his forehead. He gripped the banister to steady himself.

"Yes," said a voice with a warm, mid-western twang. "I'm looking for an old friend of mine named Bill Porter. I want to thank him . . . for lots of things." He smiled, his eyes scanning the young men in the crowded living room. "And this might sound sort of crazy," he added, "but I wouldn't know him even if I saw him. I . . . I've never seen him before."

THE TWO Ex-POWs TALKED all night. They promised to keep in touch. But life has its demands. It takes curious twists and turns, and they lost each other. In Bill's later years he couldn't remember the pilot's name, but the bond born in Ludenschide remained.

By Penny Porter, a story first related to her by Bill, and one they lived out together.

For William (Bill) Porter, Private, U.S. Army. Unit: 35th Division, 134thRegiment, Company L. Captured in Battle of the Bulge, European Theater. Interred in STALAG 11 B. Recipient of the Prisoner of War Medals Medal, two Purple Hearts and Bronze Star.

An Ammunition Shortage

IN THE LATE SUMMER of 1952 I had finished college at Ohio State University, and along with my Bachelor of Science Degree I received a Second Lieutenant's commission for artillery in the Army Reserve. It took the Army about one year to determine that they needed me to finish off the Korean War. After a few months of giving basic training at Camp Chaffee, Arkansas, I was assigned to Fort Sill, Oklahoma, to receive training in the Basic Artillery Officers' Course. After this assignment, and even though I volunteered for Alaska, I was assigned to the replacement pipeline for Korea.

"Remember to take your khakis," we were advised by the field grade officer who conducted our training, and, with apologies, I can't recall his name and actual rank now; we were intensely involved in just learning our job at the time. He continued and explained, and encouraged, "Those guys at the treaty table will have you marching in parades when this war is over in a month." We did take our dress khakis, but left them in storage in Japan. Like so many who were optimistic, we found that the war had a ways to go.

AFTER SERVING A FEW months as forward observer, I found myself as the longest-assigned officer in the battery, and was made Executive Officer for Charlie Battery of the 625th Field Artillery Battalion. We had suffered several causalities from counter-battery fire and had lost one wounded forward observer. Now the Chinese were trying to push some of our troops off of the ground that some called Sniper Ridge and Triangle Hill.

We were no longer supporting our own division troops that were in the rear (our mission was to support the infantry with our six, 105mm, howitzers) but now those of the 7th Division. We had been ordered to shift our trails about 40 degrees to the west and be in general support of troops to our left. (For the non-artillery personnel reading this, "trails" are the long steel shanks that close and allow the piece to be towed, and are also constructed to be dug into the ground to absorb the recoil of the canon.)

THE EXECUTIVE OFFICER IS in charge of the firing battery and responsible for its performance. Therefore, trading, among other things, several bottles of officers' ration of drink to provide bulldozer digging and sandbags for the construction of an excellent emplacement seemed perfectly logical when I did it. Our fire-direction center in battalion had talked to the observer and told us to not quit firing now that the dead and wounded enemy were piling up like cordwood. In order to meet the onslaught, we had for a while fired the battery two rounds every minute. That amounts to two 12-round salvos a minute. I had advised the battalion supply that we needed more rounds for the 105s. I was concerned at battalion's repeated assurances that the ammo was on the way.

We were firing through the morning and still no ammunition came to replace our used up ammo. Then at about noon the Chinese artillery found our location and was landing rounds within the battery perimeter. Our firing had stopped briefly when two two and half-ton trucks wheeled through the front gate in our barbed wire. The drivers of the trucks screeched to a stop and ran into a well-fortified ammunition bunker. The shelling scared them to the point that they didn't even attempt to report their arrival.

I ran and checked the drivers and they had the ammo we needed. We could sit there and watch the Chinese blow up our ammo or we could get it to the guns that now had only about one round apiece left for firing. I ordered the chief of firing battery (either Sergeant Belsen or Sergeant Sly, both were great soldiers) to unload the ammo for the first three guns and I would unload it for the second three guns. Explosions from the enemy artillery were all around us. We flushed the drivers out of the ammo bunkers. They drove gun-to-gun as directed. We handed down the high explosive projectiles and threw off the semi-fixed canisters that contained the powder charges. I figured we could straighten out the rims on the canisters if necessary. When an enemy shell came close to my truck I would fall on the exposed powder and hope the truck didn't get hit.

It took only about fifteen minutes to unload the ammo trucks that had come directly from the port of Inchon with no stops in between. The ammo wasn't even boxed but separated and ready for firing.

THE SKITTISH TRUCK DRIVERS had made it in the nick of time. The enemy attack was repulsed, the war continued, and you know the rest.

By Richard M. Kerr, 1st Lt. Artillery
Formerly Executive Officer, Charlie Battery
625th F.A. Bn. 40th Infantry

Skunk Hunt

WE TRAVELED AS A Light Fire Team. That meant two UH-1B "Huey" helicopters armed with machine guns and rockets. The pilot, in addition to flying the aircraft, worked the four M-60 flex guns, two to a pylon, mounted on both sides. The crew chief and I each manned our own M-60 from just inside the open cargo doors. The co-pilot fired the rockets.

We were flying a late mission, a skunk hunt. The rule was that no boats were allowed on the rivers during the hours of darkness. If we caught them out we assumed that they were Viet Cong. We'd taken off about sundown and were headed for coordinates on a map that marked a place where a lot of sampan traffic had been reported crossing the Mekong. These missions came out of MACV headquarters in Saigon after "careful analysis of the latest intelligence."

Naturally, there were tricks involved. Everybody survived on tricks. One of the tricks the old crew chief, Beany McGillicuddy, had taught me was not to go into a bad situation feeling depressed. Depression interfered with messages coming from that little voice in your head.

Beany's replacement seemed a little nervous. This was his orientation flight, his first actual experience going into something potentially "hot." Every time he looked over at me I smiled, gave him a nod and a big "thumbs up" just like I knew what I was doing.

THE GHOST-TASTE OF BREAD and wine came back to me, a memory left over from my last two-day pass in Saigon. That phantom bile came less from the food than from guilt. Guilt at bearing witness to a horrific stupidity and not saying something.

But then, maybe I was the stupid one. An alarmist. Maybe what I'd seen was all too outdated to be of any use to the enemy.

Then again, even if that were so, those papers revealed something about how we thought, didn't they? Strategy, if not specific tactics. Couldn't the generals see? But how does a nineteen-year old kid say that to a general? I couldn't find the words or the courage. The only cure for it was to keep quiet. Keeping quiet added one more small shame to the secret file I kept on myself.

THE MOON HADN'T COME up yet. Clouds hung thick and heavy just above our rotors. The other chopper disappeared behind one ragged wisp. When it emerged, all its lights were off. I noticed that our own safety beacon no longer splashed blood red across the overhead canopy.

In spite of the lack of a moon, the river below seemed to give off a gray metallic glow cutting through the utter blackness of the jungle. We began an intricate little choreography with the other chopper, forming a horizontal figure eight that invisibly linked one with the other in the night sky. Each pass repeated the pattern a little further up-river, signs for infinity that lasted for only as long as it took the blade-stirred air to return to damp stagnation. The old mantra, "Nobody Dies," came to my lips. I pushed against the machine gun's safety for the hundredth time, making sure my weapon was ready to fire.

The chopper shuddered on through the night, banking left then right. Searching.

Nothing.

Intel had it wrong again, or they were late in getting the information to us, which amounted to the same thing.

TWO WEEKS EARLIER, WHEN I'd been in Saigon, everyone there was getting ready for the *Nguyen Dan Tet,* the Vietnamese New Year. I'd stopped off at a favorite bakery, bought a warm French baguette, and then went next door for a small bottle of red wine. The plan was to spend a quiet afternoon sitting on a bench at the zoo, enjoying the peace-like atmosphere and thinking about something, anything, other than my current situation. I was getting short, a couple of months left in-country. Being a short-timer had a way of tempting things to go wrong.

Earlier that afternoon, on the way to the zoo, I had the driver make a detour. I stopped off at MACV Headquarters to scope the place out. I'd be coming there soon enough to take care of my final paperwork before boarding the "Big Smoker" for home. "Big Smoker" was GI slang for the contract 707 jets that brought you into Vietnam and, hopefully, took you back out alive, a long year later, when your tour was over. The old crew chief, McGillicuddy had gone home in one, in the cargo hold, inside a government-issue aluminum casket.

The sergeant at the gate asked for my identification. When I showed him my card, he said, "Let me guess, you're here to find out about taking home a Vietnamese bride. Don't do it man! These girls are just using you! Let it go!"

When I assured him that I had nothing like that in mind, he asked me what department I was looking for. I needed some kind of believable answer.

"Where do I go to get a firearms export permit?"

"Firearms?"

"I got an Russian SKS. I want to take it back to the states with me."

"Sweet little piece. But, you should know. They're only issuing permits to officers."

I thanked the sergeant for his information and headed for the entrance.

There was a line in front of the door marked "Permits." Instead of joining the queue I continued on, walking through the rest of the building once, just to get the layout and the location of the offices I would need to visit. Satisfied, I headed back for my cab.

Once clear of the guard at the gate, I had a change of thought and headed for a long line of street vendors that had set up along the sidewalk near one of the large white dumpsters holding paper refuse from the headquarters building. They were selling the colorful paper maché "lion head" masks that were so numerous during the Vietnamese New Year celebrations. On a whim, I chose one that appealed to me, paid in *piasters*, and walked back to the cab. There was just barely room for me and the mask in the back seat of the little Renault.

The baguette was still warm when I arrived at the zoo. I eased the mask out of the taxi's rear door, retrieved the bag holding the bread and wine, and turned toward the entrance. A zoo monkey's screech brought me to a halt. At least I had the possibility of escaping in the not-to-distant future. Today, I didn't want to start feeling sorry for anyone or anything.

I opted for an empty bench beneath a flame tree in the botanical gardens. Uncorking the wine, I took a couple of sips then eased the bottle onto the gravel next to the bench. I tore off a bit of bread with my teeth, and chewed slowly. My mood was definitely improving. There was this big bright beautiful sky, a few light fluffy clouds, children's laughter, sunshine filtering down through the scarlet blossoms on that flame tree. The wine started to kick in and the warm bread became a meal by itself. I sighed with contentment and picked up the mask.

The thing was a masterpiece of folk-art. The great convoluted face had a hinged jaw that opened by way of a pull-cord that dropped down from inside the mask. The eyes were protruding globes with pupils indicated by black paint, the brows and long beard were tufts of white fake fur. The entire exterior was decorated with black, red, green, white, and yellow paint—all the elements working together to dispel evil and bring good luck.

I turned it upside down and inspected the interior. The construction consisted of whole sheets of overlapping eight and one-half by eleven-inch white bond, typewritten in English. The sheets were held together with a whitish paste. I looked closer. Although words were streaked, and in some places obliterated by wrinkles and blotches of paste, much of their content was still legible. Below the usual military headings, there were references to units, equipment, orders for movement, and the like. One mentioned the time and coordinates of a Watercraft Interdiction mission. A skunk hunt. Each page had been stamped with large red letters. *TOP SECRET.*

The wine and bread suddenly turned sour.

I thought about hurrying back to tell someone. Who could I tell? Follow the chain of command. The sergeant at the gate. What would he do? Pass it along to a lieutenant, who would pass it along to some captain who might take the time to tell a major.

I checked the dates. The legible numbers showed orders issued more than a month ago. All those headquarters types would share a laugh about this dumb kid who thought he'd stumbled across a breach of security. I sat on the bench, watched the clouds, and did nothing. Finally, I picked up my mask, flagged down a taxi, and headed for my room at the Continental Hotel.

THE MEMORY OF THAT two-week-old bile faded as the pilot banked hard over the gun-metal river one last time then headed for our flight line back at Bien Hoa. The overcast again reflected our red safety beacon. We hadn't fired a shot.

The new guy leaned back against the firewall and took a deep breath.

I looked at him, remembered the bullet tearing through Mc-Gillicuddy, and felt less guilty. My timidity had inflicted a serious wound on my self-esteem but perhaps, on this mission at least, that paper maché lion had brought all of us a little luck.

By Lon Wolff, S4, U.S. Army
118th Air Mobile, Light

The October Surprise

I T WAS OCTOBER 1962. The sleek six-engine jet bomber, all eighty-five tons of her, groaned as she rolled down the runway gaining speed for takeoff while leaving a huge cloud of black smoke in her wake. When the B-47 reached "unstick speed" at about 167 knots, and with only a slight tug on the yoke, she lifted gracefully off the Dyess AFB runway at Abilene, Texas. Final destination: Greenham Common Air Base in England, some eight hours away. The mission was a routine overseas deployment for SAC (Strategic Air Command) in support of its global alert operation to a forward staging base. Unknown to us at the time was that this deployment was to be more eventful than others.

The three-week TDY (temporary duty) assignments, encoded REFLEX, placed the nuclear carrying bombers and their crews at forward bases where they could more quickly strike the Soviet Union and its satellites. From forward bases in England, Spain, Alaska and Guam, the REFLEX aircraft augmented the sizable bomber force on alert back in the States. With a quick launch from these forward deployment bases, aircraft could be over their assigned Soviet targets within a few short hours and *without the many uncertainties and delays of airborne refueling* with which the States-side alert force had to contend.

PRACTICE, PRACTICE, PRACTICE, I never flew a mission in SAC that didn't simulate a nuclear-bomb-carrying combat profile. These single-ship missions to our forward bases in England were no different, and gave us a great opportunity to practice our combat procedures. Immediately after leveling off at around 40,000 feet, the navigator/bombardier started a celestial "grid" navigation leg. Flying by gyros, and using only the stars and planets to keep the aircraft on track, we simulated flying over the northern polar latitudes where most of our wartime missions would take us.

We became very good at celestial navigation. Some crews could drop a bomb within 2000 feet of the target using only the stars and planets. At these very northern latitudes magnetic compasses were useless due to the extreme variations in the earth's magnetic field and the rapidly converging lines of longitude. Radios could not be counted on for navigation purposes during a wartime mission and navigation satellites and precision bombing using laser or GPI had not yet been invented. Navigation legs were an extremely difficult task for the navigator requiring many hours of arduous and focused practice to become proficient. The navigator/bombardier was required to drop a nuclear weapon, if all electronic systems failed, by celestial means alone, a daunting task at best.

Following the practice polar navigation leg, it was time to take on some "gas." This required a rendezvous with an airborne tanker, usually a KC-135 (a redesigned Boeing 707), at a prearranged time and at a designated set of coordinates. The bomber was usually low on fuel at this point in the mission and if the B-47 (receiver) pilot couldn't connect with the airborne tanker and take on fuel within a very short time, an alternate-landing field must be found immediately. We normally had only one opportunity to rendezvous, hookup at about 27,000 feet, get our fuel while traveling at over 400 knots, and get back on our navigation route, all within a very short time.

Aside from the obvious difficulties and the inherent dangers involved during mid-air refuelings, extreme turbulence, darkness and bad weather often added to the "fright factor" for the pilot and crew. From a pilot's standpoint this task separated the men from the boys. Basically the bomber was flying close-ship formation, four to five yards off the tail of the tanker. A pilot new to mid-air refueling, had a tendency to over-correct, particularly with rudder. This invariably resulted in a side-to-side swinging motion that triggered an immediate disconnect from the tanker. The whole process would then have to be started over. Aside from the psychological pressure on the pilot at this point, the aircraft was continuing to burn up valuable fuel instead of taking on the life-giving JP-4. The tanker aircraft had only limited control over this "mid-air dance" and a very small envelope in which it could maneuver the end of its refueling boom. It was pretty much up to the receiver pilot to get into position and to stay there long enough to take on ten to twenty tons of jet fuel. Normally this would take ten to twenty minutes. Pilots prided themselves on how quickly they could hookup with the tanker and take on the required fuel. It was either an ego-buster or an ego-builder for pilots; we always hoped for the latter.

After two or three more celestial navigation legs, and at least one more mid-air refueling, we terminated the mission with a simulated radar bomb run on a designated target near London. Landing after eight or nine hours of strenuous airborne activity, everyone was ready for a few hours sleep. However, sleep had to wait. First we had to debrief the mission. This could take up to an hour. During these interrogations, Wing and Squadron Intelligence personnel would delve into every minute segment of the mission from launch to targeting, including how effective our electronic countermeasures had been. I never encountered a debriefing in which tempers didn't flare a bit. Interrogators were well rested and full of questions; we were tired and irritable, and in most cases didn't see much sense to many of their questions. However, it was one of those things you learn in the bomber flying business that you have to suffer through whether you like it or not.

THE B-47 WAS THE world's first multi-engine jet aircraft, commercial or military. This gorgeous, sleek airborne delight became operational in the early 1950s and looked more like a large fighter than a bomber. But it had one huge flaw—it was not at all crew-friendly. Your left foot and leg may be freezing while the right half of your body was shoved against a bank of toasty 180-degree electronic gear. The airplane was just damned uncomfortable. Our jet helmets in those days were made mostly of metal with some plastic. They weighed almost three pounds, and after an eight-hour mission, they felt more like twenty. Helmets, in later years were molded and fitted to the pilot's head and weighed only a few ounces. The rubber and plastic oxygen mask carved into your face leaving deep lines that remained hours after landing. And the ejection seats we rode on were about as hard as a metal park bench. Despite these inconveniences, we all loved flying these sleek birds; and we wouldn't think of trading our job for any kind of high paying civilian work. The larger incentive was the pride we all felt in being in America's front line of defense as well as the awesome responsibility inherent in our job of husbanding a nuclear weapon.

Early the next morning, following a good night's rest, we reported to the Greenham Common briefing room. The Wing Commander and his staff were there to listen to briefings on our Composite War Plan from takeoff to landing. That day all went well during our briefing; however, we were unsure of our post-strike landing base. In the early days of the Cold War, we were uncertain just where our post-strike landing field would be. No one could tell us which countries might be friendly enough (following a horrendous nuclear exchange) to let us land on their soil or even what bases might be intact following initial hostilities. That day we passed our briefing and the detailed follow-up questions by the Wing Commander and received the required certification by SAC Headquarters. This certification simply stated that we were capable of striking our assigned Soviet target.

Following the briefing, we proceeded to the alert flight line, preflighting the aircraft and the nuclear weapon and signing for the weapon. Yes, in those days we actually signed for our nuclear weapon as one would sign for a loan at a bank. By noon the old crews were relieved and the new crews were in place for a week of ground alert duty. We quietly settled into a daily routine of attending classes and performing twice-a-day preflights on the aircraft and the weapon.

To keep us at peak performance, SAC initiated several practice scrambles. They all started with the shrill sound of a klaxon, an extremely loud, high decibel electric horn. This grotesque shriek could wake up the dead miles away. Years after leaving SAC, I would jump up and start to run at any sound that came close to it. It seemed to all of us that SAC Headquarters thought that these exercises would be more effective if performed in the middle of the night rather than during the day. We would be startled out of a deep sleep, jump into our flying suits and boots (laid out close to our beds) and race to waiting pickup trucks, and then speed out to our aircraft. The alert aircraft were already "cocked," that is, the aircraft equipment was already half way to the engine start position. By flipping only a few switches, the engines and aircraft systems would roar to life. With practice, we could accomplish all of this within five minutes from an interrupted deep sleep.

SAC HAD DEVELOPED A "fail-safe" system of nuclear weapons positive control. Before going on alert, the three officer crewmembers each signed for sealed envelopes that contained two sets of (sealed) coded letters and numbers. The first set of code authorized an aircraft launch. A second set of coded data permitted the actual release of a nuclear weapon. The SAC Commander could authorize a launch; but only the President could authorize the release of a weapon. The code was broadcast on a secure HF (high frequency) radio channel from SAC Headquarters. If the code for launch was initiated, aircraft were authorized to takeoff and proceed en route to the assigned target. The idea behind all of this was to get the aircraft and weapon off the ground before the airfield could be struck by a Soviet nuke. En route, another set of numbers and letters were broadcast over the secure HF frequency and again each crewmember would open his sealed packet and individually verify and confirm the code before a nuclear drop could take place.

All three crewmembers had to verify the "go code" or it was a "no-go" situation. This procedure was practiced constantly by SAC bomber crews. Crews had to be as concerned about the weapon control procedure and associated paperwork as they were about the war plan itself, for any failure with the procedures—or loss of paperwork—meant serious disciplinary action. For an officer, it meant the end of a career. Throughout almost fifty years of SAC operations and with many thousands of bomber and missile crews utilizing the system it never failed. The system was designated "Positive Control" and it worked.

The three-week tour of alert duty overseas was divided into three parts. The first week, the arriving crews were on alert. At the start of the second week new crews relieved them, rendering them free to go on R & R (Rest and Recreation). The third week they would again return for alert duty. Each crewmember was on his own for the entire R & R week. Some went to London, some found their way to Austria or Switzerland for a few days of skiing, while others chose to stay near the base and frequent the nearby small English town of Neuberry.

The week on alert went by quickly and the week of R & R was upon us. A longtime friend, Arch Murphy, and I were on the same alert cycle and decided to take the train into London and spend the week seeing the sights the city had to offer. We made reservations at a military hotel in London called the Columbia Club. The hotel, smack in the center of London was run by the British for the benefit of American and British military personnel on R & R. The cost compared to other downtown hotels was reasonable and the food wasn't too bad, even by American standards.

DURING OCTOBER 1962 WE were at the height of the Cold War with the Soviets. The night of October 22nd, President Kennedy made a speech on the worsening situation in Cuba. Through surveillance flights made by the Air Force and the CIA over Castro's communist island, the United States determined that the Soviets had placed and were placing medium-range ballistic missiles on the island. These nuclear-tipped missiles had a range of about 1100 miles making every city in the eastern third of the United States vulnerable to nuclear attack. This obviously was unacceptable. Before leaving Greenham Common on our R & R we were briefed on the situation by our intelligence personnel and told to stay close to a phone. Since we were staying in a military hotel we weren't concerned. Arch and I arrived in the center of London about noon, checked into the hotel and proceeded to do the tourist thing throughout the remainder of the day. The next morning (the night before in the States) President Kennedy in a televised speech publicly revealed the missile crisis and announced that he had initiated a naval blockade of the Island.

We somewhat kept tabs on the Cuban situation through British *telly* and newspapers, but seeing plays, shopping, sleeping, dining and touring London filled most of our time for the next couple of days. On Wednesday morning, October 24, the deadline for the blockade, two Soviet freighters drew near the quarantine line, 500 miles from the coast of Cuba. The Pentagon went to Defcon 2, (defense condition, Defcon 5 is peace; Defcon 1 is war) sending out the order loud and clear over an open channel, so the Soviets would know. All 1400 of SAC's nuclear bombers (B-47s and B-52s) immediately went on around-the-clock alert. The airborne tanker force also was alerted.

Arch and I had been trying for days to get tickets to the new London musical, *My Fair Lady.* We finally got them for the matinee performance for Wednesday afternoon. We got to the theatre early and we both enjoyed this wonderful musical. Upon leaving the theatre we managed to snare a taxi, and at about 5:00 P.M. walked into the bar at the Columbia Club hoping to tell everyone at Happy Hour about the great show we'd just seen. To our surprise, there was no one in the bar but the bartender. We ordered martinis and asked where everyone was. The bartender advised us that an announcement about an hour ago ordered all American military personnel to report immediately to their bases.

So much for the martinis. We quickly packed, checked out of the hotel and within an hour were on a train heading for the base. En route we managed to grab the front page of a discarded British newspaper and got filled in on what was taking place in the real world.

Arch and I were each in deep thought throughout most of the two-hour train trip through the rolling, green English countryside. We thought of our families back in Abilene. We both believed that Soviet Premier Khrushchev *wouldn't* back down and that President Kennedy *couldn't* back down. We were hoping, too, that there were enough airplanes and weapons left at the base for us to take part in this historic crucial event.

I realize that thought may seem perplexing and insensitive to most people but this was our job. It's what we had been training to do for years and we didn't want to be left out. In a way, we were prepping ourselves for the ultimate mission as an athlete does right before a big game—but this was not a game. We were also deeply saddened at what was taking place. As a nation, how in the world did the United States get itself into this horrific situation—this potential nuclear holocaust? There just had to be a solution, a face-saving way out of this for both Khrushchev and Kennedy. But we couldn't let our minds dwell on the political or human aspects of this momentous historical event. Our focus had to be toward mentally preparing ourselves for the mission. This was our job; and it would require every single bit of mental toughness and physical stamina we possessed.

Upon our arrival back at Greenham Common we were greeted with, "Where the hell have you guys been!" It was a rhetorical question. Everyone was too busy to dwell on slightly tardy crewmembers. Other crewmembers had already checked in, suited up and were loading their gear on the aircraft preparing for the "big one." It didn't take long to get out of civvies and into flying gear. I was at once struck by the calm and the professionalism of all involved from the enlisted crew chiefs to the bomber aircrews. As I was going through the preparation for a nuclear mission, I couldn't help but think how surreal all of this was. Only a few short hours before I was in London enjoying *My Fair Lady*, now I'm preparing to drop a nuclear weapon on a city called Murmansk. What a day this has been! Within an hour we had fourteen B-47s preflighted, loaded with 4.2-megaton nuclear weapons and ready to go. We were ordered to the briefing room.

The briefing was short and sweet. The on-scene commander, Lieutenant Colonel Hobson, assured us that this looked like the "real McCoy," and to triple-check everything, particularly the weapon in our bomb bay and our personal escape and evasion gear and procedures. The intelligence officer brought us up to date on the latest in Washington. A U-2 high-altitude spy plane had been shot down and the Air Force pilot, Major Anderson, had been killed. What we were not aware of were the diplomatic hi-jinks taking place in Washington to resolve the crisis. Some of the back-door scenarios being worked on wouldn't be made public for years. One involved Robert Kennedy, the President's brother meeting with

Soviet Ambassador Dobrynin and with Washington columnist Charles Bartlett at mid-night on two separate occasions to pass on face-saving deals to Khrushchev. Our medium-range Jupiter missiles stationed in Turkey were part of a trade-off deal.

The intelligence officer continued his briefing, updating us on newly acquired Soviet intelligence. The Soviets had in the last few days moved a partial second regiment of MiG fighter aircraft into the vicinity of Murmansk. My target was the huge Soviet home-based submarine fleet and maritime infrastructure at Murmansk. It was a good target and I could hit it within 3 1/2 hours after takeoff and without any midair refueling. I was absolutely certain that I could get in and destroy it and maybe have enough fuel to recover back to England. If not, I would look for a suitable post-strike landing field along the Norwegian coastline. The additional MiG squadron was a new and dangerous threat and would probably require added evasive action and electronic countermeasure tactics on our approach to the target. However, there was absolutely no doubt in my mind that we would get in. We had to!

The squadron personnel officer stopped us on our way out the door. He asked us to review our personnel data and most importantly our E & E (escape-and-evasion) personal authenticator code words. If we were unlucky enough to be shot down in enemy territory the search-and-rescue guys would quiz us by means of our hand-held survival radios—part of our survival gear—to verify our personal authenticator before a pickup in enemy territory could be initiated. The crewmember simply provided the intelligence folks with a short sentence that nobody else but you would have knowledge of. Mine was "The name of my first dog was Mittens." I would use this same authenticator later during my Vietnam combat missions.

We parked fourteen B-47s in echelon at about 45 degrees on the parking and taxi strips. The power carts were running around the clock. This kept power on the aircraft at all times and all we had to do to get the airplane moving was flip a couple of switches and the big bird would roar to life. The first bomber could be off the ground within three minutes. It was cramped quarters in the aircraft. We switched off-and-on every two hours with one other crew. Most of the time in the airplane was spent studying the route and target area and thinking about our families. I thought about what would happen to my family if I didn't make it back. Marcia had always been a strong person and there was never any doubt that she could raise our young family without me. She'd been a journalist with the *Tucson Citizen* before we were married and surely she could go back to that if that's what she wanted to do. I also thought about the Soviet nuclear weapons that could strike the United States.

I decided I would attempt to phone Marcia in Antigo, Wisconsin, during my next break. She had flown there with our two small children, Mike, three years old, and Carrie, a year old, to visit her parents the day after I departed for England. She was scheduled to return in two days. I needed to tell her to stay in Antigo. I was pretty sure that the little town of Antigo, Wisconsin, wasn't on the Soviet's target list and I was absolutely certain that the SAC base at Abilene would definitely be on that list. At the break I was able to reach Marcia by phone for about 45 seconds and she agreed to stay put. Knowing that my family would be safe was a big relief. Now I could concentrate totally on the upcoming mission.

THE DAY WAS OCTOBER 27, referred to as "Black Saturday." It looked as if negotiations with Washington and Moscow were going nowhere. SAC had been ordered to go to a modified Defcon 1. We would place ten percent of our alert bomber fleet with crews in their seats and with the aircraft engines running. This also required ground-refueling every hour to keep the fuel tanks topped off. We had never before gone to such an advanced alert status. With this plan SAC was assured that it would get at least ten percent of the bomber force off the ground before runways could possibly be destroyed by Soviet missiles. Our very lethal launch status was leaked to a few Washington journalists so that the Soviets would become aware of it; however, I think they probably already knew.

At the same time a cat-and-mouse game was unfolding in Washington. At about 8:00 P.M. that night, the United States publicly broadcast the President's letter pledging not to invade Cuba if Khrushchev removed all missiles from the Island. Kennedy said, *"The missile bases had to go and they had to go right now."* The United

States had to have a commitment by no later than 4:00 P.M. tomorrow, Sunday. This was not an ultimatum, but a statement of fact.

AT THIS POINT WE were getting somewhat used to the cramped airplane quarters and short naps. The air inside the cramped airplane was also becoming a little stale. After 36 hours in this venue I was also aware that my physical and mental stamina were waning. I must say, I prayed a lot. I think we all did. I prayed for my family and I prayed that God would help me be at my very best during the mission. Odd, maybe, but a lot of odd thoughts pass through your mind when engaged with something of this magnitude. You need all the help you can get. There was never a doubt in my mind that I would go on this mission, none whatsoever. And that's the mindset (also) that I had to maintain.

VERY ABRUPTLY ON SUNDAY afternoon, 28 October, the Soviets agreed to dismantle and withdraw their missiles from Cuba. They publicly broadcast over the radio, Khrushchev's declaration to the Soviet Presidium. *"In order to save the world, we must retreat."* So, abruptly, the crisis ended. As Secretary of State Dean Rusk put it, *"We looked them straight in the eyes and they blinked."*

We remained on a modified Defcon 2 for another week and gradually worked our way back to normal alert status over the next thirty days. We had all learned a lot. Krushchev had learned that he could not bully the United States—we would fight back. And the SAC system had been tested and it worked. The SAC nuclear bomber force found out that it could do the job when called upon. The threat had been taken to the very brink, and we had won. It was years, I believe, before any of us truly appreciated the momentous significance of the whole event and understood, fully, how critical to the entire world those days and hours really were. I'm so glad we didn't have to launch. But, be assured that if directed by proper authority, there would have been no hesitation on my part to carry out my mission to Murmansk.

By Robert O. McCartan
Colonel, USAF, Retired

Monkey on My Back

I HAD NEVER SEEN DARKNESS like this. I thought by now my eyes would have adjusted to the dim light but there was no light, dim or otherwise. I walked carefully, my left hand touching the structure next to me wishing someone inside would turn on a lamp or flick a lighter, anything to give me a glimpse.

I WAS ON GUARD duty. I didn't know why my own barracks in the "civilized" part of Clark Field in the Philippines should be so critical that it needed a guard at night. But they didn't ask my opinion. Just "You're it from 2 A.M. to 4 A.M. Make sure nothin' goes wrong."

I stopped. I was supposed to keep walking, all around the barracks, guarding it from—what? The Huks? The war technically was over but the Huks didn't seem to know that. They were a bunch of Communist rebels left over from The Hukbalahap guerrilla group formed in 1942, and now ongoing troublemakers. And damn dangerous you can bet.

But they wouldn't be interested in the barracks, only in the warehouse across the swamp. They would try their raids on a dark night and often there would be shooting. One pinned me down in my bunk one night, a machete at my throat while shadows went by on the way to the warehouse. "Quiet, Victory Joe. Be very quiet." I was quiet. Then, as if a dream ended, the shadows were gone. There was a brief ruckus over by the warehouse and the next day dawned quiet, bright and peaceful. The war was over, of course.

I INCHED ALONG. THE silence was as deep as the dark. I had two hours of this and I was beginning to think of a place to sit. I wouldn't get caught. Whoever came to check on me would have to use a light of some kind and I'd see it in time to stand nice and straight, carbine at the ready, prepared to call out "Halt. Who goes there?"

Except we didn't do it that way. Too many words; too much noise. The Huks could pinpoint us, pick us off if they wanted or avoid us on the way to somewhere else. No, none of that "halt" stuff. I had reduced my own challenge to a quiet "Stop," hardly above a whisper.

The Sergeant of the Guard or whoever it might be would reply with a nervous "Easy . . . *Easy*" knowing my carbine would be pointed right at him or where I thought he was, anyway.

I strained both my eyes and ears. I could hear my own feet so I knew I wasn't deaf. But God help me, I must be blind. There was just nothing I could distinguish—there, maybe. The far edge of the building. Yes, I could make it out against the sky, just barely. I started to inch forward again when—*Holy Jesus—what the hell?* Hands clawed at my eyes, something gripped my shoulder. *Damn, the Huks have sneaked up behind me and I'm supposed to* —"Dammit, let go!"

I reached up to my face, pulled at a hairy arm, another tangled in my hair. I didn't yell or anything. In fact I only remember breathing hard but no noise. I would be dead soon but by damn I wouldn't make any noise. Someone . . . something . . . grabbed me and was now clawing at my face, gripping my shoulder and neck. I stepped away and whatever it was suddenly let go. I turned and stared.

IN THE DARKNESS I finally began to discern my attacker. Looked like a monkey. A damn monkey! And a little one at that. In fact, I would learn later, a little female. *Jeez*, she felt like King Kong when she had her fingers in my eyes. But there she sat, perched in the overhanging structure, tied around the waist with a cord. She was only a shadow, not moving, not making a sound.

I took some time to breathe a little, to settle down. "Hey, you lonesome?" I kept my voice low and stepped closer. "You want to come down here with me? C'mon, c'mon." I patted my shoulder. I didn't even see her jump but suddenly her furry arms were wrapped around my head again, one hand over my left eye and the other firmly gripping my nose. Her legs straddled my shoulder. "Careful, dammit." I repositioned her arms allowing her to grip my forehead and spoke gently. "Keep your damn fingers out of my eyes. *Jeez*, be careful." She finished my stint with me on guard duty that night. Good company, too, compared to the blackness, the silence. She rode my shoulder, one arm around my neck and neither of us too uncomfortable.

THE NEXT DAY I asked around and found who owned her, a guy who soon would be headed home — so I bought her. She was mine for a year or so, an affectionate little friend who would "groom" my arm and head when I'd let her. If she yanked my hair too hard I'd pull her hair and she'd settle down. Sometimes she'd look at me, eyes full of wonder and pat my arm in apology for her roughness. Nice monkey. Well domesticated. She'd poop on my shoulder only when she was scared.

Her name was Susie and she had had many owners, I guess. The going rate for her was 20 pesos, which converted from Philippine currency to ten American dollars at the time. When I rotated home I sold her to the next guy hoping he would be good to her.

I FORGOT TO CAUTION him not to scare her.

AUTHOR'S NOTE: NOT ALL of the war was horror. Some was pure boredom and a lot of loneliness. The GI often gathered pets, tending them with a gentleness that contradicted any image of a fierce warrior. Our squadron claimed one old dog, one goat, and Susie, our monkey.

By Dale A. Adams
Corporal, parachute rigger
13th Air Force
U.S. Army Air Corps

Through the Eyes of Innocence

A s a boy, Arthur Bloomberg was shy; a quiet gentle soul, adored by his doting Jewish family. Brought up in the tenements of Brooklyn, he wanted for little for he knew not of opulence and the greatness of things. His only touchstones to grandeur were Coney Island and the cinema; and to those places he lived to escape. Today, soldiers are professionals, highly trained, but, in 1943, America found itself vulnerable, and millions of teenage boys were drafted. Arthur Bloomberg was a boy when his draft letter came.

"I asked them if I could wait to graduate High School. They let me. But when I got there, they didn't have a uniform big enough to fit," my father said. He was big. And strong. For years he'd spend his days walking, Williamsburg to Coney Island, "The City," miles and miles, unaware he was training. His first days in the army were spent at Camp Upton, Long Island. It was about as far from home as he had ever gone. "They were testing my brain, how it would work in battle," he guessed. Random I.Q. tests at all hours of the night. Finally, a uniform arrived and Arthur Bloomberg was shipped to South Carolina, Camp Croft. "They put me on a coal train. And after seventeen hours, we arrived. Everyone was ordered out for a march. I was covered in coal."

Thirteen weeks were spent in basic training—hiking, shooting, and throwing grenades. From there, five weeks were spent in swamps at Camp Rucker, Alabama, and by September, Private Bloomberg was on his way to Newport News, Virginia. There a Liberty Ship was waiting to take him overseas. The ship was very cramped, stacks and stacks of bunks, three beds high.

"There was a prankster on board who liked to play tricks," my father recalled. "The beds were canvas with metal loopholes held by ropes weaved in and out attached to a frame. I slept on top.

One night, I went to bed and heard, *pop, pop—rip!* The bed collapsed and I fell down to the bed below. Then I kept falling—onto the first bed, down to the deck with me in it. All the ropes had been cut halfway so the rope was weak. After this, I had no place to sleep. So, I slept on the weather deck of the ship all the way to Africa. As mad as I was, I forgot the incident. It was better on the deck. There was fresh air. Down in the ship, it smelled bad. And the stars were beautiful; a lot brighter and three times bigger than I had ever seen in Brooklyn. Besides, I wasn't alone. There was another boy who slept on the deck. His name was Chin, he was Chinese, a nice boy—alone and quiet, like me. After the ship, I never saw him again."

It took twenty-one days to cross the Atlantic. The ship had to zigzag all over the Atlantic to avoid enemy submarines. My father was so sick on the voyage, vomiting everyday. The food was bad. It was all pretty miserable. Finally, the ship arrived. He was in Oran, North Africa, and about two weeks were spent while it was decided where the soldiers in his unit would go next. The *S.S. Orantes* was the ship that took Private Bloomberg from Africa to Sorrento, Italy. By that time, the Americans had taken Sicily. "It was an English ship," Dad remembered. "And years later I learned that the same ship forty years before had brought immigrants to Ellis Island." He thought of his parents.

Sorrento was bombed out when their ship arrived; only rubble remained. From there his unit went to Naples. "There had been a battle and the Germans lost. So, when we got there, the whole town came out to greet us—women, men, and children. Sophia Loren was from there. She was seven. Maybe she waved." Pompeii was the next stop on his brief but dangerous Italian tour. "We slept in the street, in the mud in foxholes right by Mount Vesuvius. All the German equipment was left behind, so we took it up including the *vasser* (water).

"We then went on a four-month campaign into the Italian mountains. There was a historic battle against the Germans that were hiding in a Monastery at Monte Casino. We slept in foxholes. After a couple of weeks, we'd rotate for a two to three-day break; then right back into the same foxhole. We would fight at night, and the flashes from the bombs were like a fireworks show, but silent. Beautiful. Then in five to six seconds, you'd hear the sound because it was so far away.

"One freezing night, I was with three or four others on advance patrol and I took a wrong turn; I got separated and lost. I kept walking and walking and the next thing I knew I was in a field of dead Germans. Bodies everywhere. I could see them because of the flashes of light. I could also see the red rope. It was a rope that laid out the positions around the mines. I was in a minefield, alone in the dark with dead Germans. I followed the rope all the way down the mountain. It took me two hours but finally I saw a U.S. ambulance. I told the soldier that I was lost and separated from my unit. It was in the middle of the night so he asked me if I wanted to sleep in the ambulance. It was the first bed I had slept in and the best sleep I had in months."

I ASKED MY FATHER how scared he was. "The army training gives you a different kind of brain. I didn't think about it. I just found a way out." After a few months, the Air Force bombed the monastery.

He spent several more months in the Italian Alps. "When we were in Italy, little boys, five or six year old, would come over to us with buckets. They were starving. We gave them what we had. Fish, soup, scrambled eggs, vegetables, cocoa, fruit, meat; all mixed up into the same bucket. They didn't care. It was food. One day, we went to a farmhouse for something to eat. I don't know why, it was they who were starving. The other boys made me speak to the Italian farmers. They called me 'The Interpreter' because I knew a few Italian words. That's what happens when you grow up in Brooklyn. So, I said, *mangia,* and they gave us some Chianti. Then, they found some raw goat cheese and shared it. It was awful. We had the runs for the next four days. I don't know why we did that. We had food. I guess, we were just boys, we were curious and it was free."

AUTHOR'S NOTE: AT THIS point, it is January 1944. Most of my father's recollection regarding dates, times and places for events was fairly accurate. But he expressed a concern that some of his guesstimates may be off.

AFTER A COUPLE OF weeks of training, the troops were told that they were going on a secret mission. They were put on an LST (Landing Ship, Tank), the type of boats used in the invasion at Normandy, to pull off a baby D-Day. From there they were sent to Anzio. My father was an assistant machine gunner. The battle of Anzio was underway. Arriving two days into the fight, Anzio beachhead had already been bombed out from the invasion. All the people, the civilians and captured POWs, were hiding and sleeping in the caves. The Germans had pulled their troops out of the south of France for this battle.

"They outnumbered us three to one. And my group, about three hundred of us, were lying on the ground at night. The Germans sent up flares so that they could go on bombing. Then, fifty to a hundred of us were sent to scout the Germans, to see how many of them there were, and what they had. We lay down on the ground because they were shooting at us. Then the shooting stopped and we waited until the crack of dawn until we got up. It was a ruse. The Germans came rushing out. '*Surrendie! Surrendie*'! We had to stand up with our hands in the air. We had no choice. There were dead Americans all over the battlefield. I ripped off my dog tags. I had to. When the Germans captured me, I couldn't let them know I was Jewish. On the dog tags were the first initial of the soldier's religion, in case they needed to read you last rights. There was an '*H*' on mine; '*H*' for Hebrew. From that moment on, I was M.I.A."

AUTHOR'S NOTE: FOR MOST of my life, my father never spoke of his fourteen months as a Jewish American Prisoner of War under Nazi control. But there were two tales he did recount. The following is one of them:

THE PRISONERS WERE TAKEN to nearby farmhouses and separated, then joined with other American Prisoners of War. "There was a

German Intelligence Officer who was educated in Oxford, England. He spoke perfect English and interviewed every fifth person. Of course, I was one of them. 'What are the troops? How many? How many Americans? What is your Commander's name? Army name? Infantry? Division?' demanded the German Officer. He knew more than I did!" my father exclaimed. "I had nothing to tell. I didn't know anything! Then, he let me go."

From there the prisoners were put on trucks and were transported about forty miles to Rome. The Germans showed off to the Italians, bragging about all the Americans they had captured! But my father remembered seeing Rome's beautiful places: The Coliseum, The Forum, Circus Maximus. Their destination from Rome was Cineceti.

My father spent several months in Cineceti until, in April of 1944, the Germans moved the soldiers a couple of hundred miles north to LaTrina, Italy. There was another Italian camp near Florence.

"We were starving. For three hundred people, there was one giant bowl of soup. I had to wait in line for a tiny amount. And when I got it, the soup had pieces of a horse's head in it—the mouth with the teeth. I had to push it aside to eat. And the bread, it was made of sawdust. The coffee was ersatz, made out of burnt barley. People were fainting because they were so weak with hunger. The camp was broken into groups—Americans, English, French, and there were Arabs, I guess from Algeria and Morocco. The Arabs had the muscle and took all the bread; kept it for themselves. I was starving so one day I approached them and bargained for a piece of bread. They wanted the watch that Grandpa had given to me. I traded it and before they gave me the bread they promised, they cut off a big piece and took it back for themselves. They cheated me and I was mad but had no choice. I was starving. Then I had to hide the little piece of bread in my jacket from the other soldiers because they were starving too and they'd take it from me. I found a corner and ate it in the dark. My stomach had shrunk so much, it hurt for days just from that little piece of bread.

"It was in this camp that the Germans took our uniforms," he added. "Instead, they gave us Italian uniforms. The jacket was too short, the pants were like knickers and the shoes would squeak. I think they took the American clothes so they could fool the Americans during the Battle of the Bulge."

My father was in the camp at LaTrina for about six weeks. While he was there, Max Schmeling, the famous boxer visited the camp. He was propaganda for the Germans. They were shooting their newsreels there. Max Schmeling was a German boxer who fought in the States before the war. After he lost to Joe Lewis, he returned to Germany.

"There were American planes flying above. One of us pointed up to one of the planes and said, 'Hey, Max Schmeling, Joe Lewis is in that plane!' The jokester, Max Schmeling covered his head and ducked." Years later, my father recounts, Max Schmeling gave a lot to Jewish charities.

After six weeks, the men were moved. They were put into boxcars, about thirty to forty of them. There was no food, and one wooden kettle for a toilet for the whole boxcar. The train made stops for them to have little bits of water and food. After ten or so days, they arrived near Mooseberg, Germany, at Stalag 7A, an internment camp. My father said he had lost one hundred pounds in about eight weeks.

At Stalag 7A, there were American, British and French soldiers all in different barracks. The conditions were horrible—straw mattresses, wooden floors. Outside, there were huge loudspeakers playing German music all day—marching, singing, *Lily Marlene*. Finally, Red Cross food packages were delivered to the prisoners.

"Getting food was like New Years Eve, Christmas and everybody's birthday all rolled into one," my father said. "It was a celebration just to eat. We got back our American uniforms and every week we got packages of food; *KLIM* (milk spelled backward—it was powdered), *Spam*, canned fruit and cookies. The Germans gave us soup and a piece of bread everyday. I gained back some weight, which was good because they gave us work detail. I had to haul logs. And whom do you think I ran into when I was there—the boy that cut the ropes on the bed on the Liberty Ship. But now, he was changed. Not so much of a prankster as a POW; he wasn't laughing, wasn't happy."

After about six weeks in the camp, the prisoners went on strike. The Germans took a group of prisoners to work in a German airfield, but forcing prisoners of war to work in enemy military bases was a violation of the Geneva Convention. So the soldiers refused to work. The Germans knew the prisoners were right but they did not like their defiance and set out to punish them. The next day they took them back to the airfield, and there were trucks all around them. When the backs of the trucks were opened, there were Germans behind machine guns making like they were going to shoot us. A German General told his officers not to do anything; don't shoot. After the strike, two to three hundred American prisoners were shipped to Munich, Germany.

"They took us to a schoolhouse, Number 2, Shulstrasse. It was set up for us; triple-deck bunk beds for twenty to thirty of us in a room. We were divided into work groups of about five to six boys."

My father spent the entire summer of 1944 in the schoolhouse in Munich. It was there that he first met the civilians of this war.

"We met a lot of nice people. They took us out in groups for work duty. Work, we hardly did any. I don't know why they took us out. Maybe it was just to give us a break, some fresh air. I don't know. There was a nice Austrian soldier, Bruno, very friendly. He gave me a picture of him and I still have it at the house. Once, we were put on a trolley and went to work for this old man about sixty or seventy years old. We were supposed to dig wells but we didn't know how, so the old man did all the digging! He liked to work. After a few hours, he took all of us out for lunch—beer, cheese, bread, and potato salad. It was Munich Lowenbrau Beer Hall but there was no meat because of the war."

Sundays in the schoolhouse there was nothing to do. My father spent his days staring out the window. From there he was able to see a local store with pictures of Hitler hanging in the window, Frauenkirk which is a large church in the city of Munich, and the Deutchesmuseum, Munich's famous museum. He spoke of the German newspaper they would receive every week, printed in English. One week they read about the D-Day invasion. The Americans thought the war would be over by the end of the year.

It was from the schoolhouse in Munich that my father was able to write to his family for the first time. "They couldn't believe I was still alive. And I got letters and postcards back and sent some home. I still have those, Hitler stamps and all."

After about six weeks, the air raids on Munich began. "We had to hide in the basement every night. Once, during the day, we took a trolley to a job where the Germans were building a lot of wooden barracks. When we got there, we saw a thousand airplanes flying overhead. We knew they were American because the Germans did not have an air force that large or planes that big. They were dropping incendiary bombs. Those don't really explode but cause big fires. The Germans made us go into a makeshift shelter—just some dirt dug out and piled about eight feet off the ground. When the bombing stopped, we got out of the shelter. Every one of the barracks was burnt to the ground. After that, they took us back to the schoolhouse."

During this summer of 1944, the British were bombing Munich by night and the Americans were bombing by day. "All over Munich, the houses were on fire so one night the Germans took us into Munich to participate in a bucket brigade. It was like putting out a volcano with an eyedropper. It wasn't going to work. Besides, it was against the Geneva Convention—consorting with the enemy. We refused to do it. But one of the German guards pointed a pistol at my head and made us go into the burning house." Finally, the Germans realized that the buckets were not going to work and took the prisoners back to the schoolhouse where they were put into solitary confinement. "They put about four or five of us into a potato storage room. We had to stand on potatoes in water for about an hour. It was a small punishment."

A few days later, end of August,1944, the Germans made a group of about three hundred soldiers leave Munich. They and my father were marched through the streets. From there, the men spent two weeks in boxcars before they arrived way up north near Szczecin at a camp called Stalag 2B. "I could see outside the boxcar through small holes with wire mesh, it was a beautiful trip through mountains and beautiful grassy hills and trees, up north almost to Poland. It was cold, though, freezing cold."

Camp Stalag 2B was large. Thousands of English, French, American and Russian prisoners were there but in separate barracks. They did a lot of work duty. "One time we went to a farm house to pick potatoes. It was freezing, so cold that the Germans gave us wooden shoes from Holland to wear. We all laughed and refused to wear them. They made us. At first, they were hard to walk in but we got used to them. Never laughed at them again. Our feet never got cold."

AUTHOR'S NOTE: IT WAS regarding this camp, Stalag 2B, that I remember the second of the two stories my father recounted when I was young:

"THERE WAS A GERMAN officer who had lived in the United States for a while and knew my name was Bloomberg. I was unloading coal from a truck when he pointed a rifle at me and asked me if I was Jewish. I was so scared but I just looked at him and said, 'Isn't there a German General Werner Von Bloomberg?' He got mad and kept screaming *'Schnell! Schnell!'* That means *fast.* I had to unload the entire truck of coal myself really fast with his rifle pointing at me the whole day. Covered in coal, that night I told all of the boys that were with me what had happened. The next day another German officer came in and shouted *'Alles Juden Aufstehen!'* (All Jews stand up.) Then, like they had a signal, one of the American prisoners said 'All right boys!' And all of the Americans, about fifteen, stood up. The German officer exclaimed, *'Scheiss!'* (Sh*t!), then stormed out. There was another Jewish boy in the group. Those boys saved a lot of trouble for us, me and the other boy."

In October of 1944, the prisoners were divided into two work groups about forty boys each. They were taken to Hammerschtein, Germany, and from there, were transported to Janekow, Poland. It was for work detail and they were housed in a garage with nothing but a potbelly stove. "It was a starch factory where they made potatoes into powder to make bread and crude potato chips to feed hogs. My job was to carry giant bags of this starch labeled *Hochfein Marketfalke,* each weighing 100 kilos (220 pounds). My knees buckled just having it on my back. It took weeks to build up my strength."

My father was at the factory for four months.

"One day the Germans came into the garage with a newspaper that read the Germans were launching V1 Rockets. The soldier then held up a picture of the V2 rocket. Proud, he boasted that the Germans would win the war because the rockets were so powerful they could go all the way to England—a huge accomplishment for technology in 1944."

Christmas and New Years Day, 1945, came and went while Private Arthur Bloomberg was at the factory. "One day, we saw from the garage, people and cows and horses walking west. Then we saw a cow that had gotten loose. One boy that was with us, Harry, ran out and jumped on the cow's back and killed it—stabbed it with a dagger over and over. We brought it back and cooked it on the potbelly stove. We had steaks for a week. Harry, he was a small boy, too." In 2002, my father reunited with Harry in Scottsdale, Arizona. I heard all about the cow.

In February 1945, German officers came into the garage and told them that they had one hour and a half to get out. Everyone had to go west. "We had only a little time and we wanted to pack up our food. I took the burlap from the potato sacks and sewed shoulder straps and flaps onto it and made myself a backpack. Others saw what I did and did the same. Some found wood and made wagons. We tried to get as much food as we could to carry along. Then, we started marching. But, the bags and carts were so heavy, that we couldn't carry them. One by one we had to start throwing the food out. For about a mile and a half, there was food all along the road."

Six days a week, for six weeks, my father walked six hundred miles across Germany. "As we were walking, we saw the German soldiers heading toward the front of the procession with horse-drawn wagons pulling their supplies. Then, we knew the Germans had to be losing the war. Thousands of people were marching down the road with cows and horses and wagons. The Russians were coming and they had to get out. So many people, it looked like a John Ford epic film. We watched the Germans burn their own factories so the Allies couldn't get them."

The prisoners were starving. "We ate raw potatoes, anything we could get from the fields. We slept in barns and smelled like old cows. And we were cold, ice-cold. Our feet always were numb. And each village looked the same. We'd walk fifteen, twenty miles to another village and it looked just like the one we slept in the night before; small village, church spires."

Finally, they arrived at their final destination. "They put us into a camp and two days after we arrived we found out that President Roosevelt had died. It was really sad because he was the only president most of us knew."

The next morning, my father woke up and heard the other prisoners yelling 'They're gone!' All the Germans were gone and the door to the barracks was wide open. "We started walking out when a new bunch of Germans came in and told us that we were going to walk in the direction of the Americans. Then a German officer gave me his rifle. They were surrendering! We took them down the road like they were our prisoners. A civilian came up to us and showed us a matchbox he found on the road. It read *Philadelphia*. We knew the Americans were near. Then, the American tanks began coming toward us. They were firing up in the air, testing for resistance. There had to be at least one hundred of them. When they spotted us, all beaten up, they threw K-rations to us. Then, we saw a group of about thirty-to-forty Holocaust survivors. They were like sticks in striped pajamas. We raced into a German bakery and I yelled at the man running it to give all of his bread to the Holocaust survivors. And he did; we cleaned out the bakery. The survivors took the bread and said nothing. They were just like zombies. That night in the barracks it was our second big celebration just like when we got food for the first time in months, a year ago."

The rescued troops were taken to an airfield in France. "It was the first time I was ever in an airplane. And when the plane took off, I could see hundreds and hundreds of huge craters, each fifty to sixty feet wide. They were from the bombs and they were everywhere!" Their plane landed at a camp affectionately called Camp Lucky Strike. There, still in France, he stayed for two weeks.

"There were thousands of us and we were given a lot to eat. We were all so skinny and had things like eggnog to build up our strength. Then, we were taken to LaHavre, France, where ships were to take us to Southampton, England. There, I boarded another Liberty Ship and we crossed the Atlantic Ocean. This time it took seven or eight days, not twenty-one. No torpedoes to avoid now.

"In the distance, I could see the Ferris Wheel!" my father recounted. It was Coney Island he could see from the Liberty Ship and it was home. "When we got to Fort Dix, New Jersey, we learned that Hitler committed suicide. He was dead!" my father gleefully recalled. "There, we were given civilian clothes, new stuff," he continued on. "And when we went to eat, guess who was serving us? German prisoners of war! When we saw them, we called to them in German. They were shocked! By the way," he added. "The German POWs were well fed and well dressed."

THE RETURNING AMERICAN SOLDIERS had gotten a ninety-day furlough and my father received about six hundred dollars in back pay. In those days it was a fortune. "When I arrived at my house, my mother answered the door. She didn't know I was returning and I was so skinny, she did not recognize me. It took her a while but all of a sudden, she started to cry and grabbed me. My whole family came to the door to greet me. It was Mother's Day.

"During and after my furlough, I took an interest in foreign films because of all the sights I had seen in Europe. One film called *Open City* was about World War II and the city of Rome. Rome had been declared an open city so that no bombs on either side would destroy its magnificent ruins. There were all the incredible sights I had seen from the bus as a Prisoner of War. Another film, *Grand Illusion* had taken place during World War I. It was made way before I had gone to war. But the story and scenery had so paralleled my experience, it sent chills. The movie was about Germans who captured French soldiers as Prisoners of War. The French were put in boxcars and traveled to northern Germany. There, were the scenes of the countryside and the snow-covered mountains; trees, hills and grass until their final destination, a POW camp. It was the same mountains and scenery, I had seen from the little wire mesh hole of the boxcar. Only in the movie, I could see the outside of the boxcar as it traveled up the mountains and hills. Also, in the movie, there were two army buddies, best of friends, who came to hate each other. It was the exact opposite of my experience with the prankster boy who cut the ropes of my bed on the Liberty ship, the one who became my best friend at Stalag 7A."

After furlough, the Army sent my father to Lake Placid to get medical help and have his teeth fixed. Eighteen months of starving causes a lot of problems of which most of us are too fortunate to be aware. When he returned to Fort Dix, the news of the atomic bombs and the Japanese surrender was golden. There were parties in the streets. This terrible war had come to an end. My father spent the rest of his time in the army typing out hundreds of discharge papers. Then, in December of 1945, Private Bloomberg finally went home for good.

PRIVATE ARTHUR BLOOMBERG RECEIVED the Bronze Star, the Medal of Good Conduct, the Combat Infantry Badge, Prisoner of War Medal and the European Theater of Operations Medal. No Purple Heart was given to Prisoners of War before 1947. The scars of this war left my dad with lifelong injuries and a status of 100-percent Disabled American Veteran.

Now that he has opened up, if there was any one message my father wishes to share at this time in his life, it is this: "This is the story of just one Prisoner of War during this terrible time. But there are thousands of stories from thousands of Prisoners of War just like myself. They should all be recorded for future generations; just like the hatred of the Holocaust and murders at the 1972 Olympics in Munich, Germany."

Arthur Bloomberg lives in Florida with his wife, my mother, Irene. They met in 1949 on the Coney Island beach.

By Dr. Linda Bloomberg Simon, in tribute to and told by her father, Private Arthur Bloomberg: American Ex-Prisoner of War, Disabled American Veteran, Europe 0151 — World War II 45th Division, 157th Infantry, Company C — The Thunderbirds

A Navy Man

O N DECEMBER 7, 1941, Vera Pate and her three sons waited on the dock in San Diego, California. The *U.S.S. Saratoga* was expected that morning. Her husband, CPO (Chief Petty Officer) Clyde T. Pate, had been assigned to the aircraft carrier in 1939. During his Navy career he became a printer and was in charge of the print shop on the "Sara." The family was not reunited that morning. For the next four years they would be together only when Vera loaded boys and bags into their 1932 Oldsmobile and drove from Long Beach, California, to Bremerton, Washington, for a few precious weeks or months when the *Saratoga* was in for repairs. Japanese kamikazes, bombs and torpedoes damaged the ship during actions off of Guadalcanal, Iwo Jima, and as partners with the British near Singapore and Malaysia in the Java Sea.

In 1920 Clyde lied about his age and joined the Navy in Long Beach, California. He was sixteen. He had been left in an orphanage in Tucson, Arizona, when he was ten, and had been on his own (with a few helping hands now and then) since he was twelve. The Navy became his home, his family. Most of the time he was assigned to ships in the Asiatic Fleet. During his late teens and twenties he was a boxer, featherweight class. He won the title of Featherweight Champion of the Asiatic Fleet. He boxed for money, for prestige and just to show he could amount to something. "Bobby" Pate and "Terrible Terry" were two of his nicknames. Two of his sons would inherit those names.

While home-ported in Shanghai, China, he met Vera, a beautiful, young Russian refugee. Vera's father had been a Cossack in the service of the Czar and they fled Siberia at the time of the Russian Revolution. At first Vera refused to have anything to do with Clyde but he knew she was the love of his life and so he persisted. They married on November 13, 1931 at the U.S. Consulate in Shanghai.

Clyde retired from the Navy in 1945 when the *Saratoga* returned at the end of WWII. He had served on the *Saratoga* for the full duration of the war. He rarely talked about his war experiences, but sometimes wondered what had happened to the men he trained to be printers. He was recalled during the Korean War and served for two more years. After his second Navy retirement he worked as a printer for Hughes and Douglas Aircraft in Tucson and Long Beach.

He passed away six months before what would have been his and Vera's sixtieth anniversary. His family is proud of his service to our country, his ability to start with nothing and make something of himself. His sons and their families salute him. Well done.

By Marilyn Pate,
in memory of her father-in-law,
Clyde Talmage Pate, CPO, U.S. Navy
U.S.S. Saratoga CV 3

Hollywood Marines

F OR A YOUNG, INEXPERIENCED lieutenant like me, just keeping up with Colonel States Tomkins presented a daily challenge. Staying a step ahead of him proved impossible. No matter how new the information I served up in my morning briefing, he already knew it.

"Sir, at three this morning, the MPs reported a corporal in Fox Company molested a woman in Isabella Segunda."

"Oh, hell, Ah know that."

I hurried to the next item. "Sir, there's a disabled *amtrac* sitting on Green Beach."

"Oh, hell, Ah know that." "I" and "my" always came out "Ah" and "mah, " pinpointing his southern upbringing.

Responsible for planning the disposition of marines, tanks and motor vehicles on board our naval warships, I experienced an all-expense paid cruise to the Caribbean island of Vieques in 1953, courtesy of Colonel Tomkins and the United States Marine Corps. Just six miles east of Puerto Rico, palm-sheltered Vieques served as a training ground where our Marines and Navy coordinated landing operations and war games. Although President Eisenhower recently had ended the Korean War, short, powerfully built, Colonel Tomkins stressed the importance of remaining combat-ready.

"You stand around waiting for something to happen, and I guarantee you, it will," he preached. "The Marines Corps must be ready." When he wasn't speaking through a stubby cigar, his tongue gently massaged "Corps" into a two-syllable word.

Vieques was the ideal ground to prepare for anything the enemy could throw at us. Its leafy terrain, blistering sun and bug-nurturing temperatures made it a near twin to Iwo Jima, Saipan and Tarawa. Almost a decade had passed since the battles for those tiny Pacific Islands, yet memories of the blood spilled on them remained fresh in the minds of experienced officers like Colonel Tomkins. Their mission was to make sure we'd be ready if we ever had to face the same hellish struggles.

"Just one more, sir," I said, wrapping up my report. "Warner Brothers wants to film a landing on Green Beach. They need two-hundred troops with full packs, rifles, mortars and light machine guns."

"Hell, Ah know that," he said. Then he grew pensive. "We gotta give a party for those Warner Brothers people one of these nights. Survey some good whisky at the officer's mess and we'll get the crew and the cast over for a get-together."

"Aye, aye sir." I about-faced and thought back to the colonel's words before sailing from North Carolina's Morehead City, the embarkation point nearest Camp LeJeune, our home base. Why had he spent so much time describing Vieques as the ideal train-ing ground for jungle warfare, and not once said it was the ideal location for Warner Brothers to film a movie about jungle warfare? Yet, in pursuit of realistic war situations, busy film crews led by Raoul Walsh, their eye-patched director, overran the island. Our efforts to achieve combat readiness gave way to achieving *movie* readiness — the daily allocation of tanks, trucks and troops needed to satisfy Warner Brothers.

Although a lowly first lieutenant, I had no trouble figuring the word had come down from Washington to give them all-out sup-port. The movie, titled *Battle Cry*, was based on Leon Uris' novel of the same name. Uris, who later authored *Exodus* and *Trinity*, built his front-line war story around his experiences with a marine communications battalion that fought its way through the Pacific. I assumed that top brass backed the film because they believed it would pump enlistments the same way prior movies like *Sands of Iwo Jima* and *Gung Ho* did. The colonel and the rest of us had no choice but to see that the Hollywood people got all the help they required. For the first time, following orders was fun, even a little glamorous.

I relayed the colonel's party idea to our executive officer who immediately arranged for booze, ice, and a couple of messmen to serve drinks. Colonel Tomkins extended the invitations, and a few nights later leading man Van Heflin preceded four actors into the colonel's hut.

Warner Brothers had assigned Heflin, a Hollywood veteran who won an Oscar ten years previously, to play the part of Major Sam Huxley, C.O., Second Battalion, Sixth Marine Regiment, the outfit Uris dubbed "Huxley's Harlots" in his best-selling novel. Close behind came James Whitmore, cast in the role of Mac, the crusty master sergeant who served as the film's narrator. Tab Hunter, Aldo Ray, and a likable, little known actor, William Campbell, followed.

Hunter, probably no more than twenty, appeared respectfully quiet, even overawed, in the company of the colonel and his staff. So did William Campbell, who made headlines some years later while the first husband of Judith Campbell Exner, the beauty alleged to have had a two-year affair with President Kennedy.

Scarcely through his first drink, Aldo Ray grew boisterous. His unintelligible dirty jokes fell flat. His boast of his recent Oscar nomination for best actor in support of Tracy and Hepburn's *Pat and Mike* bored us. But Van Heflin and James Whitmore were perfect gentlemen—mature, able and eager to converse with the colonel on any level.

Talk got around to war movies, and the colonel expressed a liking for *Steel Helmet*, a 1951 low-budget, black and white film about the Korean War. He looked Whitmore directly in the eye, summoned up every ounce of personal sincerity, and said, "Jimmy, mah wife and I loved you in Steel Helmet."

Whitmore returned the colonel's look with an equally earnest gaze, "Colonel, I wasn't *in* Steel Helmet."

Colonel Tomkins never missed a beat, "Oh, hell, Ah know that." I almost choked on my drink.

The colonel's party ended quietly. Eventually, the Warner Brothers crew and cast returned to Hollywood to complete the shooting of interior scenes. I got to see more of the Caribbean while I pulled MP duty in San Juan and St. Thomas before we steamed back to Camp LeJeune.

More than 50 years later, I still have not seen *Battle Cry* from start to finish, though I have read the novel and seen many individual parts on TV re-runs. Van Heflin has passed on, and white-haired James Whitmore pitched *Miracle-Gro* plant food on TV.

Stretching out with a recent *New York Times* Sunday Travel Section, I was startled by the page-one headline—"Vieques, New Caribbean Hot Spot." I concluded that Puerto Rican citizens had won their battle to dislodge the Navy and Marine Corps. Tragically, innocent islanders had been killed by bombs and unexploded ordnance left over from the many years of maneuvers there. According to the *Times*, the military training ground is now an island paradise suitable for more peaceful pleasures.

I don't know what's become of Colonel States Tomkins, but whenever I watched a TV commercial featuring James Whitmore intoning the benefits of *Miracle-Gro*, I couldn't help imagining the colonel somewhere viewing the same commercial and saying, "Oh hell, Ah know that."

By Robert Anthony Natiello
First Lieutenant, USMCR
Force Troops, Combat Service Group

The Day the Lilies Bloomed

A STATUE OF A YOUNG fighter pilot stands in front of the old capitol building in Phoenix, Arizona. The flyer's name was Frank Luke, Jr., and his tour of duty in World War I was brief but spectacular. Downing eighteen enemy in less than a month, he became one of only four fighter pilots awarded the Congressional Medal of Honor in that war. But there's more to the Frank Luke story than brave deeds in the skies above France. A most unusual event is recorded in the family Bible. It took place six thousand miles from the war, back home at Frank's parents' house in Phoenix.

IN SEPTEMBER 1917, AT age twenty, Frank was a handsome, happy-go-lucky lad. Fascinated by the new flying machines as a teenager, he joined the army and was accepted into flight training. At the end of his training, he was commissioned as a 2nd Lieutenant and given a fourteen-day leave. He went to Phoenix to be with his family one last time before going off to war.

One day during the leave, Frank was heading off to pal around with some old classmates. On his way out the door, his mother, Tillie, stopped him. She laid a hand on his arm and said, "Frank, dear, I've been meaning to ask you to plant some lily bulbs for me. The weather's so perfect for it today. Would you mind terribly?" Tillie was known for her sweet and amiable nature, and Frank was happy to oblige her. He took the bag of bulbs and spent sometime alone in the front yard before leaving to find his friends. Just a few days later, he shipped out to join the war in France.

FRANK'S TOUR OF DUTY was uneventful until September 1918. During that month he came to specialize in the destruction of German observation balloons, as well as other enemy aircraft. In a seventeen-day period, Frank broke every record for downing enemy aircraft. Dubbed the "Balloon Buster," he destroyed one after another, sometimes with his partner and sometimes on his own. On one astounding mission, he shot down three planes and two balloons in just ten minutes. All together, in those few days Frank accounted for fourteen balloons and four German planes. He was christened the American "Ace of Aces" of his day.

BACK IN PHOENIX, THE family read about Frank's brave exploits in the newspapers. Then, on September 29, his mother stepped into the front yard to find an amazing sight. The lilies that Frank had planted on leave had suddenly burst into bloom—strangely out of season. But that wasn't all. Once blooming, it was clear that they formed the cross-like shape of an airplane! Frank was crazy about airplanes and also a devout Catholic, so his intention could have been either.

The family members gathered and exclaimed at the sight, saying those lilies should have bloomed in June, not September! And, how like Frank it was to have planted them in some special way. Word of the marvel spread. A newspaper photographer came to the house and that week the Sunday paper ran a photo of Tillie standing beside the cross of lilies.

But, from the first moment she saw them, Tillie's response to the flowers was one of sorrow. She brushed away tears, certain that something must be wrong with Frank. On November 25, two weeks after the Armistice ended the war, Tillie's fears were realized. The family received notification from the Red Cross that Frank was missing in action. They would learn much later that Frank had single-handedly shot down three German observation balloons on his last mission. He was wounded in flight and managed to land without crashing in Murveaux. But his wounds were severe, and he died later that day on September 29—the day the lilies bloomed.

By Jane Eppinga,
the account of 2nd Lieutenant Frank Luke,
Signal Corps Aviation Service, 27th Aero Squadron

And the Band Played On

IT WAS JULY 1945, on Tinian Island in the Pacific Ocean, and Sergeant Jim Glasgow was surprised to see a boyhood friend, Ed Haverstad, from Barnesville, Minnesota, on the other side of the road. He walked over to say, "Hi." and then asked him a question.

"You guys must have something special going on. What's happening?"

A look of fear flashed in his friend's eyes and, without a word, he turned and walked away. Jim didn't expect Ed's strange reaction, and wondered if there was a secret operation going on. Perhaps Ed had been instructed not to talk to anyone outside his group?

Jim knew that Ed's unit, the 509th Bomb Group, recently had arrived on Tinian and was isolated in a restricted area on North Field. Unlike the other bomb groups on the island, the 509th did not participate in the normal combat operations against Japan. Instead, they conducted navigational flights and practices with large dummy bombs. They flew specially modified B-29s that were lightweight and equipped with powerful fuel-injected engines.

What was the secret?

Jim Glasgow was a clarinet player in the 313th Wing Band that arrived on Tinian in February 1945. He had been stationed at Davis-Monthan Airbase in Tucson, Arizona, where his outfit was the 592nd Air Force Band when the band received orders to go overseas. At the airbase in Tucson they played parades for special occasions, music to greet dignitaries arriving on planes, bond-drive radio broadcasts, and concerts in Armory Park. There were two dance bands and Jim directed the smaller one and also played tenor saxophone.

The end of January, the band left Tucson by train, and traveled to San Francisco, from where they would ship out. Before boarding the transport ship, the band members lined up on the wharf with their backpacks and duffle bags. After each man gave his rank and serial number to the officer in charge, they proceeded to their quarters below the deck, where bunks were stacked five high. On ship they were kept busy with chores. Jim was assigned to chip paint off the bow of the ship.

It took the transport ship six or seven days to reach Hawaii since it had to zigzag all the way — a safety precaution to avoid enemy submarines. The servicemen had a couple of days to rest and relax in Hawaii, before boarding the ship again, still not knowing their destination.

While at sea, the band learned that they were going to Tinian — an island that the Marines had taken from the Japanese. Guam, Saipan and Tinian make up the Mariana Islands; Tinian is the smallest. Like Guam and Saipan, it was a B-29 airbase from where the planes took off for Japan, returning after their missions were completed.

When the band members disembarked, they saw Seabees (CBs, Construction Battalions) building tent barracks with wood bases and canvas tops. They worked around the clock for months, building the necessary facilities for the military and transforming an existing airfield that was not large enough to handle the hundreds of superfortresses and their crews, into the world's largest operational base — North Field, and a smaller airfield — West Field.

When the band was assigned a barracks, their instruments were delivered to them and they settled in. They rehearsed every morning and afternoon under the direction of their new band director, Jake Evans. Their duties were about the same as those at Davis-Monthan Airbase in Tucson — parades and meeting planes bringing VIPs. In addition, they entertained the troops. The band played concert music, swing music, and performed humorous musical skits. There was a large outdoor screen where the men watched movies. The band always played before a movie was shown, using the stage in front of the screen. They also provided the music for USO shows that came to Tinian.

THERE WERE HUNDREDS OF B-29s in long rows beside the six runways, four at North Field, and two at West Field. Each runway was a ten-lane highway, almost two miles long, ending at the steep limestone cliffs that ringed the island. Here the planes dropped down a short distance to cool the engines before heading to Japan with a full load of gas.

The men quickly became used to seeing the sky darkened with B-29s flying over, either leaving on a raid or returning.

A few days after trying to talk to his old schoolmate, the question Jim asked him was answered. On August 6, news came over the radio that Hiroshima had been destroyed by the atomic bomb called "Little Boy". The airplane that carried the bomb was the *Enola Gay*, based on Tinian.

On that fateful day the *Enola Gay* taxied out on to North Field Runway Able.

Captain Paul Tibbets was at the controls. The bomber was overweight and he was forced to use as much of the two-mile runway as possible. A crash would result in instant death for the entire crew. At the last possible moment, he pulled back on the yoke and the heavily laden bomber was airborne. Seven B-29s participated in the first atomic mission as support for the *Enola Gay*.

"Was Ed in one of those bombers?" Jim wondered when he realized his friend was a part of this top-secret mission. Now he understood why Ed couldn't talk to him. There was too much at stake and the information was highly restricted.

ON AUGUST 8, A B-29 nicknamed *BOCKSCAR* dropped the atomic bomb, "Fat Man" on Nagasaki. The name painted on the aircraft after the mission has no apostrophe and it is painted in all capital letters. It was named after the pilot of its regular crew, Frederick C Bock. On the day of the attack *Bockscar* was manned by the crew of *The Great Artiste*, and was commanded by Major Charles W. Sweeny of Massachusetts.

On hearing news of the bombings, all the military on Tinian felt the war would be over in a few days. With happy thoughts of soon going home, they relaxed enough to enjoy a new recreation. Navy PT boats (Patrol Torpedo boats) gave the airmen rides around Tinian and other nearby islands.

On September 2, 1945, the Japanese surrendered to the United States and signed a peace treaty on the deck of the battleship *U.S.S. Missouri* in Tokyo Harbor. The war was over and the men were anxious to go home.

A point system was devised to determine the order in which they could return. Sixty points was the total required for the first men to return home and be discharged.

Points were given for: 1) number of years of service; 2) amount of time overseas; 3) for family — wife and number of children. Each child counted 12 points. Jim Glasgow was the first band member to have 60 points. He said his goodbyes to the band and went to Saipan to join a group that was returning to the States.

The trip home didn't take long, since the ship no longer had to zigzag to avoid enemy submarines. Before docking at San Francisco, a WAC (Women's Air Corp) military band on a small boat in the harbor played songs to greet the returning servicemen, and as the ship pulled in, a larger WAC band was there to welcome them home. The Red Cross provided coffee and doughnuts for the troops as they left the ship and U.S. Army trucks were on hand to take them to barracks on a nearby airfield.

Unexplainably, Jim was given a room in a barracks on the second floor and he was the only person there. It was a strange feeling being alone. He didn't hear the call to supper and was hungry, so he went down to the mess hall and found that it was empty, except for the servers, and supper was over. The mess hall crew was a friendly bunch, and most, or perhaps all, were Japanese prisoners of war. Jim was relieved to find there was plenty of food. In fact, the servers gave him very generous amounts — more than he could eat.

The following day he boarded the train, bound for Los Angeles. There he received his discharge papers. Soon the Southern Pacific train, packed with returning servicemen, took him to Tucson to his wife, Jeanne, and the baby son he had never seen, born April 17, 1945, while his Daddy was on Tinian. Finally, Jim was a civilian again, anxious to return to college and happy to get on with his life.

Jim never saw Ed again, but, there will forever be days when his boyhood friend's face flies up through Jim's past, the fear flashing in his eyes on that far away island called Tinian. *Where is he?* Jim hopes and prays that he, too, came home to those he loved.

By Jeanne Pafford Glasgow,
her husband's story, Sgt James Glasgow,
313th Wing Band, U.S. Army Air Corps

A Confederate Soldier

AUTHOR'S NOTE: THE SUBJECT of this account, Martin Luther Morris (1846-1927), was the author's grandfather. He joined the Confederate Army in 1862, in Clarksville, Tennessee, and was paroled (discharged) in 1864, in Gainesville, Alabama. Sources are *Tennesseans in the Civil War*, Volumes 1 and 2; and *A History of Stewart County, Tennessee*, page 65, by Iris Hopkins McClain.

Official records usually are not found for an individual Confederate soldier. However, during the early 1900s, Luther recounted his memories of those years to his stepdaughter, Lillian P. Mathis, my aunt. Her written accounts, made at his dictation, are part of my family history. They are the basis for my essay presented here.

Her written accounts and other notes indicate that he fought as a cavalry rider, a scout, and as a courier under General Nathan Bedford Forrest and General John Stanley Morgan in Tennessee and Kentucky. Later, he was a foot soldier in Virginia under General Robert E. Lee, fighting, and as well, carrying wounded from the battlefield. After the surrender of Richmond, he was taken prisoner. He fell ill with diphtheria, and was released. Then he was paroled and began his long journey home to Stewart County, Tennessee.

"HOW MANY YOU RECKON we done?"

I was listening to a mocking bird singing over in the trees. "What'd you say?"

"I said, how many you reckon we done?"

"Don't know. Maybe thirty. We're workin' faster now than we was at first. We ain't diggin' as deep." I looked at the graves. "Hit don't much matter how deep we go. The varmints'll be in here after 'em, soon as we leave."

"Luther, don't talk like that!"

"Well, it's so".

"Yeah, I know it's so, but I don't want to hear about it." I nodded. It was quiet except for the mocking bird singing.

WE'D BEEN BURYING DEAD soldiers near all day—the three of us, me, Bill, and another soldier I never did know the name of. "How many you guess was kilt here?"

Bill picked up a rock and threw it at a tree. He was always doing things like that, like he was still a boy. Fact is, I reckon he was. "I cain't even guess. Maybe a hunnert. Maybe twice that, if'n you count the Yankees."

The other soldier went on. "Some I know got it. We was behind a big rock and the order come to move up and they did and got shot. I stayed behind the rock and saw 'em fall." We were quiet again, not knowing what to say. I suspect he was sorry he'd told us that. He turned to Bill. "How many men you s'pose you seen get killed?"

I knew Bill didn't want to talk about it, but he answered. "I got no idea. I hate to think about it." He threw another rock at the tree. "You been a foot soldier long?"

"Ever since I joined up. You?"

"Yeah. Luther here used to be in the cavalry."

"Why'd you quit?"

"Horse got shot out from under me."

I was quiet, listening to the mocking bird. I used to hear them back home when I was a boy. Made me feel lonesome, hearing it sing. "Truth to tell, I ain't never been much good at bein' a soldier. And I guess I ain't gettin' any better at it. When I can do it, I try to do my part movin' them that's been shot back from the firin' line. Mebbe they can get some help back there. That, and tryin' to bury the dead." It was quiet again. "It's gettin' late. I guess we better get back at it, do all we can afore dark."

WE WENT BACK TO digging graves and burying men until it was nearly sundown. It looked like we had gotten most of them in the clearing where we were. We sat down again. It seemed like nobody wanted to go back to camp. The clearing was right peaceful. The sun went down and we could see some early stars. The mocking bird had quit singing.

The other soldier still wanted to talk. "What're you going to do after the War?"

I guessed he was asking me. "Go back to Stewart County. See if I can do some farming. Marry a girl back there if she'll have me."

Bill laughed. "I swear I don't know who'd want you, Luther Morris. You can't even hit the side of a barn with a shotgun! But maybe she won't even care." He pointed to the other soldier. "What about you?"

"Don't know. Maybe go to a big town and get rich." He laughed at what he had said.

"Doesn't your family want you to stay with them?"

"I have no family to speak of. My maw died when I was a boy. The family broke up. Pa, he's a smithy, but he hardly gets by for making any money. He won't care what I do."

"I know what I'm a going to do. I'm going to get some schooling. Learn how to read and write. And go north. There's not going to be much left in the South after this War is over."

Right then, Bill had put to words what we had been thinking about, but hadn't said. "You talk like you don't figure we're going to win this War."

"Yeah, I'm saying that. Maybe I shouldn't say it but I been thinking it. I haven't said it to anybody until right now." It was dead quiet. Then he started in again.

"Well, can you picture us winning this war, after what we been through? After what we know and have seen with our own two eyes." It seemed like he couldn't stop. "And those hell-fire cannons the North has—I saw one of them shoot down a good size tree! Here we are with these old musket-ball guns and the North with their guns that you don't have to load after every time you shoot." He finally ran down.

The other soldier spoke up then. "Luther, do you remember why you joined up?"

Well sir, that was a question. "Maybe. Maybe I knew why I did at the time. But maybe not. I was just fifteen. My Aunt Polly was from a slaving family and partial to the South. All the boys around Bumpus Mills were joining up, mostly for the South. Truth to tell, I don't know why I did. I can hardly recollect; it's been so long ago. There's been so much happened to me since I did it."

He didn't let up. "What about now? Would you join up for the South now?"

I shook my head. "To tell the truth, I don't know. Maybe not, if I figured I had a choice in the matter. More of a choice than I figured I had then."

"Well, let's put it this way. Right now, would you fight the Yankees so some family on a plantation, with more money than we three soldiers ever saw in our lives, can own slaves?"

I stood up. "Maybe we better quit this kind of talking and get back to camp, if we can find it in the dark."

Standing there, I could see the soldier with us turn to the clearing where we had buried the dead soldiers. Then he said what I guess we were thinking. "You all rest in peace now." And we went through the trees and followed the campfires we could see through the trees, back to the camp.

IN MY MIND'S EYE, I get all the battles mixed up. One I recollect was at Missionary Ridge. It was something terrible, seeing what a pitched battle could do to so many men. They were laying everywhere. Some were on top of one another, laying crisscross like branches cut off a tree that had fallen to the ground. The ground was red with blood everywhere you would step. And the smell of what the body does when it dies—I'd seen that with killing hogs, and I'd heard of that from people who tended to somebody who had just died. The smell was all mixed up with the smoke and the dust. It made my gorge rise and it was all I could do to swallow it down. Sometimes I couldn't and the puke would come up.

And there were the flies. They were always around, except in winter. They lived by sucking blood, wherever they could find it. I knew about the big blue-tail fly, that you saw in cow pies and around the outhouses and on dead animals. But I didn't know how quick they come when the animal is dead. And where a battle has been fought, the dead animals are dead men. So they were everywhere on a dead body where it was wet or bloody. They were around the mouth and the nose and the eyes, if they were open, and where there was blood where the soldier had been shot. When you stepped over a body, the flies swarmed up, then they'd settle back down when you passed on. It took some getting used to, even for this country boy.

Back when I started out I figured I should try to move all the men back, away from the line of fire. But quickly I saw that many of them were dead or dying and there was no use to try. I could tell they were dead by their eyes wide open, just staring at nothing. Or by their guts spilling out. I'd been to enough hog killings to know a fair bit about guts spilling out after the belly is cut open. But they were hogs and these were men. Some of them were real bloody. If the blood was on the arms and legs I knew they were not dying, so I'd try to move them. If the blood was on the belly or the chest, I didn't know what to do. Some of them I tried to move, some I didn't. Depended, I guess, on how the face looked. Some of them been shot in the arm or leg could get up and move back with me to help.

I haven't said anything about the hospital tents. Truth to tell, there wasn't any when we were doing the hit-and-run fighting with the cavalry. Now and then there'd be a wagon or an old buggy with us with some men that would help with those that were bleeding bad. But there were no hospital tents at that time, at least that I knew of. You can tell what that means. A soldier got hit so bad he can't ride away was put double on somebody else's horse to get away or he got left behind, probably to die. Many a time, I've seen that happen. Maybe they were taken prisoner, but the Yankees didn't take prisoners that couldn't walk. Fact of the matter, the Rebels didn't either.

Anyway, after any battle I was in, if we could, we'd try to bury our dead. We did it riding with the cavalry and the same when I was a foot soldier. Sometimes we couldn't, if the Yankees had taken over the field where the battle had been. And sometimes we still had the field, but the order was to retreat, so there wasn't time to do much of anything about the dead soldiers. Many a time all we could do with a dead man was to cover him with some dirt or rocks or brush, just enough to make it hard for the varmints to get to him right away. There was no time to put up a marker. Nothing to make a marker with, except a tree limb or a piece of dead wood or a rock. So we let it go. Nothing else to do.

When we got to Chattanooga there were hospital tents and surgeons. The tents would be back of the firing line. Soldiers with arms and legs shot could be helped out of the way of the fighting and back to the hospital tent. Maybe they were not so easy to help when they got there. Probably they had the arm or leg cut off, if it couldn't be saved. There was nothing much for that kind of pain. Only hope was that the soldier would pass out when the cutting started. First time I was close to a place like that it scared the heck out of me, the man being cut was hollering so pitiful. I recollect thinking maybe it was better to be killed. But I've seen many a man without a leg or arm. It's not a good way to live, but you can do it. Better than being dead.

Some of them, when I found them, were bleeding heavily. All I could do was to try to stop it by wrapping the place with whatever I could find. Maybe the soldier's shirttail. Or maybe even some leaves. Anything that wasn't dirty. Aunt Polly used to talk about that. I recollect thinking that likely the leaves were as clean as the shirttail.

The ones I felt the most sorry about was the ones that were shot in the belly and still alive when I got to them. Likely as not, they could see where the ball went in, and if it was real bad they could see their guts coming out. They likely knew they were goners. Some of them moaned and cried out and even screamed in pain, or from maybe knowing they were dying. Sometimes they were praying. Some of wanted me to move them. Likely I couldn't or figured there was no use. Just had to pass them by to go on to somebody I could do something for.

Some were real still and real quiet, and looking up to the sky. They knew. I was asked sometimes to get word to their wife and family about where they had died. At first I didn't know what to say. But I got so I'd tell them I would, knowing that I couldn't. There was a handful of times when a soldier that was in real bad pain and knew he was dying would ask me to shoot him, put him out of his misery. I never could bring myself to do it, but I could see how he could come to ask me to do that. I'll never forget the look on their faces.

There was so much dying. All the time you were wondering if you were to be next. It was real hard on me when I'd come across a dying soldier that I knew by name or face. At first I could hardly stand that. But the more I did the more I got used to it. I guess a part of me turned it off. But that feeling came back after the war and I was home again and had to face it again when one of our babies died. That's the hardest thing I know to do. But you have to do it. There're no two ways about it.

Like I've said before, lots of us in the Rebel army didn't ever have a uniform to speak of. Maybe we'd have a coat or maybe a cap. Mostly all I had was a cap. I wore my old coat from home, if it was cold. Otherwise it was a saddle blanket on the mare. I started out with shirt and pants from home and then when they wore out, I stole what I needed from dead soldiers. Stealing pants and a coat from a dead soldier isn't easy to do. It depends on the timing. If he's newly dead, he'll be stiff. It wasn't hard to get a coat off a dead man that's stiff. If he had been dead some time, he'd turn limp, and getting his coat off was a trial. I've seen men wrestle with a dead man doing that. Boots were the same.

What I'm saying is that it was hard to tell who was on your side and who was a Yankee. Some of them had more of a uniform than us, but not always. That made it real hard in a shooting match to tell who the enemy was. I've seen with my own eyes men shot by their own soldiers. Truth to tell, I guess I've done it myself, but I never knew for sure.

One day I come across a soldier with a Yankee hat on, shot in the shoulder, bleeding real bad. It could probably be fixed up back of the battle line. I looked at him. He just looked at me, not saying a word, not asking for help or for a drink of water or anything. Without thinking about it, I reached down and took off his Yankee cap and threw it away. Then I helped him to his feet and helped him back to the doctoring line. I left him there in the grass, waiting for the surgeons. If he didn't tell who he was, nobody

could tell by just looking at him that he was a Yankee. I don't recollect exactly when or where that happened, but it stuck in my
mind. I quit trying to figure out if a soldier that was down was
fighting for the South or for the North. When they've been shot,
they all looked alike to me. The blood was just as red and the guts
looked and smelled just alike. Let somebody else figure out what
was the difference.

Another time, somewhere, maybe it was in Virginia, there was
a real big battle. Word was that we had won the battle and that
the Yankees had retreated. Men were lying everywhere, in the
blood and the stink. You couldn't see for the smoke. Horses were
down everywhere. It was a terrible picture to look at. So many
men down, I hardly knew where to start. The doctors' tent hadn't
been set up yet, or not that I could see. I come around a supply
wagon turned over and on fire. And right there by it was a soldier
in a ragged Yankee uniform that had been shot in the belly and
was bleeding something real bad. I could tell by just looking at
him that he was a goner. Soon as he saw me, he pointed his gun
right at me.

"You a Rebel?"

I nodded.

"You come to get me?"

I nodded. "I can get you to help, if you want, and if I can help
you move there."

"Likely get me sent to prison."

I shook my head. "I don't know anything about that. But you're
hurt bad. You're in need of help. You want me to help you?"

I could tell the bleeding was getting worse. It was all over the
ground where he lay. And the sweat was pouring down his face.
I could tell he was gritting his teeth, trying not to cry out with the
pain of it all. But he was still aiming that gun right at me.

"You don't talk like a Rebel. Where you from?"

"Tennessee."

"I had a buddy once from Tennessee. Got shot. He was a Yankee. Why aren't you a Yankee?"

I just shook my head. There was nothing to say. The blood
and the sweat went on pouring out. He closed his eyes, and then

right away opened them again. He was fingering the trigger of his gun, nervously, and it was still pointed at me. I just stood there, waiting.

"I'm a goner, aren't I?"

I shrugged, not knowing what to say. "Want me to help you?"

"No, it's no use. I'm dying." He looked at me and tried to sit up. "But if I'm going to die, I'm going take one more Rebel with me."

He was holding the gun now with both hands, aiming it right at me. His hands were shaking really bad and he was having trouble holding the gun still. I could see the sweat on his face, dripping down in his eyes, down on the end of his nose, down his chin.

It seemed like there was nothing I could do. There was still some gunfire behind me. The soldiers I was with were too far away for me to yell at them. And I figured anything I did would set him off and he would pull the trigger on me before I could stop him. I was maybe five feet away from him. Maybe he'd hit me; maybe not.

"What do you say to that, you bastard Rebel?"

I shrugged. "There's nothing to say. You got me to rights. You got the gun."

"Don't you have a gun?" His jaw was clenched, trying to keep talking.

"Nope. I don't fight unless I have to."

"I'll be damned. What kind of soldier are you?"

"Not much of a one, I guess." But right then, I figured he never heard me say that. His eyes were looking up at the sky. The blood kept on pouring out of his belly. So much blood I could smell it, sweet like. Flies had started in on him, where his belly was shot. I figured now that he wouldn't take a shot at me, but I knew he could have, before I got to him. My guess was right. His head slumped down, his arms dropped, and he was dead. I looked at him for a minute and went over and took his pistol away, prying his fingers loose, staying out of range in case his finger could still pull the trigger. I'd heard that a dying man can still do that.

I reached over and closed his eyes, and walked away. I had come close to being shot by a dying Yankee.

IT GOT WORSE AND worse. We walked and we fought. It would rain and the mud was knee deep, but that didn't stop the Yankees from coming at us. I don't know when we got to Richmond. Then somebody said we were not in Richmond, but in Petersburg. It didn't make any difference to me. The Yankees kept coming and coming and coming. And they had warm coats and hats. The only way we could get such was to take them off of a dead Yankee. And, if we did, we looked like a Yankee. You could sometimes rip a coat up so it would look different. Everybody tried to do that, cause it was cold, cold, cold. You never got warm. Never. The lean-tos didn't keep out the rain and the cold, and nobody had enough blankets.

And you were hungry all the time. If you were close enough to a mess wagon and if they had anything left you got a handful of cornbread. Or maybe parched corn. And maybe that was all. That and a drink of water from somewhere that might be clean; more likely not. That resulted in fever and loose-bowel sickness.

It was the fevers that were bad, real bad. They made the men real sick and maybe killed them. At Richmond I vow it was two to one—two sick to one shot. Two died of sickness to one killed. The loose bowels sickness could get you down but you had to pray that was all you got. It was when the fevers struck that you knew you were in a bad way. I'd seen soldiers keel over in the line of battle with the fevers. I'd seen them go crazy and throw down their gun and walk right into the Yankee firing line.

It got so when I was trying to get the ones that were shot out of the line of battle, I couldn't tell who was shot and who had the fevers, unless they were bleeding. But some of them dying of fever had nosebleed and were coughing up blood. So you couldn't always tell from that.

I came to know that the fevers were so deadly that it didn't matter if I pulled them away from the firing line. They were going to die anyway. And word was that there was nothing that could be done for them. I recollect a soldier working in the doctors' tent said one time that the Yankees had some medicine for the fevers but we didn't. Another nail in the coffin, I thought at the time, another way we're going to lose this War.

AND COME THE DAY I caught the fevers. It was the middle of the day, about Christmas time, as I figure it. I was in a trench, firing away at the Yankees coming toward us, and everything I looked at started to spin around. I took my gun and my powder and balls and crawled backwards maybe twenty, thirty yards. Just far enough, I figured, to be out of the line of fire.

The dizziness died down some but all of a sudden I was thirsty, God awful thirsty, more thirsty than I've ever been in my whole life. I drank all my water and all from a water tin from a dead soldier lying there close. And all from another dead soldier, and I was still thirsty. And my head started to hurt so badly that I could hardly keep my eyes open. And I knew for sure the fevers had got me.

Somehow I crawled back even more, as far as I could get, until I come to a log in my way that I couldn't get over. I lay as close to the log as I could, and that's all I knew. I woke up at nearly sunset. The shooting had died down. I felt some better. My head wasn't spinning so. But I was feeling hot and cold at the same time. And I was still mighty thirsty.

I crawled over that log and half crawled back to a doctors' lean-to. I told the soldiers there as best I could what was happening. One said he guessed I was starting to have the fevers. He mixed some powders in some water, and gave it to me to drink. He said to go on and find a place to sleep. Maybe in the morning, he said, I'd feel better.

And I did feel somewhat better the next morning, but my skin still crawled and I was mighty thirsty. I went to the mess tent just after daylight, and ate whatever they had. I drank a lot of water. And I went over to the trench to move my bowels. No trouble there, but I couldn't hardly get up from my squat for falling in the trench.

The bugle sounded for battle and I went, wondering, if this was going to be my last day at this here War. The fighting was the same as always. The officers said we were to hold the line and not give a inch. But the Yankees kept coming and we kept moving back. The shooting was terrible. Soldiers were being killed like fish in a barrel. They were dropping all around me. Both sides.

That was one time I give it my all. I hated it, but I was doing everything that had been taught me. Like crouching behind a rock and loading, then standing up, taking aim and firing. Fire at a particular soldier. Watch him fall. Then crouch again. I went from rock to tree to rock. I took to hiding behind a tree more than a rock. Rising up from a rock made me dizzy. I knew for sure that were the fevers acting up, but right then I didn't mind. It seemed like I didn't care any more. I took a lot of near misses doing that. One of them hit the tree trunk where I was hiding. I turned and saw the Yankee that had shot at me, looking my way. I shot him and watched him fall.

The call for retreat sounded and I recollect feeling mad that it had. I didn't want to fall back. I wanted to stay in there and fight. I stayed put, shooting at the Yankees coming toward me. Right then, a soldier run past me and yelled at me to fall back, for God's sake. So I did, but not wanting to. And I half ran, half crawled back maybe fifty yards, and passed out.

When I come to, I was lying in the middle of some scrub. Somebody had dragged me there while I was passed out. I knew by how I felt that I hadn't been shot. But the real bad headache was back and I had broken out in a cold sweat. When I looked up, everything was spinning around. I stood up as best I could, holding on to a sapling. I could hear the noise of the battle over to my left. I thought that I better go and fight. I took some steps and fell back down, my face in the dirt. I lay there with my eyes closed.

It seemed like I heard somebody say something, from far off. Then I knew it was me, talking. I'm done here. If I'm going to die, it'll be on my way home.

By Dr. Hughlett L. Morris
Professor Emeritus of Speech Pathology, University of Iowa.
A window to the war of his grandfather, Martin Luther Morris,
Martin's Company, Duke's Brigade, Army of the Confederacy

Steel Grip

I KNELT ON THE TATTERED sofa and pulled the curtain aside for a full view of the front driveway. John would arrive at any minute, and this would be the real and too-often-delayed beginning of our married life. It was September 1944, and the week had been lonely since he left to lead a platoon of enlisted men to New Orleans where they were to handle a munitions shipment. They would bring it back to Camp Sibert, Alabama, where he was stationed. The camp was about ten miles from the little apartment he had rented for us in Gadsden.

He'd been sent on this assignment only five days after I arrived from California to re-join him until he was shipped overseas. The army kept us guessing about when he would be shipped out and we had decided to be together at least until then.

I LOOKED DOWN AND smoothed a fold in my new blue taffeta, a swing-skirt dress he had not seen, excited about the evening ahead. I'd made a lemon meringue pie, his favorite, and the meatloaf was keeping warm in the oven of the little gas range. Hamburger was the best I could find for meat. A roast was not possible, not with the ration coupons I had, and not even available in the neighborhood butcher shop.

He said when he left on this assignment that he'd be back "about dinner time on the 25th." Once he'd overseen unloading of the mortar shells, he'd jump into our little '37 Chevy and speed home to me.

At 6:30 p.m. an official military car pulled into the driveway. Two men were in the front seat; neither was John. Another figure was in the back seat. I let the curtain fall, anxiety gripping my heart, and hurried to the front door. The man I recognized as Captain Grimes got out of the passenger side of the vehicle, took off his military cap and walked slowly, eyes cast down, to where I held the screen door open.

"Couldn't John come?" I tried to keep my voice calm.

When Captain Grimes looked up, he sent a strong waft of whiskey across the space between us.

"He . . . he . . ." Captain Grimes turned the billed officer's cap round and round in his hands. "He had . . .He was in a little accident at camp. "His . . . his hands . . ." He kept looking at his hands then glanced quickly up. "They got burned pretty bad."

"He's all right then?" I asked.

"We'll take you to see him. You'd better plan to stay at the base tonight."

"Yes, yes, I'll get my things." All the while I was thinking, *Burns heal. Only death does not heal. John will be all right*. My mind moved on two levels, the practical and the frantic. I hurried to turn off the oven and set the meatloaf in the fridge, not pausing even to cover it. Still not put away was the overnight satchel that had been my carry-on luggage for the flight to Alabama. I grabbed it, stuffed in a gown, my robe and my toiletries case, and carried it to the front door where Captain Grimes waited. We stepped out and he pulled the door closed behind me. I turned to lock it, my motions wooden. He strode ahead of me and opened the car's rear door.

"Missus Burke," he addressed the woman in the back seat. "This is Missus Simpson, the lieutenant's wife."

I slipped inside. The woman beside me dipped her chin and dabbed her eyes with a tissue.

"Your husband was injured, too?" I asked. She nodded and caught a sob with a wad of tissues.

"Sergeant Burke's not too bad," came the reassuring voice of Captain Grimes in the front seat. "A piece of wood went into his ribs but didn't reach his lung. He'll be fine in no time." Captain Grimes nodded at the driver and we backed out of the driveway.

"And John?" I directed my query to the band of close-cropped hair beneath Captain Grimes' hat.

"They're both in the base hospital." he addressed the windshield in front of him.

If John were dead they wouldn't be taking me to the hospital—would they?

Mrs. Burke (not her real name) continued to sniffle and sigh.

I had no tears. The last weeks at home had drained the tears from all of us. My mother had just died in August. By the first of September, deeply aware that this was wartime and knowing that John waited for me, my dear family assured me they would be all right and urged me to rejoin my husband. I had always taken strength from Mother's words, burned into my psyche since early childhood, "God never gives us more burdens than we are able to handle." *How could a just God give me another test, so soon?*

"The black smoke stacks of the steel mills were silhouetted against the sun-reddened sky in the late September day. The pine trees at roadside were slender matchsticks, so fragile-looking compared to the thick-trunk beautiful pines I knew from hikes with John in the California High Sierra.

Except for Mrs. Burke's sniffles and the low rumble of tires against the pavement, silence prevailed.

At the Camp Sibert entrance, the driver gave a quick salute and the sentry waved us through the gate into the maze of dun-colored barracks, one indistinguishable from another. We pulled up at another one-story building, painted white with a bright red cross on the door. The base hospital. A man I assumed to be a chaplain by the circle of white above his olive drab uniform jacket, came quickly to the car. Captain Grimes opened the back door for me. The chaplain, seeing that Mrs. Burke had now broken into loud sobs, hurried to her side and put his arm around her shoulders.

"Chaplain, *this* is Missus Simpson," said Grimes.

The driver quickly took over at Mrs. Burke's side, and the chaplain and Captain Grimes, their hands under my elbows, almost carried me into the hospital reception area. Their solicitation alarmed more than comforted me, silently announcing that John was injured more seriously than the captain had let on.

The men seated Mrs. Burke and me on a hard bench, the chaplain between us. Captain Grimes paced, hat beneath one arm, hands clasped behind his back. The driver stood at attention just inside the door.

I could hold my anxiety no longer. "Can't anyone tell me anything? Is John dead?" I blurted out and grabbed the chaplain's arm. The startled look on his face told me he thought a report had been given to me. At the sound of my voice, Captain Grimes spun around, his face ashen. "I thought . . . I thought the doctor would meet us and be able to tell it better," he said. "I guess John is still in surgery. He was injured when he helped his men unload the munitions they brought back from Orleans."

How it happened was not important at this moment and I felt like pounding the head of this evasive captain. I rose to stand in front of him. In measured tones, my teeth biting each word, I asked. "What happened to John, Captain Grimes?"

I felt the chaplain's arm suddenly around my waist.

"His hands, both hands..." Captain Grimes swallowed, his Adam's apple disappearing and reappearing above the collar of his suntan shirt, his whiskey breath filling our airspace. "Both hands," he repeated, "are gone." He shoved his own hands into his pants pockets, as though in apology for having them.

Not possible, No! The shriek came from inside in my head. I sagged against the chaplain who tightened his grip and led me back to the bench.

"But Lieutenant Simpson was great," Captain Grimes said to my back. "He sat up in the jeep all the way to the hospital. Never lost consciousness." He sounded as though I would agree that sitting up in the jeep mattered greatly. I looked up at him. Then, he ducked his head again. "His eyes were damaged too. They don't know how bad yet."

The captain's words were hypodermic needles drawing my strength with each revelation. *No hands? Perhaps no sight?*

The chaplain, his arm still around me, tightened his grip for a moment, then bent forward, elbows on knees, his hands held before him, palms together, as though in prayer.

Captain Grimes came to stand before me again. "We'll know as soon as the doctor comes."

I sat, rigid. The silence again broken with Mrs. Burke's sobs—whether for me or her own husband, I could not tell—but she reached behind the chaplain and patted my shoulder. A feeling of urgency and panic flooded me. I had to get to John immediately, tell him I was here—forever beside him whether he had hands or eyes or neither. Whatever was lost we would work it out with our love. I turned to the chaplain. "Can't I see him, just for a moment? He has to know I am here."

The chaplain took my hands. "We have to wait for the doctor."

As though in response to a summons, authoritative steps sounded in the hall and all eyes turned to the white coat-clad figure approaching. I stood. "I'm Willma Simpson. When can I see John?"

The doctor moved to the bench and indicated I was to sit again, too. "The good news is that I'm sure his eyes will be all right. We have to keep them bandaged for a few days. An ophthalmologist will come tomorrow. Did the captain tell you?" he added. "The lieutenant was helping the enlisted men unload mortar shells. A faulty one blew up in his hands."

Oh, God! He was injured because he was hurrying the job to get home to me. My heart slumped into my stomach at the thought, but I listened intently to the doctor, my eyes glued to his face, as he described the devices with the unpronounceable name—prosthesis—that would be fitted on John's arms after long hospitalization. "These are stainless steel hooks and he'll be taught to use them well before he is released—in about a year," he said. "We'll transfer him on Monday to Lawson General in Atlanta."

I grasped the doctor's cool, smooth hand. "I must see him, speak to him, so he'll know I'm here with him, no matter what."

"He knows we sent for you, Missus Simpson. He's under sedation now. In a few minutes, I'll have the chaplain bring you to his room. You can stay until he regains consciousness." He rose, laid his hand for a moment on my shoulder before turning back along the hallway.

I looked down at my fingers clasped together on the skirt of the new blue taffeta. Finally tears came, blurring my hands into the four they would become.

AUTHOR'S NOTE: JOHN ALEXANDER Simpson graduated from officer candidate in March 1943. He was elevated to First Lieutenant some time during his hospitalization at Lawson General in Atlanta, Georgia. I remained with him, living near the hospital in Dunwoody, Georgia, from September of the accident until August of 1945. We drove home to California in our little '37 Chevy, arriving on the day of the Japanese surrender.

By Willma Willis Simpson Gore,
her husband's story,
First Lieutenant John Alexander Simpson,
U.S. Army, Chemical Warfare Service

A Clash of Patriotisms

Tom Huestis was as American as anyone, and more than most. Indeed, he belonged to a long-established colonial family. Not like that arrogant rabble-rouser, Thomas Paine, who had hardly arrived in America before he was spouting sedition and rebellion all over the place. That was far from Tom Huestis' take on politics and government.

Calling the rebels of 1776 "patriots" infuriated Tom; *he* was patriotic, *they* were rebels and outlaws. A man had duties and responsibilities to God, to the King, and to his family. If some of those obligations were inconvenient or onerous, you didn't just abandon them. They were the pillars that supported civilized society, creating law and order. Anything else was anarchy and mob rule. And there was plenty of that going on in Westchester County.

Family obligations had constrained Tom as he grew up. He had been born at White Plains on Christmas day in 1759, the eldest son of Joshua and Abigail Huestis. As such, he had important responsibilities and could not run off on his own whim. By 1780, his next brother, Benjamin, was old enough at sixteen, to take Tom's place, which meant Tom had the freedom to join the Tory cause. He and Ben, and even twelve-year-old Joshua, quarreled about it, but Tom paid them little heed. He would follow his heart and fight for King and Country.

It hadn't been long before that brought him trouble. Rebel forces captured him, took him across the Hudson to the Tappan area, and held him with other Tories until they could be exchanged for prisoners held by the British. It was the fall of 1780, and Tom was still at Tappan when they brought in British Major John André. The Americans had caught this elegant gentleman within American lines, in civilian clothes. He was using an assumed name, and carrying in his boots traitorous papers from

General Benedict Arnold—no less than the plans for West Point. On General Washington's orders, despite anguished pleas from the British, they hanged André as a spy. Tom respected what he had heard of Benedict Arnold as a soldier, but felt only contempt for his treachery.

All the same, something important happened to Tom during his forced stay at Tappan. He fell in love. The young lady was actually a couple of years older than Tom, but that didn't bother him. Phoebe Mabie came from a prolific Dutch/Huguenot family that had been in America since New York was Nieuw Amsterdam, nearly as long as Tom's own family. It was out of the question for Tom and Phoebe to marry at that time. Tom had no land, no immediate prospects, and the endless war interfered with such things. They promised to wait for each other. Soon, in a prisoner exchange, Tom returned to Westchester County.

Despite family misgivings, objections, and more quarrels with his brothers, Tom left home again in the spring of 1781. This time, he joined the major local Loyalist regiment, Colonel James DeLancey's Westchester Refugees, serving as a light horseman in Captain Samuel Kipp's troop. With him in that same troop were Peter and John Mabie, cousins of Tom's girl friend Phoebe. Both were now on their way with him to Nova Scotia.

The Refugees were an active unit, better led and organized than most of the rebel forces in the area, but only loosely supported and not actually paid by the British. Still, they wore uniforms, and when on raids were supervised by officers. But the unit had to support itself. This it did not only by raiding and capturing Patriots, but also by driving off cattle and horses, which they then sold to the British. For this, they were derisively known as "DeLancey's Cowboys." In fact, rebels, and others who adhered to neither flag, did the same thing, as it was a ready source of cash. After the war, with the victors writing its history, DeLancey's men got blamed for most of the raiding and theft of livestock.

The war waxed and waned in Westchester County, depending on the seasons. Farmers kept their livestock hidden far from the roads. After some demonstrations of strength in the summer of 1782, the British withdrew to New York, and in the fall, Washington's army settled at West Point. After the peace agreement at Paris in November, DeLancey's Refugees were the only British unit outside New York City. In January 1783, the Patriots made a final effort to capture DeLancey, but he was not where they expected him. After back-and-forth fighting on the Hudson River ice, the engagement broke off. News of the war's end reached Westchester in March of 1783. Overt operations then ceased.

The Refugees were allowed to stay together and proceed by King's Bridge to Manhattan Island and New York City. During one of the many delays along the way, Tom re-connected with Phoebe and married her.

Tom well knew there could be no life for him in Westchester County. It was the same for DeLancey. But the colonel was a powerful and influential man. Though he had to leave his native land, DeLancey would be able to re-establish himself with little difficulty—as indeed he did at Annapolis, Nova Scotia. For Tom, and for others of the rank and file, it wouldn't be so easy. Tom had nothing but his family, and he was leaving them. He was also leaving the land his family had lived in for nearly a hundred and fifty years.

Two small sailing ships, the *Thetis* and the *Nicholas and Jane*, creaking and rolling in the long Atlantic, conveyed DeLancey's veterans northward. Seeing to his bride's comfort provided little outlet for Tom's restless energies, and the ship didn't offer much in the way of deck space. As he paced the gun deck, stepping around blankets and capes set up to provide a little privacy, Tom wished he were on a good horse again. He thought about his family too. Funny how he differed from them in the strength of his convictions. They, like many in Westchester County's no-man's-land, stayed neutral as much as they could. Some openly adhered to the Patriot cause.

Tom and his Phoebe reached Nova Scotia by midsummer of 1783, where they were recorded as man and wife with no children. They had no notion of exactly where in that wilderness they were going to settle. At Fort Cumberland, which lay between present-day Sackville and Amherst, the authorities were by no means prepared for an inundation of Loyalists. Besides Tom and his fellow Refugees, about half of them married and some with families, tens of thousands of other Loyalists were arriving that summer. The government had to find them places to settle, and provide food and shelter. It was too late in the year for crops of any sort to be planted.

The Refugees spent about a month in tents at Fort Cumberland, growing more and more restless and anxious about the forthcoming winter. Finally the government selected an area for them. This was a few miles west of the established village of Tatamagouche, on the north shore. The site, known by its Micmac Indian name, *Remsheg*, lay by the Northumberland Strait separating mainland Nova Scotia from what is now called Prince Edward Island.

The settlers had brought with them a good supply of farm implements and tools, plus bulk iron for things like nails and horseshoes. The British provided this from military stores at New York. From Fort Cumberland they also received tents, wool and linen for clothing, muskets, ball and powder, flints, blankets, and leather. They drew food from military stores: salt beef and pork, flour, salt, sacks of dried vegetables, molasses, tea, coffee and, of course, barrels of rum. All these were carted overland with the settlers the twenty miles or so to Baie Verte on the north coast. A coastal schooner then took them to Remsheg Bay, where they had just enough time to erect temporary huts before the winter snows blew in. It wasn't too hard to put logs together for a 150-square-foot cabin, moss-chinked, and pole-roofed with a bark or canvas cover, a shuttered window, and a mud and stone hearth. It would be dark, stuffy, and soon smelly, but good for a couple of winters.

In the fall of 1783, the word went out to the Loyalist settlers that the British Government was going to compensate them for "losses sustained by their adherence to the Crown in the late dissentions in America." Unfortunately, a March 1784 deadline made it impossible for many of them to submit their claims to London in time. Some never received news of the compensation.

Two years later, the opportunity arose again. This time, a roving two-man commission would hear claims in America at the principal Loyalist settlements. Tom Huestis' claim, along with those of the other Remsheg veterans, would be presented to the Commissioners at Saint John, in the newly established Province of New Brunswick. On March 29, 1786, Tom appeared before his former captain, Samuel Kipp, now a Justice of the Peace. He swore out his Memorial, along with an explanation of why he had not submitted it in 1784. Tom's claim was received April 6th and rejected April 18th.

The reason Tom didn't receive compensation was most likely that he had not suffered financial losses, such as confiscated land, houses, livestock, or furniture. The new authorities had not penalized his Westchester family as a result of Tom's services to the Crown. His Uncle James, who had been a Loyalist officer and had his property confiscated, emigrated to Montreal and later to England, where he, too, presented a Memorial. But James did not submit it to the proper office or in the correct form, and thus received nothing either. Such things were held to all legal niceties.

Tom was a good farmer with an easy and friendly nature. A responsible citizen, he served in various civic capacities at one time or another. In 1794, for example, he was an assessor as well as hog-reave and pounder (responsible for rounding up stray livestock). Both he and Phoebe were literate and there were no schools yet, so the children had to be home taught at first.

Tom's original assignment had been on the Malagash peninsula, between Remsheg Bay and Tatamagouche. He soon dropped that for a piece of land to the north of the Bay, where he had found a spring that allowed him to dig a well with good, clean water at a depth of only six feet. The land at Remsheg also was good and, once past the first few winters, the farms there did well. Their biggest problem was the dismal state of the roads connecting them with other villages and towns. Road improvements were slow; years later the settlers were still complaining to Halifax about them.

In about 1810, the village's Indian name was abandoned in favor of *Wallace*, to honor a prominent provincial official. Tom's land was across the bay to the north, in what is now called North Wallace.

Worn out by bearing and raising five children in primitive conditions, Tom's wife Phoebe died in 1811, at age 54. The next year, Tom married Elizabeth Smith and sired another six children, the last in 1828 in his sixty-ninth year. Joshua Huestis received a letter in 1822 from Tom's younger brother, another Joshua, in Westchester, saying: "I have to tell you of the death of your grandmother. She said she died in the Lord and we buried her body in the first Methodist graveyard in Marmoneck [sic], N.Y." Abigail Huestis had out-lived her husband by more than forty years. Interestingly, the letter was sent to Joshua, not Tom. Perhaps the Westchester Huestises still considered Tom *persona non grata*.

Tom died in the summer of 1851, in his ninety-second year. He saw at a distance the development of the new nation to the south, but seems to have had no inclination to visit it. He and Phoebe are both buried in the Methodist cemetery at Wallace. He never again saw Westchester County or his relatives there.

AUTHOR'S NOTE: THOMAS HUESTIS was my great-great-great-grand-father. Some of my information about Tom's life is from articles written by his grandson, Martin Bent Huestis, in the *Halifax Evening Mail* in 1927. Some can only be classified as family tradition. Tom's Memorial, in his own fine handwriting, is a matter of record. Data about DeLancey's Westchester Refugees and their emigration and settlement at Remsheg, Nova Scotia, is mostly from Gerald R. Vincent's book *The Civil Sword: James DeLancey's Westchester Refugees,* Cobequid Press, 1997. I have allowed myself to add Tom's probable thoughts about things that obviously mattered a great deal to him, and have filled in the gaps as best I could. He did not leave large footprints in the historical record.

Tom's branch of the Huestis family spread from Wallace to other parts of Canada, and some moved back across the border, as I did. Only one person bearing the family name still lives in the Wallace area. The more numerous Huestises who remained in the United States have likewise spread about the country. They remain entwined in the history of Westchester County. There, during the Revolutionary War, the family was split by two opposing concepts of patriotism.

By Doug Huestis
The recorded and family oral history
of Tom Huestis, a patriot on the other side
in the American War of Independence

Military Men in My Life

PATRIOTISM WAS A GIVEN in my family. According to our family history, the last four generations have participated in wars. We can document my great grandfather's service in the Civil War; my father's in World War I, my brothers' service in World War II, plus my husband who served in Korea.

Great grandfather, Isaac B. Howland, age 36, enlisted in December 1863. He was a private in the 7th Regiment of the Iowa Volunteer Infantry, assigned as a replacement to Company B. During the eighteen months of service he fought his way through thirteen major engagements, taking part in the battle of Kennisaw Mountain outside Atlanta, and eventually into the city itself. He was mustered out of service on July 12, 1865, in Louisville, Kentucky. He returned to his farm in Iowa bringing his musket with him. As a child, during Memorial Day ceremonies, I laid garden flowers on Isaac's flag-draped grave.

My father, Harold King, considered it his duty to leave the farm, and enlisted in an Iowa Regiment during World War 1. He was inducted into the Army on July 26th 1918, and was assigned as a private to Company C, 99th Divisional Training Camp I, in Macon, Georgia. He served only six months and was honorably discharged in December 1918. Like Isaac Howland, he returned to his farm in Lime Springs, Iowa. Dad spoke of hardships on bivouac in marshes, bad food, snakes in bedrolls, surviving the great flu epidemic, and yet he held a great admiration for the camaraderie and experience of being a soldier. His discharge carried the comment, "recommended for Corporal if re-enlists."

MY BROTHERS, ROBERT W. King and Royce A. King, eight and ten years older than me, were just the right age to be caught up in World War II.

Robert was content to work in the family business after high school with his father. He tried to enlist when war broke out but was several pounds underweight. The recommended weight-gaining strategy at that time was for the enlistee to gorge himself on bananas and water for a week before weighing in. Unfortunately it didn't work. His disillusioned remark at the time was, "They can just come and get me."

The local draft board called his number in September 1942, and he reported to the Army at Ft. Leonard Wood, Missouri. Now an army private, he was stationed first in Kentucky, then sent to a new base near Sedalia, Missouri. He stayed there for twelve months serving as a company clerk in a hospital unit attached to the Air Force.

Christmas Eve 1943, he was transferred to the 438th Troop Carrier Group that carried paratroopers and supplies for many campaigns throughout Europe. Robert was a replacement clerk, traveling by train to New York, and with his unit, boarded a troop ship bound for England. He was assigned to an air base near Newbury, England, and served as an administrative and technical clerk in the medical detachment. General Eisenhower spoke to paratroopers at this base on D-Day.

Some months after D-Day his medical unit moved through various areas of France, but he does not talk about what he did, or what he saw during that time. Sometime after V-E day, May 8, 1945, he rotated back to the U.S., and while home on leave, the city bells and whistles announced the Japanese surrender on August 14, 1945. We sat on the front porch steps and cried, because now he would not be reassigned to fight in the Pacific war. He was honorably discharged in September 1945 as a Corporal and returned to work in the family business.

My brother Royce was obsessed with all things aeronautical as a boy. He built balsa wood model planes and hung them from his bedroom ceiling, wrecked them in mock battles, and once set fire to a model plane and launched it out his bedroom window.

In September 1942, Royce entered Iowa State College, where all freshmen and sophomores attending land-grant schools were required to take training as reserve officers, (ROTC). In December

1942, he left school to enlist in the Army Air Corps. Just 20 years old, he had to have his parents' permission. In February 1943, he reported for basic training at Jefferson Barracks, Missouri, then was accepted for cadet training. His pre-flight training took place at Michigan State College, and then came more cadet training at bases in Texas and California. He received his pilot's wings from Ft. Sumner, New Mexico, in May 1944.

His first orders as a C-47 pilot assigned him to George Field in Lawrenceville, Illinois. After more training in these cargo planes, he carried troops around the U.S. that were headed to the Battle of the Bulge in December 1944.

In March 1945, he was headed overseas via South America and Africa, to India.

He was assigned as replacement pilot to the 3rd Combat Cargo Squadron in the Imphal Valley, India. He flew 226 combat missions over "The Hump" from India, Burma, and into China, hauling mules, Chinese soldiers, volatile gasoline, wounded soldiers, and military supplies. These missions continued from a base in Kunming, China, and after the Japanese surrender included flying relief missions to a prison camp in northern China and supply missions south to Canton and Hanoi.

After a long wait in Calcutta, India, for repatriation, his ship arrived in Seattle in February 1946. Discharged in Kansas, he returned to work in the family business, but chose to remain in the active Air Force Reserve. He retired in August 1972, as a Lieutenant Colonel.

JUMP NOW TO THE 1950s when another war, this time in Korea, and called a Police Action, was uppermost in the mind of a different young man who was at Iowa State College taking ROTC. Jesse D. Chapman graduated in June 1952, and was commissioned a 2nd Lieutenant in the U.S. Army Corp of Engineers. He reported for active duty in October 1952, at Ft. Belvoir, Virginia. After completing training there, he was assigned to the 884th Engineering Aviation Maintenance Company, (EAMC), attached to the Air Force, at Wolters Air Force Base in Mineral Wells, Texas. By June 1953, this newly married soldier received orders for Korea.

In Korea he was assigned to the 919th Engineering Aviation Maintenance Company, which was headquartered in Suwon. These EAMC's maintained the construction equipment used to build and maintain airfields. His platoon was assigned to bases in Taegu and Pusan. He was promoted to 1st Lieutenant while in Korea and later, in summer of 1954, the unit moved to Yokohama, Japan via LSTs. He was stationed at Showa Air Base for a month waiting for a ship to return home. It docked in San Francisco in July 1954 and he was discharged from active duty at Ft. Sheridan, Illinois in August 1954.

MERCIFULLY THE MILITARY MEN in my life returned physically unharmed. Their lives had been changed by their experiences. Their honorable service was of varying durations, under vastly different circumstances, yet it demonstrates their courage while taking part in the dangerous and frightening realities of war.

By Marylyn K. Chapman
A chronicle of four generations
of a family's service to country

The Marines of Midway

IN JUNE 2002 AT Fort Mitchell, Kentucky, on the beautiful grounds of the Drawbridge Inn Estate, former World War II Marines gathered to share their stories. I met several of the Midway survivors celebrating this 60th anniversary of that fateful day in Midway. A salute to those attending this 26th reunion of the Sixth Defense Battalion:

Byrl Bragmer, from Pennsylvania. "H" Battery;

Donald Drake from Virginia, "G" Battery —Sand Island;

Walter S. Funk, from California, 3rd Defense Battalion

Don Henson, from California, "H&S" Squadron;

Robert Hendrick, from California, "B" Battery;

Leo Moore, from California, "D" Battery;

Ed Sharber, from Tennessee, "G" Battery;

and H.R (Chris) Swaggart, from New Mexico, "H" Battery.

I must say that as I spoke with each of these gentlemen and met some of the wives, their stories touched my heart. They shared happenings like it was only yesterday. Most of them were young men in their late teens or early twenties then. Even with the horror of the happening on Midway, their stories told of wonderful memories. I saw the twinkle in their eyes as they remembered these events. God Bless the Great Warriors who kept their cool, who were there to protect the mainland...to preserve our freedom and rights of liberty and justice for all.

Found in one of the many scrapbooks brought to share their memories was a copy of the Battalion Instruction Memorandum from Headquarters, Sixth Defense Battalion, Fleet Marine Force, issued to the Marines on Midway early the morning of May 30,1942, and signed by Colonel H.D. Shannon, U.S. Marine Corps, Commanding Officer. It read in part: ". . . our President, our Country, our Corps, and the Commander-in-Chief of the Pacific Fleet are depending on us and we will not let them down." Col. Shannon's final statement "We'll hold Midway 'till HELL freezes over," appeared on coffee mugs presented to Reunion attendees that year.

One of those scrapbooks holding copies of these priceless copies of orders included Memorandum Number 3-1942 paragraph 2, issued on May 30, 1942, and it reads: "Our job is to hold Midway. We are to have assistance of other forces to help us to do our job. Our aviation forces have been strongly reinforced. Daily long-range patrols are made to locate hostile forces and track them to within striking distance of our air force. One of our most important jobs, therefore, is to protect our aircraft on the ground and in the water against hostile attack. As long as we keep our aircraft flying, we can work on hostile carriers, transports and other surface craft. We must not let our aircraft be attacked while on the ground, taking off or being serviced. We must also be careful not to fire on our own planes. Keep cool, calm, and collected, make your bullets count."

FOR ALMOST THREE DECADES, the Sixth Defense Battalion Association has been a reality. Not the oldest of the Defense Battalion Associations founded following the end of World War II, but surely one that is unique. Its uniqueness is that it's the only organization of its kind to remain static at one location throughout the entire war in the Pacific. It was the only Battalion that continued under the organizational structure; Sea Coast Artillery, Anti- Aircraft artillery, and machine gun units composed of both 30 and 50 caliber guns. The alert that started the night of December 7, 1941, a frightful time for fewer than 500 young Marines manning gun positions, and with no air coverage, became a memory.

In interviews and stories printed in the newsletter of the Sixth Defense Battalion USMC and Defenders of Midway Islands Association, *Midway Mirror*, the author notes:

JOHN GARDNER RECOUNTS THE following story. "On the night of December 7, 1941, the men and facilities on Midway were exposed to a baptism of fire. Two nasty fast-striking IJN destroyers swept from the northwest and opened fire with 4.7-inch naval cannons. Japanese naval records indicate that they fired some 700 rounds. There seemed to be dozens of ships firing even more rounds than they claimed. We lost three good men to their attack. We knew, as did those in Pearl Harbor, Wake Island and Guam, we were at war. A deadly serious business, but little did we know how serious and how long it would take to win. We were young, confident Marines, and no one mentioned or envisioned losing to the most unlikely nation known for its manufacturing of cheap tin toys."

John Gardner shares more: "There were many Navy corpsmen and men that worked on torpedoes, repairing and servicing our fabulous submarine fleet. We enjoyed them as if they were one of the Sixth Defense Battalion men. They contributed as much or more during the struggle to defeat Japan, as did the Marines on Midway."

ANOTHER STORY SHARED WAS by Walter Grist as he recalls: "I remember the evening of June 3, when Major Henderson mustered the squadron and said that the Japanese were on their way and it was up to us to defend the Island at all cost. As we launched our planes on the morning of the fourth, we knew that we were as ready as we could be. We were ready for a big fight with the memory of Wake Island still on our minds, and the many friends we had lost there.

"As our planes got into the air, we went to our assigned battle stations and just made it as the bombs started to fall and all hell broke loose. It lasted for 25 minutes. After the bombing and strafing was over, the dust and smoke filled the air to the point where it was hard to get a good breath. They hit all the surface structures on Eastern, hit the PX, and beer that had been in the reefers was scattered all over the place. I'll bet if you looked even today, you could probably find a can.

"As the fighters that survived began to land, we were busy pulling wounded pilots out of their planes. Then our divebombers came in to land, and were badly shot up. Two of the B-26 Army bombers made it back and landed. And finally, Bert Earnest, Harry Furrier, and Manning landed in the only TBF to survive. Manning was already dead in the turret, and both Harry and Bert were wounded. We immediately started to make repairs on our SBDs and SB2Ds that were able to fly. About 10:45, a flight of SBDs from *Hornet* landed to refuel and that was when we learned that the Pacific Fleet was on station, and we were not alone. As they say, "the rest is history."

H.R. (CHRIS) SWAGGART, 1ST Gunner, tells of being dug into the dunes. Chris was one of the 30-caliber machine gunners, and his friend of many years, Don Drake, manned the searchlights right behind him. "The battle started well for the Japanese, but the Americans caught the Japanese fleet off guard. Waves of divebombers, launched from carriers that had escaped detection, emerged from the cloud cover overhead. Our bombs hit all the Japanese fuel and ammunition. The Japanese carriers became raging infernos.

"Being out on the edge of the island was not much fun then. We had dug our foxholes and waited. We knew that soon there would be an attack, but we didn't know when. Food supplies were short. Sometimes we only had two meals a day."

Chris also reported how the coral was harvested, crushed into fine pieces to create a runway for our Midway planes. Midway was where the China Clipper refueled during her long trips. The island also had become an all-purpose advance station for the submarines.

Chris arrived on Midway Island in September 1941 and remained stationed there until the summer of 1943. "Once you've been on Midway, you absorb the environment of it, the simplicity and it grows on you so you just can't wash it away."

THEN THERE ARE THE more humorous stories by Rudy (R.J.) Heinle, who arrived after the actual bombings and shared stories of how 1300 cases of beer seemed to just vanish, or how a Quonset hut just seemed to mysteriously disappear only to turn up completely repainted and designed to the hilt in another location. One of Rudy's famous quotes was "the purpose of us being here is to secure the island . . . not to keep track of the beer." Of course, this was his reply when questioned about the 1300 cases of beer by the Commanding Officers.

Then there was the story of the missing steel Army bunk beds, of course only suggestions were made about what truly happened, but Battalion Chairman, Don Drake, wanted to know. "Does anyone know where the Army steel bunks went?" and only a smirk appeared on Rudy's face.

Stories flowed about the "gooney birds," which of course are the famous Albatross. One of the funniest stories was the arrival of a new Commanding Officer. He had called for a drill and noticed all the Marines were carrying sticks as they drilled, and when the occasion presented itself they would swing these sticks wildly at the gooney birds. Being very upset over this type of attack on the birds, he ordered all sticks dropped immediately. As the great Divine Justice would have it, they once again began their cadence. From out of the beautiful blue Pacific sky, one of the largest Albatross to be seen set his target and christened the Commander right on top of his head! The platoon was noted upon return to be "all carrying sticks."

Gooneyville Island—yes that was the new name. Among the stories of those gooney birds was that there were so many of them in one location that it would be difficult to land or take off in the airplanes as the birds would fly into the propellers. They even had a song called "The Gooney Bird Hop" about birds that did not make it into the air.

WALTER LORD SUMMED IT up in the foreword of his book, *Incredible Victory:* "They had no right to win. Yet they did. And in doing so they changed the course of a war. More than that, they added a new name—Midway—to that small list that inspires men by example . . . like Marathon, the Armada, and the Marines . . . There is something in the human spirit—a magic blend of skill, faith and value—that can lift men from certain defeat to incredible victory."

By Dr. Nomi Sweetfire
Remembering and honoring
The Marines at Midway

Flying the Brownie Camera

"LET'S SEE NOW. ACCORDING to these directions, we fly south for two and a half hours until we come to the coast. Then turn left," radioed the pilot over the intercom.

"It would be nice if someone had remembered to bring the map," came the voice of the makeshift navigator.

THIS WAS THE CONVERSATION between Lieutenant "Wally" Simerly and his P-38 pilot buddies who were having their first experience flying a four-engine bomber. They had borrowed the General's B-17 for a short vacation from Italy to Cairo, Egypt.

"You fellows can take the plane. Just don't get sick on the upholstery," was the General's comment. The bomber had been converted into his "private" transport.

Toward the end of World War II, the skies had been cleared of enemy planes. It would be safe to take a jaunt south over friendly territory for a little R and R. The fact that none of them had ever flown a B-17 didn't present a problem once they figured out what the extra controls were for. However, the one thing they had forgotten was the map! All they had were hurriedly scribbled directions from the General's regular pilot who wasn't flying with them.

"I can see the coast up ahead. What's next," asked Simerly, flying as co-pilot.

"Turn left and follow it. You'll cross a big city and then come to a river that looks as if it might be flowing the wrong way, but it isn't. That will be the Nile," the pilot's intercom crackled.

"I can see the city," came the navigator's muffled voice.

"It might be Alexandria," said Simerly.

"Look, there's the river. Now what?" asked the navigator.

"Turn right and follow it until you lose visibility. Then you'll know you're over Cairo," the pilot answered.

MOST OF LIEUTENANT WALLACE J. Simerly's experiences weren't as easy as co-piloting a B-17 to Cairo. Usually he was flying missions from Italy north over enemy territory as a photoreconnaissance pilot. The only "shooting" his modified P-38 Lightning fighter could do was with cameras. His only defense was high speed, and maneuverability.

He related, "I remember, as a young boy, riding in an old Ford Tri-Motor airplane. But my first *real good* ride was in a stagger-wing Beech of about 1932 or 1933 vintage. I hitchhiked forty-five miles for that ride. I must have been about twelve years old. After that flight, I always wanted to fly. I joined the Civilian Pilot Training program in Bishop, California. I no more than got my pilot's license than war broke out. I joined the Army Air Force when I was eighteen."

After initial training at Thunderbird II in Scottsdale, Wally advanced to Marana, then to Williams Field and P-38s, all three fields in Arizona. From Williams Field, he flew coast patrol along California to Washington for about three weeks.

As Simerly expressed it, "People might say I was crazy, but I always volunteered. That's how I got into reconnaissance photography." After three weeks of aerial photography training in Oklahoma City, Oklahoma, he was shipped overseas by troop ship to Naples, Italy.

Some folks referred to this duty, not always affectionately, as "flying a *Brownie* Camera". While maybe not as spectacular as shooting at the enemy and getting swastikas painted on the side of his plane, the job was essential to military intelligence by enabling bombers to locate and destroy targets that would cripple the enemy. Attacks were delayed until the latest pictures taken by photoreconnaissance pilots could be developed for up-to-the-minute locations of enemy strongholds, tank movements and enemy airport construction. It is accurate to say that a pilot's pictures could be responsible for destroying hundreds of airplanes and armaments, equaling more symbols than could be painted on the side of his ship.

"From there we were loaded onto cattle cars and shipped to the 15th Photo Recon Squadron base. I flew one practice mission down to the toe of Italy, across to Greece and then back," Simerly explained. After that, he went to work.

"Our operations shack was directly beneath the 15th Air Force Headquarters. All the General had to do was hang his head out the window and yell, "Send me up a pilot."

One of us would dash upstairs and get our assignment," said Simerly. His missions sent him all over enemy territory. "We covered everything from Munich to Russia, Romania, Greece, Austria, Hungary, Czechoslovakia, Eastern Germany, and a seven-hour flight to Berlin and back." (He received the Distinguished Flying Cross after that flight.) "We took fire but we got out okay." He flew 44 or 45 missions from three-and a half to six-and a half, and occasionally seven hours. "Seven hours is a long time to stay up in a P-38," he explained.

"Our planes were being repaired and checked all the time," Simerly continued. "We never knew which plane we were getting until we were on the flight line. There was a period of time for about three months when I almost always had the same ship. It helps. It's just like driving a car; they can all be by the same manufacturer but each one handles a little differently. I decided that because I was switching around all the time I didn't want to fall in love with one particular plane. They were so beautiful to fly it was easy to love all of them. I got acquainted with them before they even lifted off the ground. Every airplane I got in, I'd pat 'em and talk to them. They became part of me. They *better* be part of me."

Simerly told of how he "caught" fear.

"It was quite an experience. At first I had no fear. But then some of my buddies got killed. Then my ship would be hit. There was a German gunnery school in southwestern Austria. I went over that thing one day and got some pictures at 21,000 feet. Some flak exploded about 50 or 75 feet below the ship. Some of the shrapnel came up through the bottom of my cockpit. I knew the ship was hit but I wasn't. I didn't pay much attention until I looked up and I noticed a little crack in the glass. I took my glove off and reached up and felt where something had hit it. I made it home without an emergency landing, but the ship had been holed several times."

When Simerly landed, his crew chief was waiting for him.

"My mechanic was right there checking me out. He was always right on top of things, right in my lap, immediately with, *How you doing, how you doing? We heard you over the radio, that you were having trouble.*"

I said, "It's okay, it's okay. It's been hit a little bit, but it's not bad and I'm not hit."

The crew chief looked down and started moving stuff around and said, "Hell, there's shrapnel all over down here."

A lot of the shrapnel had come through and hit the dashboard and rudder pedals but it was "spent" and had dropped down on the floor. The one that had hit the glass had come right between Simerly's legs, through his electrically heated flying suit. It had missed him by a hair's width.

"I had to get the suit sewed up where it had been punctured. After that, I began to *catch* fear," said Simerly.

His last wartime flying was photographing General Patton moving along the Danube River.

"We sent two or three pilots out each day to photograph him on his way to Berlin," Simerly explained. "He was moving thirty-five to forty-five miles a day, traveling so fast that gas supplies couldn't keep up with him. He had to steal it from anybody he could. I flew those last missions about four or five days in a row."

SHORTLY AFTER THAT, PEACE was declared. Simerly's P-38 love affair wasn't quite over. After the war, he spent three months photographing the coastline—Greece, Italy, France —at 100 to 200 feet off the ground shooting at 45 degrees, mapping the topography of the coast.

Simerly felt that the saddest experience for him came on his final landing: "When I finished with that assignment, we landed our P-38s (in Italy) and taxied them across the runway where ex-German soldiers were in charge of dismantling them. They were practically new planes. I climbed out, kissed it good-bye and as I walked away a German climbed in the cockpit with a little hammer and broke every one of the instruments. Some other men cut off the propellers and poked holes in the tires. I just couldn't watch that. I hated to see those beautiful planes ruined. The entire 15th and 8th Air Force was junked right there where they landed. They could never be flown again."

"I never flew another plane," Simerly concluded. "The P-38 was the only plane worth flying, anyway."

By Sam Turner
An interview with Wallace J. Simerly
Lieutenant, U.S. Army Air Forces
15th Photo Recon Squadron

Count the Rivets

Bainbridge Air Base, Georgia. June 1957

I TAXI INTO THE TAKEOFF position and hold the brakes on with my feet pressed against the top of the rudder pedals. Today, it's a solo flight to practice coordination maneuvers and aerobatics.

The plane in front of me has lifted off, so I apply full power. The big radial engine has a comforting sound and I feel the propeller torque trying to turn me to the left. I press in right rudder and keep the Trojan headed straight down the runway. The prop seems to be turning very s-l-o-w-l-y, but it's a typical illusion of the T-28's two-bladed propeller and not at all like the smaller T-34 in which I soloed. The airspeed is increasing normally and I lift off at around 85 knots. I say out loud to myself, "Gear up," and climb straight ahead to 500 feet, increase the airspeed, raise the flaps and then make a right, then a left climbing turn and I'm clear of the traffic pattern. I check the cowl flaps closed and set the power for Climb.

A BEAUTIFUL SPRING DAY. Big woolly clouds against a clear, blue Georgia sky. But I don't daydream—I've work to do. I clear the sky to my left to see if anyone else is close and continue climbing and turning to 8000 feet. The farmland underneath, as indeed most of the land in the U.S., is laid out in sections with the boundaries running north, south, east and west. As I climb, I practice staying lined up with the section lines.

Using an imaginary line that I mentally draw across the windshield, I practice steep turns. We have not been taught to fly on instruments yet, and I refer to them only to check my ability to maintain altitude while looking outside. I talk to myself while turning.

"Throttle up a bit. More back pressure on the stick. Keep that imaginary line on the horizon. Oops, I can feel I'm losing altitude! Add power. Raise the nose a bit. I'm skidding. Ease out some bank and use a little top rudder—keep the ball centered, keep it coordinated. Now, more bank again, back to 60 degrees. Fly the plane, don't let it fly you!" I work at turns for about 15 minutes till I'm tired of it.

Now for some chandelles. This maneuver, that I seem to have little trouble performing, feels like flying is meant to: a rapid change in altitude, pitch angle, speed, and the sense of a rapid climb out of some dangerous situation. I imagine myself flying into a fjord or into a box canyon and finding that I must immediately reverse direction and climb back out. This is a situation that can easily happen and indeed, several years later, I put this maneuver to good use when flying in Greenland.

Next, snap-rolls, horizontal reverses and the exhilarating Cuban Eight. I don't know why it's called a Cuban Eight but it is two loops joined together like an infinity sign. I try to remember what the acrobatic section of the flight manual says as I talk myself through the maneuver: "Mixture . . . Rich; Prop . . . Full forward; Airspeed . . . descend to increase to 200 knots."

I begin to dive and enter a loop. Easing in the backpressure, I feel the gravitational force—"Gs"—as I begin the loop looking over my head to keep the North/South section lines fore and aft. Over the top, back on the throttle and dive upside down at a 45-degree angle until the nose passes through the horizon. Then I half-roll till I'm right side up and commence another loop all the time keeping the plane properly aligned. Over top again, down at 45 degrees and roll out at my original entry altitude. *Wow! Fun, fun, fun. Oops, lost a thousand feet or so—better do another, and another.* I'm charged!

BEFORE I REALIZE IT, my two-hour solo is almost over and I'm going to be cutting it pretty fine to land in time so that the next student can have the plane. I can see the field from this altitude and also can see that the line of trainers preparing to land is stretched out five or six miles. *Yikes! How will I squeeze in?* Like the "tiger" I'd like to be, I make a high-speed descent, parallel to the 45-degree entry for the southeast runway. I see a gap and whip into a steep 180-degree turn and bully my way in front of another T-28 that has left a bit wider spacing than usual. What I don't know is that the ship I have pushed in front of has a student *and an instructor.*

I turn right 45 degrees on to "initial" and can see I'm too close to the plane in front, so I extend my pitch-out point a bit further down the runway. What I *don't* hear is the mobile control tower saying to me, "Solo T-28 on initial, go around." They can see I'm extending the pattern too far, but my attention is already divided with spacing and landing. For all intents, I'm deaf to their request and I begin my 60-degree "pitch-out" to the right.

"Throttle back until the horn sounds, Gear down, Horn silent . . ." I say aloud as I turn.

Suddenly I become instantly aware of a blur ten or fifteen feet above my canopy. I can almost count the rivets in the underside of another trainer's fuselage. I have barely survived a near miss at less than 1000 feet. If we'd hit, nobody would have survived; we would both be a pile of burning metal at the end of the runway.

I continue my descending turn toward the runway, but something doesn't feel right. I'm descending too fast. I add power, and the descent slows. I touch down much faster than usual and do not make the first turn off, but taxi further down the runway causing the next T-28 to go-around.

While "cleaning up" after landing, I realize why I landed long and fast. After the near miss with the other plane, my train of thought was interrupted and I forget to put down "landing flaps." *What a tiger I am*. More like a pussycat.

Entering the line shack, I decide to say nothing about the near miss to my instructor, Earl Wederbrook. Glancing out of the window, I see a short instructor walking very quickly toward our building. Earl also sees him coming, and flicks his eyes toward the parachute loft. I take the hint; beat a hasty retreat. I put it together! The approaching instructor is my old nemesis, P.D. Bridges, the southern boy who doesn't like slow Yankees with an Australian accent, and it was he whom I cut out of the pattern and with whom I almost shared a common pile of burning rubble.

Five minutes later having checked in my parachute, I look inside the line shack. P.D. and Earl are nose to nose, except that my instructor is about six inches taller, fifty pounds heavier, and is looking down on a red-faced Bridges who obviously is yelling. My protector is saying nothing, and shortly P.D. turns on his heel and leaves.

Earl has a wry smile during the debriefing and after I discuss my maneuvers, Earl says, "By the way, next time you cut someone out of the landing pattern, be sure he's shorter than me. I'm a lover, not a fighter."

Back in the barracks before supper, I look at my log book and realize that I have just passed 100 hours of flight time and in an airplane which 15 years ago would have been considered a high performance machine.

AND I AM SAD knowing that neither my mother nor father will ever know their grown up son.

By William (Bill) Critch
2nd Lieutenant
Military Air Transport service

Finding Life at the Bottom of the Pool

ARM RESTING ON THE side of the pool, body immersed in water, checklist thoughts flashed through Steve's Gladish's mind: Army of One . . . Coronado Island . . . Twin 80 tanks strapped tight . . . frogman flippers on snug . . . lead-weight belt on tight . . . SEAL bubble mask on tight . . . life vest on tight, lollypop string puller accessible for Sergeants-only instant inflation . . . tread water . . . scissors kick . . . hands above water . . . five minutes . . . FIVE MINUTES!

SERGEANT HOOPES' IMPOSING SPECIAL Forces demeanor and no-nonsense shades appeared above and in front of Steve. Only Hoopes had the timer watch and the whistle, to start and finish the exercise. *Absolutely nobody else can wear a watch, least of all, us,* Steve thought. *I can't even monitor my progress, as I did in my running days.*

Gladish, ready? It was a challenge, not a question.

Steve swallowed and nodded, "Yes, Sergeant."

Hoopes went down the line, prepping the other three ROTC cadets. "Okay men, give me your best five minutes! I want to see your hands above water at all times, you got that? Starting . . . " he glanced at his watch, "NOW!"

Chilled from the ninety minute long, total muscle-fatigue physical training drills and the cold mile swim in the ocean, Steve pushed off from the side and began the dreaded tank-tread test, his feet scissoring powerfully front to back, his hands above the water, trying not to bob up and down. His first surge of exertion got him past his initial fears and nervousness. But it wasn't long before his legs began to ache and his lungs began to burn; pain began to construct multiple freeways for the truckloads of chemical messengers warning his brain of the coming pile-ups. One . . . two . . . three . . . four, he counted; mentally measuring his water strides each time his feet arced farthest away from each other and then changed positions.

Fourth day, he thought. *Two of my cadet cadre already sent home. How can I keep up?* The water was cold, the air had been cold, and he was cold. He set his jaw and steeled himself.

"Do the task or stay down trying," the sergeant's voice from earlier instruction floated through his consciousness. "Don't even think about coming to the surface unless you have completed your assignment."

Steve remembered two instructors the day before diving in to push two cadets down to the pool's bottom—cadets that were starting to come to the surface. He glanced at the pool deck. Sure enough, against the wall were defibulators available for restarting his heart. Trained Army Special Forces medics were on hand for CPR and water ingestion—any emergencies. *But woe to the man who needs them,* he thought. *You might as well cash it in.*

He closed his eyes for a moment, shutting out the images of failure. His mask began to fog up slightly, alerting him to change his breathing. He looked up and over to Sergeant Hoopes, wishing for a signal showing a minute's time, knowing he would not get it. Disbelief showed through his mask, and the sergeant frowned.

His disapproval registered, "Keep your hands above the water," he yelled.

All of a sudden, the twin eighty tanks, weighing close to a hundred pounds, seemed to be pulling Steve backwards and down. His feet were screaming with pain, the bruised muscles and tendons of his ankles and feet protesting, with every forward and backward push, against the weight of the huge Navy SEAL flippers, eighteen inches long. *Get a-hold of yourself,* he command-ed. *Assume you got one minute down. So take one minute at a time,* he began to say in his mind, in cadence to his leg swings: *Not one test, not one day, not one hour, just one minute at a time.* Kick after kick followed in tortured monotony. Every second now seemed to last a minute. He went back to counting: one . . . two . . . three . . . four . . . . *How can I keep this up,* he asked himself after the tenth count sequence.

He thought that nobody would ever understand all the pain involved. *Nobody I know has been in a position where you can't quit, you can't call in sick, and you can't beg the boss for mercy. Nobody sets himself up to be tested to his limits, because nobody wants to face failure. This is what the Army's doing,* he thought, *because on our own we would not do it. The Army needs to know they can count on us to get the job done. So I'm either an A student, or an F—for failure. The pain has nothing to do with it. Can I live with pain and get the job done? Can I will my body to do what I know must be done?*

Steve felt his heart pounding and thought *There must be a better way to kick. Why didn't they teach it? I heard one of the sergeants talking about an eggbeater kick, doing figure eights sideways, not up and down. Why did they hide the technique?* His logical mind seethed at the unfairness.

I can't learn anything new now. Wait, he thought: *initiative, that's what they want. They want proactive combat divers, not trained dolphins.* He remembered his dad saying, "Life is not just another video game. You can't wait for the bad guy to appear on the screen. The real bad guy will be behind you."

I am an Army of One, Steve reminded himself. *If it is to be, it is up to me. I know I used to be laid back. There's no social promotion here, it's "Get it, or die, GI."* Feet flailing ponderously through the water, neck arching the hands desperately out of the water, he looked up at Sergeant Hoopes. Steve remembered two days ago during his timed exercise in the pool, Hoopes had walked across the deck toward him! He had glanced at his watch, and pretended to start blowing the whistle. And then he smiled and walked away. *Jeez,* Steve thought, *I hope he doesn't do that to me again!*

Fear squeezed his gut, and he felt a tremendous need to urinate. Concern seized him temporarily, and he fought the childish urge to excuse himself and climb out of the pool as he had been taught at home. *I've got to go, sir,* he imagined himself being able to say to the sergeant, as if urinating in the pool were a death-penalty infraction, and of course the sergeant would let him go.

Shaking his head, Steve came to his senses. He noticed Sergeant Hoopes' glowering face and push-off motion with his huge hands, "Get away from the edge, Gladish!" he shouted. Steve heard him only faintly, as if he were in a dream. *I'm gonna make it to halfway, and then I'll go to three minutes,* he determined. *I can't let everybody down.*

Jensen and Todd have washed out, he thought. *Ventry is being swallowed up with the water; there's no hope left in his eyes. I'm all we've got left. I've got to do it.* He pedaled madly on, like the ill-fated boy in "The Rocking Horse Winner," obsessed with winning for his family, unaware that with victory comes death and defeat.

Count, count, count, he reminded himself, his lungs aching and gasping with the effort of both keeping fully inflated for life-saving buoyancy and gulping in new life-saving oxygen, his throat ragged and close to spasm, his hands constantly wanting to go underwater to help stay afloat. Suddenly, he swallowed water from bobbing down too low, and began coughing and gasping, trying to clear his freaked out lungs.

"Keep your hands above the water, or you start over!" Sergeant Hoopes yelled. Steve felt excess water pooling around his eyes, not knowing if they were tears of defeat, or reaction from the coughing. *Count, count, count.* He looked over through a foggy mask and saw Sergeant West in the pool, easily treading water as if he hadn't a care in the world. *West is my lifeguard,* Steve thought. *Of course Hoopes isn't going to dive in to help, he's keeping times.* Steve saw Ventry on his right, struggling with courage and fatigue. At the same time, he almost swallowed another lungful of water. *I'm not swallowing any more water,* he told himself fiercely. It's Army "Go-No Go" training. You get it, or it gets you.

He willed his legs to keep scissoring front and back, remembering his dad trying to tread water four weeks ago at the University of Arizona's pool alongside him, with just the sixteen pounds of lead-weight belt. "I can't even do this for a half-minute," he had shouted, "and that's with both hands and feet! How in the world do you do it?" He remembered the look of admiration his dad had shot him, and thought of all the training he had gone through with Sergeant Klein and Sergeant Carden in the last two months.

None of that is helping me here, he thought. *I'll bet I'm barely past three minutes. A whole galaxy could be born before my five minutes is up. I've got to keep trying,* he thought. *There's no give in giving up. They want me to do five minutes, I'll do five minutes.*

Count, count, count. Where does all this pain come from? My legs, my legs, my feet, my feet! Don't die on me! I've never done anything this hard before. I've never failed at anything I tried before . . . soccer . . . track . . . hurdles . . .Oh, no, who's that over there hanging onto the edge of the pool? He's crying and shaking his head. He's totally lost it. The Sergeants won't respect that one bit.

I'm going to fall over backwards, he thought. *Sergeant West has somebody behind me pulling at me, trying to harass me and annoy me, trying to make me give up. These tanks are dragging me down. They are much heavier than they told me. I'm not going to quit, but I've got to use my hands. It's that or die . . .* He kept on, his heart pounding out of his chest, his lungs exhausted, his legs leaden and unresponsive. *Where does all this pain come from? I know Sergeant West is disappointed in me,* he thought. *I know he can see me with my hands underwater. But I'm not quitting, I'm not crying, I'm not giving up. I'm not going home early.* He opened his palms and began moving his hands in forty-five degree arcs, back and front, to stay upright, to keep from going under permanently. *It's working,* he thought. *Maybe I can get my breath back . . . Somebody must be behind me, pulling on my tanks. I can't seem to stay upright any longer. How can the sergeant let somebody do this? Everything is so cold here at Coronado,* he thought . . . *It should be* Cold-a-rado. *We wear only tee shirts, and the air is cold; the ocean is fifty degrees cold; the pool is cold. Everything is so cold. Am I still upright? Where's the sky? Where's Sergeant West?*

I can't see East, I can't see West, he thought drowsily. *I can't breathe this stuff. I can't stand straight any longer. Am I really falling backwards? The tanks are so heavy; the lead belt is pulling me down Are there magnets on the bottom, or what? Everything is slowing down. I must be floating—or am I still falling? Everything is so easy now. . . West is just floating around up there.*

Hey, Ventry is looking at me. He's watching me go down . . . his face is all twisted . . . he thinks I'm in trouble–He's crying. For God's sakes, Ventry, don't give up! I can get back to the surface.

"Just give me a few minutes; I'll get my strength back and finish the job. I'm not giving up, Sergeant West, Steve murmured in his mind.

I'm just resting, sir. I'm seeing these beautiful colors — yellows and blues and greens, I never noticed them before . . . Can't be the sunset, but it reminds me of two or three . . . I can almost touch these colors.

Wait a minute — who is that floating next to me? He looks pale. I can't touch him, and I can kinda see through him . . . he looks like dad. No, he has black hair and a mustache — it's Grandfather. He was a doctor in the Navy . . . he's been here at Coronado . . . never got to meet him . . . he was long gone . . . he helped everybody else, now he's gonna help me . . .wait a minute. Am I . . .?

Okay, I'll take off the lead belt. Wait–he's putting his finger to his lips . . . pressed together. Be still. Don't say anything — is that what he means? Okay . . . He's smiling. Everything is going to be okay — and Steve floated out of consciousness.

SUDDENLY A SWARTHY HAND grabbed the lollypop, pulling the cord, and his life-saving vest inflated, lifting Steve off the bottom of the pool. It was Sergeant West, finally diving in to get his student. He propelled Steve to the surface, swiftly unhooking the tanks, and began slapping Steve, and yelling, "Gladish, breathe! Gladish, breathe!"

After a few slaps and shouts, Steve opened his eyes, and opened his mouth to breathe. As groggy as he was, he thought, *Air! Blessed Air!* The colors faded from his consciousness, and he began taking huge drafts of air, trying to clear the dreams and slow-motion life away. But he still felt as if he were in a dream, unable to move, unattached to his body. *Nobody will understand this pain,* he thought. *It's worse than death; it just goes on and on . . . no mercy.*

The world of Combat Diving slowly came back into focus. Sergeant West peered closely at Steve and said, "Now get out of the pool! Nobody's gonna do it for you."

Steve felt foolish and awkward, regaining use of his limbs once again, as if he were a baby just learning to swim. He slowly went arm-over-arm to the side of the pool, dizzy, exhausted, trying to get to the ladder that seemed a hundred feet away. Finally, he clambered out of the pool, all in slow motion. He swayed at the top, and Sergeant West yelled, "Gladish needs a buddy! Get over and help him with his gear!"

Burfield from Wisconsin rushed over and grabbed Steve's elbow. Slowly Steve made his crooked way to his gear bag, and Burfield helped him remove all gear, slowly, painfully, one item at a time, except his swimming trunks. "Even if you don't have to," Burfield murmured, "head for the men's room." He didn't have to say that twice. As he held open the door, Steve staggered over to a bench, and sat down heavily, surprised his legs were still there, feeling that they had died hours ago. "Hang out here while I watch the door," Burfield said.

Within ten minutes, Steve got to his feet and walked out to face the sergeants. "I'm ready for the drown-proofing drill, Sergeant West," he said. "And I'll tackle the tank test again tomorrow."

I'll believe that when I see it . . . Burfield's your buddy, so get to it," Sergeant West replied. "You know the drill, Burfield, don't cut him any breaks. Tie his hands, and tie his feet . . . tightly, and get Gladish back in the pool."

At graduation the following Tuesday, when Steve made it into the final ten candidates for the Key West Army Combat Diving Qualification Course, Sergeant West shook Steve's hand. "You made it. Eight didn't. You did it the hard way. Not many come that close to drowning and then stick with it. You earned your nickname, 'Stone-Cold.' I never saw anybody so calm in the face of failure and drowning. You really hung with our motto, 'It's better to drown than not getting the job done.' Next time we meet, and it's not instructor and student, the first beer's on me."

By Stephen G. Gladish, Sr.
About his son Lt. Stephen Gladish II,
an Apache Pilot, Army National Guard,
deployed to Afghanistan January 2007.

Memories of World War II

ALTHOUGH I WAS TOO young to really grasp the overall worry and strain that World War II placed on my family, there are a few memories that remain vivid even today. My father, Frank Interrante, was drafted shortly after the birth of my sister and I remember asking my mother the same question, day after day.

"Where's Daddy?"

"He's in the army with Uncle Joe and Uncle Al," she always answered, those uncles being Joseph and Alphonse Interrante

Joe and Al were my dad's brothers. They were identical twins and did everything together. I always had trouble telling them apart. I guess the army couldn't tell them apart either so they separated them. Uncle Joe was sent to Italy and Uncle Al got shipped off to France.

My mother used to take us to grandma and grandpa's house a lot so that everyone could pray together. Mom didn't drive so we had to take the streetcar. We were there the night the telegram came from the War Department. It said that Uncle Joe had been wounded in action. That was it, no other information; and for weeks and weeks we all waited for the army to tell us more. Finally, Uncle Joe was shipped back to the States. He had been wounded in the leg and could no longer fight.

My dad had never left the United States. He was drafted despite the fact that he had asthma and perforated eardrums, so the army sent him to Louisiana and taught him how to cook. His letters said the army had one special dish he had to make all the time for the men stationed at his base. It was creamed chipped beef on toast and everyone called it S-O-S. Dad then explained what S-O-S stood for, but my mother wouldn't read me that part of the letter. She did read me the part where Dad said he was glad to be serving his country, but that he missed us very, very much.

Since Dad's car was just sitting in front of the apartment building where we lived, my mother suddenly decided that she should learn how to drive it. That way, she wouldn't have to take my baby sister and me on the streetcar all the time.

Now that Uncle Joe was home and couldn't work because his leg was healing, my mother asked him to teach her how to drive. I was sitting on the floor listening to the radio when they came home after mom's first lesson. Uncle Joe came into the house and collapsed into the nearest chair.

"I'll go back and fight the Nazis again before I get into another car with your mother," he shouted.

I didn't understand what had happened, but whatever it was, it didn't faze my mother. The next day she was back in the car driving up and down the streets in our Chicago neighborhood. The car had wide running boards, and after awhile all the neighborhood kids would ride on them as mom practiced her driving. Fortunately, with all the men away at war, there was no other traffic on the side streets.

Then, my father's cousin who was a violinist got his draft notice. My mother always said that cousin Frank and his wife, Barbara, were high-strung. I thought that had something to do with the fact that he played a violin. Since my mother was an experienced driver now, she volunteered to take Frank and Barbara to the station where the troop train would take Frank off to boot camp.

There were a lot of tears that day, but Frank finally got on the train. He found a seat by the window and waved to us as the train pulled out of the station. However, his wife did not wave back. She took one look at him passing by on the train, and fainted. Some nice strangers helped my mother and me revive Barbara and get her back to the car.

After all of that, Frank was back home within a week. The army discharged him saying that he was too nervous to remain in the military.

Uncle Al came home and he and Uncle Joe started doing things together again. Only now, I could always tell the two of them apart. Uncle Joe was the one with the limp.

My dad stayed in the army the longest. When I'd ask my mother why he wasn't home yet, she would say. "He's such a good cook, the army can't do without him."

I REMEMBER WHEN THE war ended and everyone was running into the streets shouting and laughing, but that is not the memory I treasure the most. My fondest memory was the event that took place a few weeks later, when I woke up one morning and found my dad, dressed in his uniform, standing beside my bed.

By Carol Costa
Accounts of her family
at the front and on the home front
of World War II

The Military Gender Gap

(Circa 1952-1972)

"There is an appointed time for everything." Ecclesiastes 3:1

She pioneered a role in the young free-spirited U.S. Air Force
when dietitians yet numbered few.
This ingénue 2nd Lieutenant charged forth undaunted,
ignoring logistics that placed her in managerial positions
ill befitting her relative youth and limited experience.
Nor did she wince at the all-male makeup
of the foodservices she supervised.

Upon inheriting an operation deeply in the red
at the 400-bed Keesler AFB Hospital, Mississippi,
with economy-minded fortitude she dared to serve Milk Toast
    for breakfast
to GIs accustomed to and expecting SOS.
Not her proudest moment!
She addressed the vertical learning curve with dispatch.
Her red-necked Executive Office Major wrote in his *official*
    evaluation:
Even though she is female, she has proved ability to manage.

Early in the second decade of her career, she was tossed
into the fray of flagrant gender thinking
at the 1000-bed Wilford Hall USAF Hospital in San Antonio.
Countering the Hospital's decision that
only a man could handle Big Willie's Foodservice problems,
her Corps superiors in Washington resorted to subversive action.
Accordingly, she was routed to the infuriating scene,
theoretically to head a subdivision, but ultimately
to land the prized Head position.
That opportunity presented itself without delay.
The scheduled male officer was downed enroute
by a heart attack and retired before ever appearing.
Presto, Big Willie's Foodservice was headed by this female
   officer.
And never again was there talk of a *man being required* for the job.

By Shirley Chaska Baird (autobiographical)
Lt Colonel, USAF, Retired

A Doughboy's Adventure in World War I

WILLIAM LEON ROPER WAS attending Drury College and working part time in Heer's Department Store in Springfield, Missouri, when the United States entered World War I. He enlisted in the Missouri National Guard. His unit was mobilized as Company B, 130th Machine Gun Battalion, 35th Division. Pfc. Roper became part of the American Expeditionary Force sent to France in the spring of 1918.

"In early September, 1918, we knew we were moving up for the big showdown battle that we hoped would end the war," Roper wrote in his memoir. "We knew, too, that the great offensive would take its grim toll, and that some of us would not be going home again."

PFC. ROPER AND HIS fellow doughboys were young and self-confident, and they didn't talk much about that. They were eager to get it over with, and do the job they had been commanded to do. But "just in case," he did write a farewell note to his parents and put it in his jacket pocket.

In preparation for the "big drive," the battalion moved in night marches. Daytime rests were in wooded areas where they would be less visible to German pilots on observation flights.

"Crawling forward in the darkness in the center of the highway was a seemingly endless chain of trucks, tanks, artillery, ambulances and field kitchens competing for space with our machine gun carts," Roper related. "Our muleskinners walked beside their mule-drawn carts, carrying machine guns and ammunition, but I and most of the company splashed along on the right side of the road."

Adding to the discomfort of the thousands of foot soldiers was a cold, continuous drizzle on the night of September 11, as they sloshed along on the muddy, troop-congested highway toward Saint Mihiel.

"As we plodded forward at a snail's pace, the darkness was frequently punctuated by flashes of light far ahead—artillery fire, exploding shells and parachute-suspended German flares that shed an eerie, greenish glow over the army moving forward," Roper recalled.

The battalion didn't get a chance to participate in the Saint Mihiel battle as it was opened with an intense artillery barrage by Captain Harry S. Truman's regiment shortly after midnight. The 35th Division was ordered to lie in reserve in a wooded area. The men bedded down in pup tents for the rest of the night. Pfc. Roper's heavy pack contained, among other items, an extra pair of hobnails, two cans of bully beef and emergency rations.

The next morning, September 12, the men received word that the Americans' attack on the Saint Mihiel bastion had been successful and the mopping-up procedure was continuing.

Company B, after the men helped the French celebrate their Independence Day July 14, left Saulxures for the Vosges trenches, marching during the night up a winding mountain road to the Gerardmer sector. This was to be their home for the next 45 days. During July and August, the Germans often shelled during the early evening. In one trench raid a new member of the company was killed. Pfc. Roper and another soldier were sent down the mountain trail at night to find out what was taking place at a forward-emplacement and mistakenly were fired on by one of their own machine gun posts.

When Company B marched out, Pfc. Roper and another liaison private were left behind to serve as guides for the French troops coming in to replace the company, and obtain a receipt for the equipment turned over to the French.

"In preparation for this responsibility, I spent an hour with my French phrase book, memorizing and practicing my French," Roper related. "But when I saluted the French lieutenant leading the first group, he smiled and said with an Oxford accent, 'We're familiar with this sector and I speak English.' Then he added: 'I hope you have left us some good American magazines to read.' "

The American soldiers rejoined Company B that afternoon. After a brief stay at Charmontois, the Company, making night marches, proceeded toward the Meuse-Argonne front, arriving at the top of a barren, shell-battered hill on September 25. The men were to occupy these trenches for the night and use them as the jumping-off place for the all-out Meuse-Argonne offensive.

"We set up our machine guns and began calculating data for the barrage we were to lay down in advance of our infantry the next day, when our assault began," Roper recalled. "It was getting dark when Lieutenant John H. Helfrecht sent for me and handed me his large, silver-cased, open-faced watch and said, 'I want you to go to headquarters and get my time synchronized with that of the battalion commander.'"

Pfc. Roper set out under artillery fire from the Germans. Some shells contained shrapnel, others poison gas, so when he smelled gas on his return from headquarters, he put on his gas mask. In the darkness, his visibility further reduced by the mask, he fell into an old trench, filled with gas. He had to remove his mask to find his way out. He felt a burning sensation in his lungs and throat, but was more dismayed to find that Lieutenant Helfrecht's watch had been broken and had stopped. Fortunately the lieutenant was able to get another watch with synchronized time.

During the night of heavy German bombardment, the earth trembled with the detonations of both exploding shells and the firing of the Americans' own artillery. The 35th Division moved forward the morning of September 26 as part of the great Allied offensive.

"In this first phase of the advance, the 35th Infantry regiments bore the brunt of the fighting, with the Division's artillery batteries pounding the German trenches and pockets of resistance," Roper related. "During part of the first day's advance I was with a group under the command of Lieutenant Tony McBride, but in the afternoon all units of Company B converged on Cheppy, a well-fortified German food and munitions supply center, from which the enemy had been routed earlier in the day. I accompanied Captain Frey as he inspected the food stored in the underground hillside rooms."

The men were preparing to go forward with their machine guns, tripods and munitions when a plane of questionable identification appeared but its motor had the distinctive intermittent whine of a German plane. The pilot released a bomb. Pfc. Roper saw it dropping from the plane.

"It seemed to be coming straight at me," Roper recalled. "In high school track meets, I had done a 100 yards in almost 10 seconds. As that bomb fell, I sprinted at top speed to get out from under it. Other company members were also scattering. The bomb, carried forward by the momentum of the plane, hit about 50 yards from me, blasting a crater. Circling, the plane came back. We could see the pilot had another bomb, and now we were firing at him with rifles and pistols. He dropped the bomb, apparently his last. It was a dud. He then flew away. None of us had been hurt."

Sometime after midnight, Pfc. Roper crawled out of his foxhole to stretch, and found Captain Frey standing alone. (Frey and Roper had been friends and fellow employees of Heer's Department Store before the war. Roper was a clothing and shoe salesman; Frey was the floor manager. During the war, sometimes when they were alone, Frey would call Roper "Leon" instead of Private Roper.)

"Leon," Captain Frey said, "I've got an errand that ought to be done tonight but I hated to wake any of you boys up since we've had a hard day." Pfc. Roper said he felt rested. Captain Frey asked him to go back several kilometers to where the mule carts and the rest of the transport section had been left, and give the officer in charge an order to move up. Roper said he'd be glad to take the message.

"It was a dark, drizzly night, not a star in sight," Roper related. "Twice I fell into shell holes, one partially filled with cold, stiff bodies, and one with a phosgene gas odor. I also passed a field hospital set up in a wrecked dugout, where wounded were groaning and screaming with pain. But I was lucky as usual in finding the transport outfit and delivering Captain Frey's orders."

During the days that followed, Company B suffered several casualties, including close friends of Pfc. Roper. Despite a shrapnel wound to one eye, Captain Frey carried on his duties, refusing hospitalization until the Company was relieved. All the men had close calls and those who survived felt fortunate.

"Company B repelled a slashing counterattack on September 29, and underwent numerous strafing attacks by German planes," Roper recounted. "At three P.M., October 1, the 130th Machine Gun Battalion, along with other 35th Division units, was relieved by the First Division. At approximately the same time I was being admitted to a field hospital for treatment for poison gas inhalation and exhaustion."

While recovering from those ailments, Pfc. Roper caught the flu, then epidemic in the U.S. as well as overseas. He spent the winter in three Army and Red Cross hospitals at Mesves-Center, France. He was awarded the Purple Heart.

AFTER THE WAR, ROPER moved to California and married Violet May Corwin in 1923. He was a news reporter on the *Progress-Bulletin* and later became a staff writer for the *Los Angeles Herald-Examiner* and the *Los Angeles Times.* He was the author of several books, including the biography of William Spry, Governor of Utah, and *Winning Politics.* He was the Southern California publicist for Lieutenant Governor George Hatfield. Roper was a regular contributor to *The California Highway Patrolman*, and had essays and articles published in more than 100 magazines. William Leon Roper died January 7, 1990, in the Veterans" Hospital, Loma Linda, California. He was survived by a daughter, Rosemary (Mrs. Anthony) Ivins of Thayne, Wyoming, who provided this information to SSA member Faye Brown.

By Faye Brown
Based on the Memoir of Pfc. William Leon Roper
Company B, 130th Machine Gun Battalion, 35th Division
American Expeditionary Force, WWI

The Last Midget Submarine

Pearl Harbor, December 7, 1941

JAPAN'S SURPRISE ATTACK ON the United States was in full swing, with bombers, fighters and ships all in place. A small part of the Japanese Navy's plan included five midget two-man submarines, each with two torpedoes, released just outside the harbor to gather intelligence and sink any U.S. ships trying to leave once the bombing had started.

Fifty midget submarines were built by Japan. They were 78.5 feet long, 6 feet wide at the beam, and 10.2 feet high; and were designed for a depth of 100 feet, surface speed of 23 knots and a submerged speed of 19 knots.

Of the five midget submarines used at Pearl Harbor, one is believed to have made it into the harbor; one was captured in 1941, the others were considered lost or sunk. By 1960 the Navy considered the submarine chronicled in this story to be the final one in the attack on Pearl Harbor.

Pearl Harbor, fall, 1960

JIM CONNOR WAS STATIONED in Pearl City, Hawaii, at EOD (Explosive Ordnance Disposal) Unit #1, that was developed for the purpose of searching out and disposing of underwater bombs or explosive devices, including those placed by an enemy, our own wayward ones or those carried by planes that crashed in the ocean. EOD is the defensive part of this specialized branch of the services. The offensive group is UDT (Underwater Demolition Team) that plants the underwater explosive devices.

Jim's unit operated out of West Loch, one of three lochs in Pearl Harbor, and took care of the Pacific waters. Of the many interesting operations he participated in as a Navy Lieutenant, JG, the Japanese submarine event was at the top of the list. It caused a large stir in the media at that time. A charter boat with sport fishermen and snorkelers discovered a strange vessel on the floor of the ocean near the entrance to Pearl Harbor.

Jim had the duty at the time the call came in, and took a team of divers to investigate. It was definitely a two-man midget Japanese submarine, intact with two torpedoes, left over from the infamous 1941 attack on Pearl Harbor. It was sitting upright in seventy feet of water, no more than fifty feet off the channel into Pearl Harbor. In the clear Hawaiian waters, it was amazing that no one had discovered it in twenty years. The sub was totally encrusted with coral. Two 17-inch diameter torpedoes, one stacked on top of the other and protruding from the bow, seemed intact. Certain of what it was, Jim's team marked the location with a buoy. What they had found sent shock waves all the way to Washington.

Dwight Eisenhower was President at the time and was on a much-publicized visit to Japan, a country we had helped rebuild after the war. The discovery of the two-man sub with its connection to the vicious attack in 1941 that brought the United States into the war could stir up a political maelstrom for the President. The Navy was told to wait on any action regarding the sub. After the President had returned, the word came down from above to retrieve the vessel. A salvage ship was assigned and the divers focused on methods to raise the sub.

At a meeting with the officers from the salvage ship and EOD diving officers, a plan was settled on to dig two holes under the seventy-five foot sub, one fore and one aft. Cables then would be lowered from the ship and the divers would loop them around the sub, forming a saddle that could be attached to the hoisting crane. The recovery team explored the rocky, coral crusted bottom with picks, crowbars and probing tools. Most of the team worked on the project for three days. Finally the cables were rigged.

Care had to be taken with the ancient torpedoes. Effects of explosives underwater are more powerful than on land, and old explosives with corrosion and salt etching could be unstable.

As the cables were secured, the team waited while the salvage ship's crane hoisted the seventy-five-foot boat to a depth of about twelve feet below the surface. Considering its forty-six ton weight, the sub could be maneuvered more easily under water. The salvage ship towed the sub very slowly toward Pearl Harbor, keeping it in the water until they reached the main docks at the shipyard. A barge was brought into position next to the salvage ship and the crane lifted the sub from its watery berth. Salt water poured from it as it was set onto the barge. Reporters, photographers and a good many interested Navy people were on hand to watch.

The entire sub was crusted thick with coral. Only the bottom of the boat, which had not been protected with coral, was thin and rusted. Jim prodded with a tire iron at the hatch, carefully at first, and then with increasing muscle, pounded all around the edges, knocking barnacles and seashells flying. Apparently the hatch wasn't locked from the inside, because finally after several minutes of pounding and prying as though it were a stubborn bottle cap, it popped open. The skipper of the EOD unit, Lieutenant Commander Vince Lovett, clad in flip-flops, shorts and a Hawaiian shirt, peered inside, as press and official Navy photographers snapped away.

No human remains could be seen on first inspection, but the sub was so small that it was difficult to see much of the interior. "They're probably driving cabs in Honolulu," one of the men joked.

The serious international concerns were a matter for the Washington politicians and the top Navy brass. Eventually it was decided that the front part of the sub would be separated—in other words, sawn apart—removing the section with the torpedoes. Further testing on the explosives assured the Navy experts that the torpedoes were still viable even after twenty years, and still could explode. It also was discovered the midget sub contained a 300-pound scuttling charge that had to be dealt with. Once the sub was open, a detailed search was made of the interior and assurances were made the Japanese crew had gotten out. Whether they had made it safely to shore or had met another fate was never known.

As a gesture of good will, the U.S. returned the remainder of the sub to Japan.

By Norma Connor,
as told by Lieutenant JG, Jim Connor
U.S. Navy Explosive Ordnance Disposal Unit #1, Hawaii

A Naval Aviator in Desert Storm

I HAD LONG BEEN INTERESTED in military aviation, and at one time or another explored the possibility of serving in every branch of the armed forces. Every branch that is, except the Navy. Living on a ship for months on end seemed monotonous to me, and I was looking for excitement. After college, I quenched my thirst for adventure by working as a police officer and taking civilian flight lessons. I learned that the Air Force was offering pilot slots to anybody less than 27 years of age with a bachelor's degree, and having just seen the movie *Top Gun*, I wondered if the Navy had a similar program. The movie made a Navy flyer's job seemed more exciting than that of their Air Force counterparts, and the Navy also offered something that the other branches lacked at that time, the potential to get into an honest fight with somebody! The only shooting being done in this era of peacetime was by Naval Aviators. It turned out that the Navy did have a similar program, so I bought a study guide to bone up on my deteriorating math skills, and managed to squeak by with a test score high enough to qualify for the program.

At Pensacola's Naval Aerospace Medical Institute, I was cleared for training as a Naval Aviator. Two months later I was sworn in as an E5 and headed to AOCS (Aviation Officer Candidate School), considered the toughest officer basic school in the U.S. armed forces. I joined class 06-89, denoting that we would be the sixth class to graduate in the year 1989. The day I graduated from AOCS, I was commissioned an Ensign in the United States Naval Reserve and headed a few miles north to Naval Air Station Whiting Field for primary flight training.

I began flying the T-34C Turbo Mentor, a tandem-seat turbo-prop that could fly at 280 knots, was fully aerobatic, and resembled in many ways a scaled down WWII fighter. Everyone wanted to fly jets after graduation, and for that you needed to graduate in the top of your class, accumulating about 30 "above average" grades throughout the primary syllabus. I was up to 34, and my instructors all started to relax and give me tips on how to excel at jet training. But I got nervous or cocky or something, and faltered slightly at the end, ending up second in my class. The Navy employed what it referred to as "quality spread," a mechanism to ensure that good pilots ended up in every community of the service regardless of their preferences, and I was selected to fly helicopters, my second choice,

I was then assigned to another squadron at Whiting Field, HT-8, for advanced training in the TH-57 Sea Ranger. This was the military version of the Bell Jet Ranger single engine turbine helicopter. That syllabus turned us into rotary wing aviators, and emphasized low-level flight, tactical operations and instrument flying. After a few practice ship landings, I earned my gold wings and was designated a Naval Aviator.

Although I'd hoped to move to the West coast and fly the new SH-60 helicopter, the Navy again put its needs ahead of my desires and sent me to Jacksonville, Florida, to fly the 1950's era SH-3H Sea King. It was just slightly smaller than a school bus, with pontoons on the side so that it could float if needed. I liked the Sea King because it was old and proven; all the basic problems that could kill you had been worked out years before, and now the thing just plugged along like a faithful but tired old dog. Sea Kings also were the helicopters that deployed on carriers, and if you're going to be a naval aviator, you might as well live on the big boat.

I was assigned to Helicopter Antisubmarine Squadron Nine, a squadron of Carrier Air Wing Eight, deploying aboard the *U.S.S. Theodore Roosevelt*, CVN 71. Things were heating up rapidly in the Persian Gulf, with Desert Shield well underway and the deadline for Saddam's withdrawal from Kuwait approaching fast. We deployed days after I joined the squadron in December of 1990.

My first days on an operating carrier were busy and confusing. Just finding your way around on a carrier can be bewildering at first. Each space is placarded with its deck or level number, its frame number telling how far forward or aft you are, and a number designating how far to port or starboard you are from the centerline. It's not as easy to get a grasp on as it sounds, and I gave up exploring pretty quickly; else I might never find my own room again. General quarters was even worse, requiring you to move "up and forward on the starboard side, down and aft on the port side" to keep folks from banging into one another. I just stayed out of the way,

Not much flying is conducted during the *trans-lant* (across the ocean), but one incident did harshly remind us of the dangers inherent in Naval Aviation. One of our EA-6B aircraft snapped an arresting cable on landing and went over the edge of the deck and into the drink. All four guys ejected in time, but we lost a sixty million dollar aircraft and some of us started to think that our cruise was already jinxed. Shortly after that I was flying plane-guard near the ship on a dark night as the fixed-wing guys were lining up for their turn to land. One F-14 inadvertently let go a sidewinder, an IR (infrared) heat-seeking air-to-air missile designed to home in on the hot exhaust from a target aircraft's jet engine. Our helicopter was the slowest moving, highest IR signature target around, and directly in line with the path of the missile. We got down really close to the water and pointed our exhaust away from the coil of aircraft descending to the landing pattern. I waited for the boom, but it never came. The war hadn't even started and I was getting shot at by my own guys!

A few days later the Air Boss tasked us with a new mission. He wanted us to fly out 15 miles from the ship and investigate an Iraqi amphibious assault ship. Rules of engagement required that we visually identify the ship as an enemy before the fleet could attack it. We felt unprepared to say the least; we had no flak vests, no guns, no chaff, flares or other countermeasures. In order to get within visual range of the enemy ship, we had to get well within its weapons range, and thus were sure to be blown out of the sky! It was around sunset, so we cut the lights and dropped down to 40 feet and 100 knots. We saw the target ship on the horizon and made our sea skimming tactical approach, coming out of the sun like in the movies. Luckily for us, the ship turned out to be a friendly, so we didn't end up the first casualties of the war after all.

On 17 January I briefed at 0400 as part of an alert-crew, standing by to fill in as needed. The shooting had started, and the best source of information on the hostilities seemed to be the BBC, which was broadcast over a pictureless channel on the ship's closed circuit TV. Details were sketchy, and our intel guys really couldn't tell us any more than the BBC. We learned that this conflict would be known as "Desert Storm," and we heard Hussein say we had started the "Mother of all wars," whatever that meant.

On the 18th we transited the Strait of Hormuz, and were officially in the combat theater. That meant tax-free status and $110 per month "imminent danger" pay. We were told at that point that the allied forces had flown 4000 sorties and had lost only seven aircraft to the enemy. That may have been a good ratio for the military but didn't sound so hot to me. On January 21st, aircraft from the *T.R.* fired their first-ever shots in anger. The early morning strike was delayed due to poor weather and the presence of a particularly annoying SA-2 missile site. An EA-6B Prowler from the VAQ 141 Shadowhawks launched a HARM (Homing Anti-Radiation Missile) to take out the radar that controls the missile site. The HARM homed in on the emitted radar signals and destroyed the facility. That first shot cleared the way for the rest of the strike package, and we were finally in the war,

Our carrier flew night strikes, while other carriers flew day missions. The first aircraft to fly was always the helicopter, which launched to cover the launch of the other aircraft. We flew in a D-shaped pattern on the starboard side of the ship, always prepared to rescue a pilot who had to eject on launch or while landing. We were always the first to launch and the last to land.

Takeoffs from the deck after dark could be intense, as the nights were often pitch black with no discernable horizon. We performed what were called ITOs (instrument take offs) where we pulled into a hover visually, then switched our eyes to the instruments and flew off into the blackness. The first few were pretty scary, I must say. The Persian Gulf is a hazy dismal place to fly at night; as my father would say, it's dark as a tax collector's heart. We started flying with NVGs (night vision goggles) but the practice was in its infancy and we weren't really equipped to take full advantage of the technology. The cockpit lighting in the Sea King was red, intended to help preserve the pilot's night vision. But NVGs picked up light in that spectrum and amplified it immensely, causing the goggles to wash out in blinding light. Newer helicopters were equipped with green backlights for the gauges, which were compatible with the NVGs. We jury-rigged our system by turning off the cockpit lights, and then duct-taping green chemical light sticks all around the instrument panel. The green light wasn't visible to the NVGs, so we could fly without being blinded. The procedure in those early days was for one pilot to practice with the NVGs while the other kept an eye on the gauges the old fashioned way. After a while we'd switch off. It was sure nice to have the goggles on those really black nights. These days all Navy helicopter pilots fly with goggles all the time at night.

I remember those first few days of the war as being rather confusing. We got very little input back from the intelligence guys about how the war was proceeding. We didn't know if we were winning or not, or even if we were accomplishing our own mission objectives. The only TV station the carrier's satellite dish could pick up was CNN, and after a while the powers that be stopped piping it into our ready rooms. We didn't have much time for TV anyway, or anything much else for that matter. On the ready-room blackboard was written in big letters "Eat, Sleep & Fly," because that was all we had time to do. I had less of a handle on what was going on than did the folks back home, who could watch twenty different channels and had as many daily newspapers to read.

The operating procedures were confusing as well. We tried to communicate as securely as possible; using a code list promulgated each day. I remember spending an entire flight trying to find four other ships to deliver them the day's codes. But our call signs for them were outdated, as were their reported positions, so we never found some of them. With so many counties involved in the allied effort using the same radio frequencies, we often couldn't speak to our own guys or spoke to someone else by mistake.

An excellent example of all this confusion occurred on January 24th, when we were briefed that an FA-18 pilot had ejected about 100 miles from the carrier. We took off for the SAR (search and rescue) and soon after were told through various mumbo-jumbo code words that there was a missile inbound toward the carrier. One of our jobs was to drop chaff in such a situation to spoof the missile. The chaff we carried was a cylinder containing thousands of strips of a material akin to tin foil, with an explosive charge that would blow the foil into a large cloud. The cloud of foil had a large radar signature, hopefully big enough to convince inbound radar-guided anti-ship missiles that the cloud was the intended target. So we completed the weapons checklist and headed out the bearing line in question to get between the ship and the missile and head it off. My aircraft commander went on the NVGs, and then all hell started to break loose.

A tongue-tied German started screaming for us to make clear our heading, and someone kept yelling for *Jaguar* to turn a certain direction, but the voice was British and not from our carrier. Our call sign was Jaguar, but the Brits flew a jet strike-fighter called the Jaguar, so we couldn't tell just to whom they were talking. Then the guys in *Strike* on our own carrier started to adopt that stressed-out voice as they yelled for all aircraft to scramble west. Strike is the division that coordinates tactical operations, and soon we heard them scream "Mom's hot" and the sky started to light up. "Mom" was the call sign for the carrier, and "hot" meant that she'd started shooting. The *U.S.S. Caron*, a Spruance class destroyer, was less than a mile ahead and started blasting a salvo of rockets in our direction. The rocket blasts were far too bright for the HAC's (Helicopter Aircraft Commander) NVGs, and he was instantly blinded. I quickly took control of the helicopter, trying in vain to keep from flying through the chaff cloud created by the exploding rockets. As the other pilot waited for his eyes to readjust to the dark, I got down low to the water and decided to get outside of CIWS (Close-In Weapon System) range, still prepared to dump our countermeasures if the call came. The CIWS is a 20mm Vulcan canon that can vaporize a target close to the ship, so I didn't want to be close! It turned out that the alleged inbound bogey was hundreds of miles away and no threat at all. But once again, I had been shot at by my own guys.

On February 2nd we lost an A6 Intruder and her crew, shot down while returning from a massive strike on Iraq. I manned aircraft 612 when the call for "Operation Falcon" came down, indicating the need for a strike rescue mission. This helicopter is equipped with DALS (Downed Aircrew Locator System), a James Bond sort of box that homed in on a downed aviator's portable radio beacon and steered you right to him for the rescue. We then got word that 616, our forward deployed aircraft, had launched on the SAR, so we wouldn't have to go. Later, I went for my debrief and listened to 531's wingman recounting how he had lost contact with his playmate. I had been confident that the crew would be rescued, but I learned then that they had been lost. These two men whom I barely knew were our first casualties of the war, and I started to brace myself for the time when my friends started to get killed, and wondered if I'd survive myself.

But the war wasn't over yet, so we resumed flying our combat support missions, consisting of starboard D, mine sweeping, logistics, and target identification. Mines were a big threat, as the *U.S.S. Princeton* and the *U.S.S. Tripoli* both had suffered damage from them. One time we were vectored to a suspected mine, which turned out to be just a trash bag. But we still needed to dispose of it; otherwise it might be mistaken again and cause an interruption to flight operations as the carrier turned away from it. I pulled out my Astra 9mm pistol and pumped a few rounds into it, but the thing wouldn't sink. The next time we found such a bag we opened fire with our M-60 machine gun to no avail, the trash bags just didn't want to sink. Another time an S-3 aircraft reported a mine and fired a bunch of smoke rockets at it to mark it for us. I flew over to the smoke and discovered an ancient, barnacle-encrusted sea turtle paddling his way out of the fiery water. Poor guy, he almost got himself blown up. Forward deployed helicopters from my squadron ended up deploying SEALs to destroy ten floating mines, but I never did happen upon a real one myself.

On February 24th the ground war began. We heard it was coming about 12 hours in advance and I was in the air, covering the strike when it began at about 0400 local time. The A-6s on the deck were loaded with ordnance for close air support, quite an impressive sight. As the ground war progressed, I was at last anointed with my official call sign: "Blitz", as in Blitz Craig (Blitzkrieg). Something to do with my gun happy nature I think. Pilots had been issued handguns for the first time since Vietnam, and I had provided some training due to my experience as a police officer. Contrary to popular belief, pilots don't get to choose their own call signs; rather they are bestowed on them by other members of the squadron. Most don't get exciting ones like *Maverick* or *Iceman* either, so I felt pretty lucky to end up with Blitz. One man with a big noggin ended up with "Bucket Head", a guy from Wisconsin became "Cheese Head." and a pilot who seemed too liberal, became "Flower Child." Our XO (executive officer) inadvertently had deployed a large cloud of chaff, and so became "Tinsel Town." Yep, Blitz was just fine for me.

By February 28th the ground war was over. Our strike guys got a lot of action providing close air support for the advancing troops, who were leery of Air Force cover after some nasty friendly fire incidents by Air Force A-10s. The skipper treated the crew to a "steel beach picnic" on the flight deck, and issued each man two beers in celebration of our victory. We even got a short port call in Dubai, in the United Arab Emirates. Back on the ship I did some informal math and added up my combat support points. By my calculations I didn't quite have enough for an Air Medal: 19.768 out of the needed 20 points. One more flight and I would have logged enough "green ink" time to qualify. Combat hours are recorded in your logbook, in green pencil actually, to differentiate them from non-combat sorties. I thought I would be the only pilot in theater to go home without an air medal.

We soon steamed out of the Persian Gulf, hung around outside the Strait of Hormuz for a couple of days conducting flight ops, then started heading south toward the Red Sea. During that time I was promoted to Lieutenant, JG, which meant a small increase in pay and a commensurate increase in respect. Around that time there was an awards presentation for the squadron held in the ready room. Admiral Frost was on hand to award each pilot and air crewman with an Air Medal for our operations during Desert Storm. My notoriously poor math had been in error, I did indeed qualify for a medal myself; and it looked damn good on me I must say. The admiral cracked quite a smile when told that my call sign was Blitz.

After leaving the Red Sea we ended up on station in the northeast corner of the Med, between Cyprus and Turkey. The task force was poised to strike Iraq if they decide to interfere with Operation Provide Comfort, an operation protecting the northern Kurds from Iraqi oppression. Some called it Provide Muffet, after Little Miss Muffet in the nursery rhyme, ensuring the Kurds get their "way." After more port calls in Haifa, Israel, and Rhodes, Greece, we turned over Mediterranean operations to the *Forrestal* battle group and headed back across the Atlantic for home. My father joined the ship in Bermuda for the last few days trek back to port as part of the Navy's traditional "tiger cruise" for sailors' families.

IT'S HARD TO EXPRESS to an outsider how it feels to participate in a war. I didn't charge up a hill with a rifle or really become an active combatant in any way. But it was still a surreal experience to simply be a component of the effort, ever conscious that my small part could at any time become a significant one. I flew constantly, most often in pitch-blackness, sometimes without a chance between flights to shower or eat. Crew-rest regulations went out the window the first day, and I was tired, confused and struggling to stay ahead of the power curve. People that I ate breakfast with were dead before dinner, my own guys were shooting at me in all the confusion, and I had absolutely no indication whatsoever of when it all might end. I remain fiercely proud that even though I was not a front-line fighter, I managed to do whatever was asked of me; that fresh out of flight school I was able to hold it together and make a positive contribution to the effort.

By James S. Craig, Lieutenant, USNR
Helicopter Antisubmarine Squadron Nine
Carrier Air Wing Eight
U.S.S. Theodore Roosevelt, CVN 71

A Gallant Woman of World War II

A U.S. ARMY HOSPITAL IN 1944 was as real to my aging neighbor as the spacious living room where she described it to me sixty years later. In her recollections, she would revisit that army hospital in Western England—a thousand beds in row on row of concrete block buildings, and tents for five hundred more. She would recall keeping the joints and muscles of wounded GIs from atrophy, training body parts to take over from those lost to shrapnel, bullets, burns and air crashes. My friend was worlds away from the days when she and an assistant set up a physical therapy clinic to treat casualties from a conflict that was at that time just a rumor. A gigantic buildup of men and material in the surrounding countryside, "The Yank Invasion" as the locals called them, signaled a major battle on the horizon, didn't it?

It did.

Supply ships dodging German U-Boats in the Atlantic meant delayed equipment, forcing the staff of the budding hospital to improvise. Gertrude's crew of enlisted men poured cement into empty tin cans to produce weights for rope and pulley exercises. When heat lamps finally arrived, they dismantled the crates and built treatment tables with the precious lumber. Gertrude and her assistant searched a village dump for bottles to hold rubbing alcohol and soothing oils. They set up forms for patients' records on a quarter-sheet of paper each. Even now, Gertrude seldom wasted anything. Her handwriting was still minute, virtually illegible.

In my months of fascinating conversation with her, Gertrude's then six-by-ten-foot personal space in a concrete block hut shared with six nurses and a reluctant coal-burning stove became as real as the house around us, these current rooms filled with mementos of her studying dance at Julliard School of Music, earning her doctorate on the GI Bill, twenty-five years as a university professor of dance, travel, retirement in Arizona. With hands deformed by advanced arthritis, she pulled the collar of an imaginary field coat to her chin and described periodic dashes through freezing drizzle to the bathhouse across the hospital grounds—three tubs for fifty women, five inches of lukewarm water three times a month. Wolf whistles from GIs who gazed from windows of the wards as she went by were far behind her, but she still smiled at the memory.

These and other stories inspired me to bring a yellow notepad to our sessions. I begged Gertrude to slow down so I could take notes as she described D-Day.

"Britain shot plane after plane into the skies. Seaports spewed out countless vessels filled with combat forces and material. We thought the departure of three of our surgeons and three enlisted men meant they were on a short leave. Not until they came back two weeks later, having been through hell and looking like it, did we learn they had been part of a flotilla that carried a half-million men and their equipment across the Channel. Within days our hospital filled the regular beds and overflowed into the tents."

DURING HUNDREDS OF AFTERNOONS on Gertrude's sofa, I filled my notepad with tales of men who arrived direct from field hospitals or aid stations, still in muddy combat clothes. The story of a patient whose orders read, "Exercise for fractured femur," occupied a full afternoon. This soldier, a boy really, had trouble following Gertrude's orders to work specific muscles in the broken leg. Suggesting he try practicing with his other leg, she had lifted the blanket to find 'the good leg' had been amputated. *"We'll just have to work harder with the injured one,"* she said to the young soldier. *"Let's see if we can get it right because you'll need to have this one good and strong when you learn to walk with your prosthesis."*

"How I regretted not being informed!" she told me. "How I struggled for words of optimism instead of pity." Turning philosophical, she murmured, "The first adjustment to amputation is an agonizing ordeal, but the soldier who survives that battle has character outranked by no one. I witnessed many such campaigns in the months to come."

Another patient became real to me as Gertrude remembered a GI with a back injury—a gunshot wound to lumbar spine, possible resection. Over time she was able to straighten his legs, help him sit up, move his legs until he could extend and eventually stand on them. "He did it!" said Gertrude. "He took a few steps, and said, 'Well, I guess I can meet my wife since I'll be able to walk after all.' "

MY FRIEND TOLD TALES of herself as well as patients, describing the misery of thin cotton uniforms in a chilly English spring, and delight with a suit of red underwear in a Christmas package from home. She told of the day she and her assistant hitched a ride to London in a B-17 bomber, following a rumor of warm field coats, size Men's Small, at a PX there. "Once in the plane, we took turns crawling into the tail-gunner's turret on our hands and knees, glad we weren't fat and glad we weren't tail-gunners," she said. Her description of walking past bombed buildings on the way to a stage play in the city, coming out of the theater into the blackout, asking an MP for directions to their billet and being taken for prostitutes, seemed a story from a fairy tale to me, I who had spent the war as a heedless child complaining of sugar rationing and skinned knees. My parents read the war news. Gertrude lived it.

The excursion to London had taken place as Gertrude waited for word of a pilot from Airborne Infantry, a soldier who caused her to break her resolution not to be "a women who spent the war waiting for a man she loved." A participant in a glider landing behind enemy lines, her Dan was missing in action.

Almost as painful as her heartbreak over her lover was Gertrude's story of the day when orders came to empty the hospital. "All our patients were to be transferred elsewhere," she said. "We were always saying goodbye to infantry units, artillery units and air corps engineers being sent to France. It seemed to be our turn until the Colonel read us our orders. Our own GIs had been cleared out for a convoy of fifteen hundred German prisoners of war, patients from a hospital cut off from their unit during the Allied siege at Brest. We were to stay here in this fourteenth century cow pasture and take care of the damned bastards who started this mess!"

Body trembling with fresh indignation, Gertrude described the weeks following the POW arrival. No fraternizing. No conversation. Strict instruction to maintain a dignified coldness with homesick young kids as well as heel-clicking officers who tried to pump the staff for information, unmitigated joy when the POWs were sent away as abruptly as they had come.

"Allied planes roared overhead on bombing missions over Germany every night now," said Gertrude when a plane flying low over her house reminded her of other flights. "One clear night I ran outside as a distant hum became a drone. Planes came from all directions. They circled, fell into a pattern and flew off toward the East. It looked like all the stars were moving."

IN TIME AND WITH age, there came a health crisis of Gertrude's own. She tried a nursing home but checked herself out and took a taxi home declaring, "Everybody I met there was boring." Thanks to a team of willing neighbors, she never moved back, but she was no longer independent. Friends and relatives brought her groceries, took her to doctors' appointments, balanced her checkbook. Always "crusty,' she became confused and argumentative during multiple hospitalizations where her heart faltered, failed. On a chilly April morning at age ninety-two, it stopped.

By Janet Sabina
Recounting the story of her friend,
Second Lieutenant Gertrude Mooney,
Nurse, U.S. Army, WWII

Christmas at Bougainville

A T DUSK ON CHRISTMAS Eve, 1943, the South Pacific island of Bougainville was a dim line far off to starboard as the ship, an Attack Transport, sailed in a northwesterly direction parallel to the island coast in fairly calm seas. At dawn on Christmas Day the 164th Infantry Regiment, part of the newly created Americal Division, was aboard that ship, preparing to land on Bougainville. Our mission was to relieve a Marine unit that had made the initial assault and established a beachhead for us.

Below decks in the troop compartments, the men were reading, playing cards, talking, sleeping, or just loafing. I went down to remind the NCOs that quiet hours tonight start at 2000. All games and chatter are to stop then and everyone is to be in his bunk. The NCOs are to have their men ready to disembark at 0600.

How many of the men slept, or how much they slept, I don't know. I do know my sleep was broken with repeated worrisome thoughts and uncertainties. I knew our landing area was inside the Marine perimeter, so there was little possibility of enemy resistance other than that of artillery fire, but what about my men? Has their training been effective? Can they all get down the cargo nets into the landing craft without mishap? If someone falls into the water, has he learned enough about how to shed his gear and get to the surface before he drowns? Questions like that plagued my thoughts before I finally did get to sleep.

Next morning, my first conscious thought was that a storm had come up. The ship was rolling heavily. My second thought was that we had arrived and anchored. The only reminder that it was Christmas Day came at about 0500 hours when a voice came over the ship's loudspeaker:

"Gentlemen, we have about four hours to get this ship unloaded and out of here before the Jap bombers get here from Rabaul. We wish you good luck and Merry Christmas!" My next thought was, *Merry Christmas, indeed!*

I dressed quickly and went out to the nearest weather deck and there was Bougainville, a mile away. The late moon did not reveal any detail, just a black line above a white line of surf. Other officers were out now. It was not light enough to smoke so we went into the Mess to catch some coffee and cigarettes. The ship came alive, winches grinding; the squawk box sounding orders. Navy people were busy with their tasks. Landing craft with their crews aboard were being dropped over the side and I heard engines starting up and saw the cargo nets being thrown down the side of the ship.

It was time for me to check my men. Down in the troop compartment I caught a glimpse of my platoon sergeant in the crowd milling about. He reported all men up and ready to go on deck. Then the call came, "Now hear this. First wave to your boat stations."

The rifle companies were on the first wave. Successive waves took the Heavy Weapons Company, Battalion Headquarters Company, and my Anti-Tank Platoon.

Boat stations were on the lowest weather deck as close to the water as possible, but still required a climb of fifteen or twenty feet down the cargo net to reach the landing craft.

Climbing down the nets with full combat equipment was an art. We had practiced many times ashore and several times aboard ship, but this was real. Most nets took five men abreast down at a time. As soon as one man disappeared over the rail the next man in line climbed onto the rail and started down. With the ship rolling, and as many as fourteen or fifteen other men hanging on to the net at the same time, each carrying forty to sixty pounds of pack on his back, his rifle trying to hook itself on the net, and the bayonet on his belt doing the same, I have often wondered why so few people are killed or injured in this part of the landing.

The next problem was getting from the net to the boat. Each man had to judge just how far to climb down the net to reach the best spot to drop off into the landing craft as it reached the top of a wave. He could only pray he didn't get so far down the net that the boat rocked against the ship and crushed his feet before he had time to jump into it. Worse yet, he hoped he wouldn't let go the net and land on his head in the boat or in the water between the boat and the ship. On the other hand, if he did not climb down far enough, or misjudged the rise of the boat, he could end up with a long drop and serious injury. Senior Commanders figure on having a one percent casualty rate on unopposed landings.

Fortunately none of the men in my landing craft were hurt and that was the best Christmas present I could have hoped for. We landed safely ashore. Our 37mm anti-tank guns, along with the jeeps to pull them, would come later.

We celebrated Christmas on the beach sitting in foxholes that had been dug by the Marines we were replacing. There was no festive dinner for us; the cooks and their field kitchens were still aboard ship. We ate the same old K-rations we had eaten yesterday and the day before that and the day before that. There were no Christmas trees to decorate. The only trees we saw were a few ragged palm trees that survived the barrage from the initial assault. There were no church services; the chaplains also were still on the ship waiting their turn in the landing craft.

We were just a group of sweaty, weary soldiers, glad to be alive, missing our families and friends back home and wishing we were anywhere but here.

By George Isenberg
2nd Lieutenant, "E" Company, 164th Infantry Regiment, WWII
"H" Company, 38th Infantry Regiment, Korea, U.S. Army

Stars and Bars in Vietnam

November 1967

AFTER A TEN-HOUR FLIGHT from Hawaii, the coast of Vietnam finally appeared on the horizon. I could feel the adrenalin beginning to flow. Finally, I was going to war.

For years, growing up in a small Wisconsin village, I had listened to the vets from WWII and Korea recount their experiences. My step dad and mom were active in the VFW (Veterans of Foreign Wars). I often attended VFW functions with them, so I had many opportunities to listen to war stories. Most vets chose not to speak of unpleasant events, but they all agreed that going to war was a crucial step in becoming a man. It taught courage and self-confidence. Although none of them had made a career of the military, for some, their war experiences seemed to be life-defining moments.

I had spent six years in the Army already, but most of that time was in schools. I was itching to get out into the real Army and do something. Now I was going to get a chance to prove myself. In the real Army. In a real war.

WHEN THE ARMY OFFERED me a promotion from staff sergeant to first lieutenant, they told me I would have to do a year in Korea. At the Fort Devens Intelligence School, however, I met a fellow lieutenant who had come on active duty just to do his time in the Army and then return to civilian life. He was scheduled to be sent to Vietnam. I saw a chance to help a buddy and get a piece of the action. Who knew; the war might be over before I got a chance to participate. I had been too young for Korea. So my new buddy and I arranged to switch assignments and now here I was, about to land in a war zone.

Most of the passengers on the plane also were on their way to the war for the first time. I wondered if they felt the same nervous anticipation I felt. The ribbons on the uniforms of other passengers showed they were headed back for repeat tours.

As we began our initial approach to Tan Son Nhut airport, my excitement increased when I looked out the window and saw explosions on the ground. Oh, no! What was going on down there? Suddenly the engines began to roar and I felt myself being pushed back into my seat. The plane was climbing again. It banked to the right and continued to gain altitude. It then leveled off. In a few minutes, the captain came on the intercom to reassure us.

"Sorry, guys. We've been told we can't land yet. Something goin' on down there. We'll just circle around for a little. I'll keep you posted."

The plane continued to circle above Saigon, sometimes climbing, sometimes descending. I could do nothing but look out the window at the explosions on the ground and the sporadic pyrotechnics in the Vietnam sky and wonder what was happening down below. I tried to relax, but couldn't help getting more nervous with each passing minute. Desperately needing to talk, I turned to the sergeant sitting next to me.

"I've done this before," I said. "Circled twice above New York City and once above Chicago."

"Me too," grunted the sergeant, "but then there wasn't no war going on below."

"I remember circling O'Hare once until we started running out of fuel and had to land in Peoria."

"Probably ain't much fuel left in this plane either. Wonder where else we could land."

Finally, the captain announced we were cleared for landing. When the plane taxied toward the terminal, I barely could make out the silhouettes of the runway lights that had all been turned off. By now, clouds had appeared and concealed the moonlight. I could see huge searchlights dancing across the area, but they carefully avoided our plane.

One by one, we stepped from the door onto the platform and into an ominous scene. American soldiers in jungle fatigues, flak jackets, and helmets were waiting at the bottom of the ladder. Each was carrying an automatic weapon; one had a grenade launcher slung over his shoulder. Four dark-colored busses were nearby. Ambulances with their roof lights flashing were parked in the distance. Gray figures were running across the tarmac. People yelled out orders. The *wop-wop-wop* of several Huey helicopters dominated the spectrum of night sounds, while the blinking of their running lights added an eerie hue to the airfield.

Now, as we stepped down onto Vietnam soil, someone called out to us to hurry to the busses. "Officers on the first bus! Forget your bags. They'll come later."

We quickly ran to our bus. Four armed MPs followed us on board. The bus windows were dirty and had bars on them. The door had been removed. The bus lurched forward. As we sped across the tarmac, one of the MPs addressed us.

"Welcome to Nam, Sirs! Y'all landed smack dab in a hornet's nest. We had a mortar attack here about an hour and a half ago. Now listen up real good! We're gonna be takin' you to a hotel for the night."

"What about our bags?" asked an officer at the front of the bus.

"Your duffel bags'll be sent over before morning," the MP answered. "First, we gotta go through some Vietnamese villages and we don't know what we'll find there tonight. Charlie's definitely in the area. In case we come under enemy fire, I want y'all to hit the deck and stay down till I give the 'all clear.' Don't worry about getting your uniforms dirty. Don't worry about nothing, except keepin' your heads down."

"Hey Sarge! How about giving us some weapons in case we're attacked?" another officer yelled.

"Ain't got no more. Besides, y'all are probably safer without 'em for the time bein'."

We all fell silent and tried to get a glimpse of the scenery that whizzed by. Or as much of it as we could see in the dark, through dirty windows, and with our heads tucked down. The first village was right outside the airfield. The night air was heavy and the smell of fish and garbage wafted in through the opening that had been the door of the bus. We passed through two villages, both dark, as though no one lived in them. From time to time, a dog was heard barking as the bus sped through the narrow, dirt streets. Explosions from artillery and the crackling of small arms fire continued, but by now it seemed a natural part of the soundscape.

After a twenty-minute ride, the bus pulled into a compound encircled with concertina wire atop high walls of dark green sandbags. Guards manning 50-caliber machine guns were situated every 20 yards just behind the wall. Inside the hotel, a middle-aged Vietnamese woman greeted us from behind a desk counter in the dark, shabby lobby. Down the hall appeared to be a bar. Registration was simple; the senior MP went up to the desk, said something to the woman, and collected a handful of keys. After passing one out to each of us, the MP again addressed the group.

"Hope y'all have a good night's sleep. Be down here at 0800 tomorrow and there'll be someone here to give you further instructions."

The elevators were not working. I climbed the stairs to the third floor. Inside my room, I stood and wondered how I would look and feel in the morning, since my toothbrush, razor and clean uniform were in my duffel bag. I took my shoes off and lay down on the bed without undressing and tried to doze off. But I couldn't keep my eyes closed. I had to admit to myself that I was a little shaken by the events of the last couple of hours. I took some solace in the belief that it was only natural to feel this way. I now realized that all my impressions and images since the moment I arrived in Vietnam were at the same time fuzzy and exhilarating. But not exactly what I had expected. *A mortar attack at the airfield? Welcome to your war, Lieutenant!* Finally, after an hour of failing to get to sleep, I decided to go downstairs to see if that really was a bar I had seen, and if so, whether it was still open.

When I entered the "Saigon Tea Room," I saw that the only lights in the room were behind the bar. Two people were sitting there, drinking. As my eyes became accustomed to the dim lighting, I saw a couple of the officers who had ridden in from the airport with me, sitting at a table in the corner with two young Vietnamese girls. I took a stool at the bar.

I then noticed that although both my neighbors at the bar were in uniform, one was a woman. I looked closer. Hell, it was the actress Martha Raye! She was wearing tiger fatigues with colonel's eagles on both collars. The man was dressed the same way, except he had crossed rifles on his left collar. I assumed he was a real colonel. Both were wearing Special Forces shoulder patches.

I ordered a beer and listened to the two "colonels" talk.

" . . . at Tan Son Nhut tonight, you mean?" Raye was asking.

"Yeah, no one's safe in this goddammed country! At least when we're out in the boonies, we're always expecting something. And we're ready for it. But you'd think a guy could come into the city and relax once in a while."

"I heard there were some K-I-As," said Raye, casually dropping the military abbreviation for "killed in action."

"That's a roger. And I knew one of the guys. He was just about to enter the plane when he took a mortar fragment in the head. Can you believe that? The poor bastard spent twelve months with the 1st Division fighting the Cong down in the Delta. Not even wounded during all that time. Then he buys the farm within one step of being inside the Freedom Bird. We spent some time together at Bragg. Sonofabitch!"

"Did he leave a family?"

"I'll say! A wife and five kids."

"Christ!"

"Yeah. He was being assigned to West Point as an instructor. Hey, Martha, let's have another one. This one's for Joe."

I GAZED AT MYSELF in the mirror behind the bar. There sat a new lieutenant who was about to realize his dream of fighting in a war. But what had he gotten himself into? Was war beginning to lose some of its luster? My stomach began to act up. I stared at my beer for several minutes. Finally, without taking another sip, I left two dollars on the bar and returned to my room.

By J.R. Holbrook
Lieutenant Colonel,
U.S Army Intelligence

A Ranger and the *Tet* Offensive

January 30, 1968

A T 0300, THE NVA/VC (North Vietnamese Army and the Viet Cong) simultaneously launched major offense maneuvers throughout the country. It was the *Tet* Offensive—Tet, the Vietnamese New Year. Within forty-eight hours communist forces attacked thirty-six provincial capitals, five major cities, countless military headquarters, airfields and combat bases. It soon became clear that Saigon and the ancient capital of Hue were primary targets. Seventy-two thousand of the enemy, 5000 Americans and over 10,000 South Vietnamese civilians were killed before it ended two months later. At that time the young soldier, Gene Sprouse, was stationed in Saigon at the Tan Son Nhut Air Base adjacent to the city.

The allies, or United Nations Peace Keepers, mostly Americans, were caught unaware. The NVA/VC operation was well organized with infiltration of men, weapons and supplies that had been pre-planned over a period of months. The Viet Cong had come into Saigon on laundry trucks, disguised as vendors, and even in mock funerals. Later it would become clear that there was a sizable cadre of communist sympathizers scattered throughout Saigon. Not only had the enemy assembled in secrecy, they actually tested and fired their weapons during Tet fireworks displays.

GENE SPROUSE, A RANGER in Special Forces, was among the twenty percent of U.S. Army personnel who were armed at the time of the attack at Tan Son Nhut Air Base in Saigon. He was positioned with other Rangers in a bunker that was part of the thirty-mile defensive perimeter around the base. The soldiers carried M16s with eight magazines, each with twenty rounds. Mounted on the rifle was a NOD (Night Observation Device), also called a "Starlight Scope," enabling a soldier to see in the dark. Everything appeared green. Along with magnification, the NOD captures movement of a body by reacting to its generated heat.

Because of an amnesty program called *Chieu Hoi,* American soldiers had to follow certain rules of engagement during conflict. Chieu Hoi allowed NVA/VC troops to surrender to the U.S Army without the threat of disciplinary action, making it necessary to require identification whenever the enemy was spotted. Indeed, it was impossible to identify opponents by sight because all Vietnamese looked and dressed alike. It was also true that women and children served side by side with men in the NVA/VC.

The Vietnam War frequently was fought after dark. There was an extensive network of underground tunnels from which the enemy would emerge at night. The NVA/VC, effectively camouflaged in their black clothes, attempted to discover flares, claymore mines, and booby traps emplaced by the U.S. forces. They were very good at disarming them. They would even turn the mines around to explode toward the Americans. During the Tet Offensive, communist forces were so certain of victory that many discarded their peasant clothing, donned uniforms and marched in a parade, as battle raged throughout Saigon.

Around the perimeter of Tan Son Nhut Air Base was a fence topped by circular razor wire. An infiltrator from the NVA/VC could drag a ladder to the fence, throw a mattress over the barrier in order to climb over it, and jump to the ground inside the army installation. Gene was in position in his bunker to see, through his NOD, people crawling toward the perimeter fence. Because of the limiting rules of engagement, these people had to be challenged because they may have been turning themselves in to gain amnesty.

Gene challenged the people in the distance by shouting *"Dun lai, dun lai,"* meaning "Halt." He could see very well they had not yet made the fence but they were close enough to hear him. Fortunately for Gene, one of the enemy made a tactical error. While looking through the NOD, Gene saw a muzzle flash and knew someone had fired. He sprayed the area immediately with eighty rounds, using up four magazines.

Suddenly the sky lit up with rocket-propelled flares. So many bright flares attached to parachutes shot into the sky lighting up the area. Gene was blinded but he kept shooting toward the place where he had seen the enemy. Instinctively, he fired his weapon from left to right and back again, over and over. Gene's heart began to pound and he thought he was going to die.

By the time he was able to see again, about 30 minutes later, U.S. Army helicopters were all over the sky and the gunfire was deafening. However, the episode was over quickly. Later that morning he learned that this was to have been a major attack on Tan Son Nhut. The NVA/VC plans were found on the bodies of the men whom Gene had killed. They had accurate maps of the base that showed that if they had penetrated the perimeter they could have damaged many airplanes, ammunition dumps, fuel storage areas, and containment or housing areas. U.S. casualties would have been overwhelming.

It took time to gather intelligence since very often the dead bodies were booby-trapped. It was discovered that Gene had shot three NVA/VC soldiers, one of whom was only fourteen years old. Of the dead and wounded it was learned that four enemy soldiers had been barbers on the base. They had cut the GI's hair and at the same time, were gaining useful information on the base's security.

The next morning Gene was debriefed and told by his superiors that his action had saved the base. During contact Gene had no time to think; it happened too fast. He did what he was trained to do, which was to lay down intensive firepower as fast as possible. He learned there were incidents all around the perimeter and a total of twenty-six NVA/VC were killed that night, all of which indicated a major attack had been imminent. Gene was required by mandatory regulation to speak to a psychiatrist and was back in a different bunker position the next night. Reports were sent to MACV (Military Assistance Command Vietnam) headquarters in Saigon.

Gene would be twenty years old on March 24, 1968. One day before he was to celebrate his birthday in Vietnam a buddy announced to him, "Hey Sprouse! You're going to be getting a special birthday present! You're getting the Silver Star for bravery in action."

He received it in a ceremony about a year later.

By Charlotte J. Rickett Wykoff,
The story of Private First Class Gene Sprouse
377 Combat Support Group
U.S. Army, 1st Cavalry

A Nice Ring to It

GRIM AND FORBIDDING IN her somber gray, the *U.S.S. Mobile Bay* loomed overhead. The American flag fluttered from her mast. White "E's" on each bridge wing and a golden anchor chain were her only decorations. As I stood waiting for my grandson, Lieutenant Commander Joseph James Ring, to sign us in I thought of how he had come to be stationed on this guided missile cruiser.

Joe worked for a grade point average that would qualify him for a Navy Reserve Officer's Training Corps college scholarship. He received a B.S. in Engineering at the University of Southern California, Los Angeles, and joined the active Navy after graduation on May 12, 1995. The Navy is his family tradition: Joe had drunk-in his great-grandfather's story of hanging over the edge of a destroyer with a security rope his only connection to the destroyer riding out a typhoon. Joe's young mind marveled at the tale of his grandfather as crew on a gunboat patrolling the Yangtze River to keep U. S. treaty ports safe from Chinese warlords.

His own acclimation to the service started with training at sea on the *U.S.S. Lake Champlain* from November 1995 to November 1997. Ensign Ring was assigned duties as Damage Control Assistant, and qualified as Surface Warfare Officer during this tour. From a base in Hawaii he spent ten months serving as Repair Officer for Commander, Naval Surface Group Middle Pacific. He attended Hawaii Pacific University at night during this tour and was awarded an M.A. in Organizational Change, with distinction, in December 2001. As a Lieutenant, he next did a tour in Pearl Harbor, Hawaii, as Flag Aide to Commander, Navy Region Hawaii. From here he was sent as a student to the Naval War College in Newport, Rhode Island. This assignment was a bonus for him; Joe's father was born and grew up in Newport, and it had been his great grandfather's Atlantic Coast homeport. There were friends still living there. He realized that the Navy is a large and extended family.

At age 30 Joe received the rank of Lieutenant Commander and was designated Combat Systems Officer on the *Mobile Bay* from October 2002 to October 2005. The ship had been his home in the North Arabian Gulf for two tours. At the time of my visit much of the activity and information about those tours had been declassified. We signed the daily log and clambered over the gangway to the upper deck.

JOE RECOUNTED THE EVENTS that marked his service to country and to his ship. President Bush gave the order for Iraqi Freedom on March 19, 2003 and major air strikes began two days later. Using a launch system from the cells located in the deck, the Combat Strike Team successfully completed multiple strike missions into Iraq, mostly at night. For this combat action in Iraqi waters LCDR Ring received the Navy-Marine Corps Commendation Medal and was selected 2003 Commander, Naval Surface Forces Tactician of the Year.

In September, 2005, the citation accompanying the Meritorious Service Medal awarded to him stated that LCDR Ring's perseverance, ingenuity and tactical genius were directly responsible for the second consecutive Battle 'E" earned by the *Mobile Bay.*

As OUR TOUR OF his ship moved to the wardroom, Joe explained that his second tour was also part of Iraqi Freedom in support and defense of Iraq's major oil platform. Using the *Mobile Bay* as home base, the Combat Team had completed security sweeps of tankers and tugs operating at the platform. Joe and his team developed complex quick-reaction drills for oil platform defense, and trained personnel in the procedures. The whole ship united behind the Combat Team and helped provide hot meals for oil platform personnel and fuel to keep the coastal patrol craft in operation.

"What I am proudest of," Joe said, "is hosting four Iraqi Naval Officers for dinner, a movie and conversation about our homes, families and hopes for the future."

On the way home the *Mobile Bay* had stopped in Australia and Joe met Nada Blumfield when she came aboard as Quarantine Officer. She had been a member of the Australian Navy and she understood the demands of Navy life. After a brief courtship they had decided to marry on October 2, 2005. They planned a trip across country on the way back to Newport and the Naval War College where Joe became a student for the second and longer time in order to earn a Masters in National Security and Strategic Studies.

IN MARCH 2006, LIEUTENANT commander Joseph James Ring was posted as Executive Officer of a guided missile destroyer, but no matter how far up the naval ladder he ascends, he will always be My Grandson, First Class.

By Helen E. Gallant
Proud grandmother of
Lieutenant Commander Joseph James Ring, U.S. Navy
U.S.S. Carney, DDG 64

Home of the Brave

EDITORS' NOTE: DURING THE War of 1812, it was the valiant defense of Fort McHenry by American forces during the British attack on September 13, 1814, that inspired a poet to write the poem that we know now, when set to music, as "The Star-Spangled Banner."

Presentation of this historic poem is the single exception to the claim on the rear cover of this book that all contributors are members of The Society of Southwestern Authors.

The Defense of Ft. McHenry

Oh, say can you see, by the dawn's early light,
What so proudly we hailed at the twilight's last gleaming?
Whose broad stripes and bright stars, through the perilous fight,
O'er the ramparts we watched, were so gallantly streaming?
And the rockets' red glare, the bombs bursting in air,
Gave proof through the night that our flag was still there.
O say, does that star-spangled banner yet wave
O'er the land of the free and the home of the brave?

On the shore, dimly seen through the mists of the deep,
Where the foe's haughty host in dread silence reposes,
What is that which the breeze, o'er the towering steep,
As it fitfully blows, half conceals, half discloses?
Now it catches the gleam of the morning's first beam,
In full glory reflected now shines on the stream:
'Tis the star-spangled banner! O long may it wave
O'er the land of the free and the home of the brave.

And where is that band who so vauntingly swore
That the havoc of war and the battle's confusion
A home and a country should leave us no more?
Their blood has wiped out their foul footstep's pollution.
No refuge could save the hireling and slave
From the terror of flight, or the gloom of the grave:
And the star-spangled banner in triumph doth wave
O'er the land of the free and the home of the brave.

Oh! thus be it ever, when freemen shall stand
Between their loved homes and the war's desolation!
Blest with victory and peace, may the heaven-rescued land
Praise the Power that hath made and preserved us a nation.
Then conquer we must, when our cause it is just,
And this be our motto: "In God is our trust."
And the star-spangled banner in triumph shall wave
O'er the land of the free and the home of the brave!

By Francis Scott Key
In praise of unnamed American heroes
that successfully opposed the British siege
of Ft. McHenry, Baltimore,
The War of 1812

A Pacifist in the U.S. Army Medical Corps

July 16, 1958.

INTERESTING NEWS ON THE *TV that night,* my wife Janice and I thought, as the announcer described the landing and explained that President Eisenhower had responded to the request for help from President Camille Chamoun of riot-torn Lebanon. The announcer went on to explain the magnitude of Eisenhower's response, emphasizing the importance of the oil-rich area in the Cold War, stating that was why several units in the Midwest had been put on alert. Interest turned to apprehension when we both recognized that one of the units put on alert for immediate overseas combat was the medical unit at Fifth Army Headquarters.

"I HAVE A PROBLEM, Colonel," I blurted.

"Sit, Captain," said Colonel Charles Ward as he put on his fatherly smile and motioned to the chair in front of his desk. Colonel Ward, chief medical officer for the Fifth Army headquarters outpatient dispensary, indeed was fatherly. In a way, he had to be, for he had six young physicians under his charge. "It can't be that bad. I have a meeting with General Arnold soon, so...."

"Sorry, Sir." Gen. Arnold's name only made my reticence more entrenched. "I don't want to do anything to embarrass you or seem unappreciative for the kind way you have helped all of us greenhorns." I forced a nervous smile. "The alert to our unit means I must go down and sign out an officers' combat pack." His eyebrows met, my heart raced. "I'm a pacifist, and I can't take the revolver that comes with the issue." There, I had done it. The alert referred to the orders the staff doctors, nurses and corpsmen received that morning to pick up combat gear from supply and be ready to ship overseas with a twenty-four hour notice.

Not dread, but relief came over me when Colonel Ward picked up the phone and told his secretary to tell General Arnold he would be a few minutes late. Pulling up a chair next to mine, he leaned forward and said, "I had no idea. Tell me about your problem. You are here, so you can't be a conscientious objector."

"No sir, but I am a pacifist. When the Korean War broke out I was a freshman pre-med student. My religion professor at Albion College said my fundamental belief, 'thou shalt not kill,' meant I was a pacifist and I could be in the army, but not carry a gun, but as a corpsman I could still serve my country. He told me that is what the Quakers did in World War II." In World War II the Quakers were pacifists, but joined as corpsmen, refusing to carry a weapon. They lost more men per capita than any other group.

"And the college exemption test saved you from the draft. Correct?"

"Actually, I told my parents I was going to join as a corpsman and not wait to be drafted."

Colonel Ward glanced at his watch, said, "And so after all the years of avoiding standing up for your faith, you are determined to do so now."

"Yeah. I should have joined in 1950. Now, I have a wife and two kids, and I'm embarrassing you."

Without removing his warm eyes from my face, he stood, helped me up and grabbed my upper arm. "Don't worry about embarrassing me. You must not deny Him again. I understand, and I will be disappointed if you do. Go down to supply and ask for your issue." A glitter appeared in his eyes. "Tell the supply sergeant you refuse to take the revolver."

I SMILED AT THE supply sergeant. I had tended to him as a patient two weeks previously. "Captain Humphrey, here. I have come for my combat pack. But I will not…"

Big smile. He waved a hand before me and said, "Whoa, Captain. Just look over the contents and sign the paper."

No revolver. I searched again, carefully. Nope. Not there. I raised my head. The sergeant had a peevish smile. "I don't understand, since . . ."

"Captain, my personal doctor, just sign for what is there." His Irish cheeks appeared redder than usual.

I checked off each item as I placed it back in the pack. Never found a revolver, but on the paper a green line had crossed it off. *Curious, indeed.* Of course, back in the dispensary my friend and associate physician Bob Williams took me aside and asked, "Did you sign for a revolver?"

"I signed for everything in the pack, Bob." At home a relieved wife and I pondered the disposition of one pacifist officer's revolver. I decided to let sleeping revolvers lie. But before discharge eleven months later I would hear about the missing gun.

Perhaps it is well to point out that the physicians who served the required two years seemed to be respected by the career officers; not upset that we were not very "military." On the other hand, the tolerance of many line officers seemed to be strained. Mind you, we never purposefully disobeyed an order. In fact we respected the officers, as most appeared professional soldiers. Perhaps they tolerated our sloppy salutes, our focus on medicine, and seeming poor understanding of their gung-ho attitude for all things military. We discussed these different cultures, and it was a Major, a career army officer, who put our discussion to rest when he allowed as how they all recognized that some day they might need us as their doctor, maybe in dire circumstances.

SIX WEEKS AT OFFICERS' indoctrination can in no way prepare one for decision making when a medical emergency is thrown into the teeth of military protocol. In February 1959 I learned, in several incidents all within one 24-hour period, that even with 18 months experience at a bustling dispensary and trading "clinical war stories" with seven other young medics almost five days a week I did not have the knowledge to keep me from breaching several military rules.

The particular day was in the middle of the week when Colonel Ward's adjutant came into the dispensary and asked if I would do a favor. It seems in the park located across from headquarters building a man had shot himself. The police had come and asked the Colonel if a military doctor would go over to the park and pronounce the man dead. For the physicians not from Chicago that seemed outrageous. I smiled for I knew if we did not oblige them Chicago's finest would have to take him to Cook County Hospital, wait in a long line before depositing the stiff in the County Morgue. I volunteered. The adjutant and I walked out the front door, crossed the busy street, and headed for a small crowd gathered around a park bench. I had only a white coat over my uniform. The adjutant was bundled in his heavy gray-brown military coat. As we approached the crowd he fell behind me. A burly policeman in the typical dark blue, mid-thigh length winter coat stepped from the crowd. Taking me by the arm he explained that they had been called about a suicide and found the man as he appeared to be. He effusively expressed his thanks for my help, asking me to pronounce the man dead. Bodies stepped back, making room for the man in blue and his white-coated friend. I knelt over, looked at the ashen face, the cold stare, and fixed pupils, and peered closely at the top of the gray head, finally resting my scrutiny at the open mouth. Such scenes always bring a rush of sadness, seeing the remains of a human who blew his brains out.

I stood, looked at the cop with my most professional face and stated, "You may record that Captain Loren Humphrey from the Fifth Army headquarters dispensary pronounced the man dead at," I paused to stare at my watch . . ." at 4:21 p.m."

After he jotted down the words he leaned close and whispered, "Aren't you supposed to listen to his chest? Listen for the heart?"

Bending over, I retrieved my stethoscope from my coat pocket, stuck it inside the man's shirt, wincing at the coldness of his bare chest. I rose to my feet, faced the smiling cop and told him, "I did not need to do that. He has brains floating in the blood in his mouth." I thought I said it softly, but the gasps around me belied my intention.

So that was the beginning of a long, tedious night. I was medical officer of the day. The sojourn across the street was a routine civilian medical activity, sanctioned by the adjutant taking me to the park, although technically a break in protocol.

At 4:30 p.m. on weekdays the physicians who are not "Medical Officer of the Day" flee just as do the non-medical personnel. We all agreed to do this even if walk-ins sat in the waiting room. Actually, we violated this several times, especially during the Asian flu epidemic in the winter of 1957-58, or when an inordinately large number of patients were in the waiting room. This evening I had seen a few, mostly dependent children with strep throat, flu or some type upper respiratory infection. Around 10 o'clock, after a lull of some 45 minutes, Sergeant Vega, who was corpsman on call, poked his head in the dispensary coffee room, making a sign that the phone was for me.

"It's the general duty officer. Some major. He's perturbed, anxious, something."

Strange, I thought. I had been at the headquarters for almost 18 months and never once was called by the officer out front. They tended to act as though we did not exist. I eased out of the chair, sipped the now lukewarm brew and picked up the phone on a wall in the hall.

"Captain Humphrey here, sir. What can I do for you?"

"Captain, I have a man outside my office. Said his son, who just happens to be AWOL, is in the back seat of his car. Said the boy has been ill for some time since arriving home, but today became confused. Said his boy passed out as they left Gary, Indiana, and approached Chicago's south side. Captain, I went out and took a peek. He don't look too hot to me."

"Major, let me buzz around front and check him. If he's dead we can send him directly…" I paused as it occurred to me I did not know where to send an expired soldier. I grabbed Sergeant Vega, and on the way to the front I asked him where to send the boy, if dead. To Great Lakes Hospital, he answered. That made sense. I passed the Major's office that stood by the front entrance, nodded in recognition and was immediately in the clutches of a small distraught man.

He prevented my advance to the car, spewing unintelligible gun-bursts of some foreign tongue. I held him by the shoulders, reassuring him and asking for a slower version of his remarks. He stammered in a heavy Slovak accent that his boy wasn't a deserter, a good boy, only quite sick. He begged me to tell me he was just in coma, going to be all right. *Not again,* I thought as I opened the back door of the car and surveyed the form in the back seat. Motionless, no chest movements, eyes fixed to one side and a strong odor of urine. Right away I knew if I told the unsuspecting father his son was dead, without some preparation, I might have two corpses on my hands. "Sergeant Vega will climb in back and tend to your son while you drive him around back to the dispensary so I can examine him better."

That worked. The man was eager to do anything, and Vega understood my ploy. The couple hundred-yard trek to the dispensary gave me time to design a plan, one that would let this father down gently. Sergeant Vega had arrived and with a helper put the dead boy in an examining room, the father hovering close behind the stretcher.

"Take this tired looking man into the Colonel's office, give him a cup of coffee while I see what can be done for his son." Vega nodded and disappeared with the man toward Colonel. Ward's office across the hall from the dispensary. "Come help me, Private," I said to a confused looking baby-faced soldier.

In the room I went through the routine, the one we did many times in the emergency room or on the floor during internship. No heartbeat, with dilated, fixed pupils, pronounces death in a finite way; the cold skin and stiff limbs adding emphasis. I recalled the father had told of headaches, and with the odor of urine I reasoned he had a head injury, maybe the cause of his AWOL status. I grabbed an ophthalmoscope and peered into a dilated eye. The optic nerve revealed that he had increased pressure in his head. I shuffled into Colonel Ward's office. The agitated man jumped to his feet.

"Well, well. What?" I motioned for Vega to help him sit. I went behind the colonel's desk, my mind racing, searching for a way to cushion the grim news. Hesitantly, I reviewed the boy's medical history, any past headaches, the present illness, letting the man answer. With each dramatic symptom described to me I would shake my head and say, "Worrisome, what did you suspect?" All during this part of my plan the phone on the colonel's desk was flashing, persistent, demanding, but I had the man following my path, a gentle path to grim reality about his boy. At this most inauspicious moment the Major appeared in the doorway.

"Didn't they teach you to answer the phone in med school, Captain?" He stood, hands on hips, quite irritated.

At that precise moment the father's face lit up, eyes big as saucers. "Doctor, are you telling me my son is dead?" Such anguish, a pitiful whimper, and he buried his head in his hands.

I nodded to Sergeant Vega. He pulled the man to him and held him. I sprang for the door and faced the Major. His mouth still hung open. I stared, waiting for him to tell me what was so important that he felt it necessary to violate one of man's most hellish moments, the instant you realize your son is dead.

"Sorry, Captain, but I have the control tower at Madison, Wisconsin, on the phone. They have a medical emergency in a military transport plane that is circling overhead. They want permission to land in Chicago. I can't make that call. You find out if it's an emergency." He pointed to the flashing light on the colonel's desk. "They're on that line."

Vega had heard this and came by, ushering the man out of the office. My mind was numb, but the father's red, tearful eyes screeched at me, stopped my move for the phone. "You did right bringing your boy here, " I told him. "He's no deserter. He had brain damage from a head injury. Go with Sergeant Vega and give your boy a last hug." Apprehensive, I returned to the Colonel's desk and eased the phone to my ear. "This is Captain Humphrey. I am medical duty officer for the Fifth Army headquarters dispensary."

A voice on the other end said, "I am transferring you to the pilot of the military plane circling over our field here in Madison." He paused, and continued, "Go ahead, sir. You may speak directly to the medical officer in Chicago."

I BEGAN TO REALIZE a problem was unraveling for which I had no experience and not the foggiest idea what medical problem could evoke such a peculiar communication. The voice continued amongst the background noise of a propeller driven aircraft. "I have 172 soldiers returning from Korea on the way to Langley Airfield in Virginia. Several are ill. A couple of them passed out and one is unconscious in the aisle. The corpsman on board thinks they some need immediate attention; doubtful they will make it to the east coast."

My palms were sweaty. *Why me?* Great Lakes Naval Base is nearer and they have a hospital. So I verbalized my question, and received some reason why they couldn't land there. I believe the reason was that due to lake effect a blizzard was dumping huge amounts of snow at the station's field and Chicago's Midway was clear. *Great!* I could feel the noose tighten.

"If you can obtain permission to land at Midway, sir, I will have a medical team there by the time you arrive," I said, calculating the distance, the route and absence of traffic at midnight.

A pause. I heard crackling voices in the background mixed with engine noise. "All right, Captain. I have permission to land at Midway Airport. Should be there within sixty minutes."

I found Vega returning through the back door, a dour look on his face. "I just sent a destroyed father to Great Lakes, accompanying his boy's body."

"That call you heard, the call from the Major, was forwarded to me from a plane loaded with 172 GIs returning from Korea, some quite ill, some unconscious. They're over Madison—can't land at Great Lakes—so they are going to land at Midway Airport in about 55 minutes. Get two teams, two ambulances, out back in ten minutes. We are about to have a live medical triage." I was astounded. I expected concern, reticence. Not so. Vega was excited. I guess his tour at the dispensary had been too boring for this battle-worn veteran.

Twelve minutes later I climbed in the passenger seat of the first of two drab green ambulances, ones without the usual light atop the roof. The brass had refused our request because we were in a big city; I never understood their reasoning. Sergeant Vega was driving the lead and started out like a racecar driver. I told him fast was okay but no speeding through intersections. On the west side of the park we both spied at the same time a black and white sitting by the intersection with parking lights on. *Aha,* I thought. *We can get them to escort us.* No vehicles approached the intersection so I said, "Floor it through this one. I see our escort." The ambulance leapt forward and we zoomed past the cops. They blinked their headlights and watched both ambulances race down the street. So much for an escort!

We arrived in record time, my nerves a bit raw. We parked on the tarmac facing the terminal building. I instructed my team about the coming airplane, setting a triage with two corpsmen to check vitals, and two to follow with a stretcher in case we needed to carry a critical soldier off the plane. I sent Sergeant Vega to the building to set up an area to place the stretchers if necessary. They carried intravenous bottles and paraphernalia into the building. Within minutes we saw the lights of an approaching plane. It taxied over to our location; the thundering engines whipping sand particles, remnants of the last dusting of snow, in its wake. The door just behind the cockpit opened and a middle-aged man in khakis bounded down the steps. I glanced at the hardware and noted he was a staff sergeant with many medals hanging over his left pocket. Nearing me, he saluted. I returned my best. He told me he had two soldiers unconscious in the aisle and three more slumped over in their seats, but responding to commands. I sensed Sergeant Vega at my back as the man answered my questions regarding length of illness in the different men, drug use and any epidemics at the camp in Korea.

The last query brought out a snort, accompanied by a look that told me I was either naïve or stupid. I ascended the steps and knelt over the lifeless body of a young man, perhaps early twenties. Shallow breathing and fast pulse led me to his face. Pinpoint pupils gave me the clue. I turned my head. Sergeant Vega's head was at my shoulder. "See that?"

"Yes, sir. Drugs," he said as I turned my gaze toward the back at the next body, some ten feet away. "We'll get his pulse and B-P while you check the others." I found the next one, moaning, and covered with sweat. He had a bounding pulse, but did not respond to my voice. His pupils were normal size and reacted normally to my light. His eyes roamed back and forth, and holding an eyelid open for my exam I noted his skin was very hot.

Sergeant Vega rubbed against my side, studying the ruddy-faced man. "Different, no?"

I nodded and told him, "Pneumonia or some infection with bacteremia. Have the guys check his vitals and move both to the building. Start I-Vs. Then come to the back."

Vega slipped by the medal-adorned sergeant who eased up to me. "What ya think, Captain?"

"First, drugs. Second, pneumonia or some systemic infection. We'll get I-Vs going in the building, and then I can do a more definitive exam. Where are the others?"

He guided me to one after another, three in all. They all seemed to have some gastrointestinal problem, in acute distress, but not life-threatening. I instructed him to have them brought to the building.

The plane emptied, the young soldiers milling about the vending machines in the terminal building, and the sergeant hovering around like a mother hen. He informed me that they had about seven hours to their final destination. "How soon can we depart?" He stared past me at his sick men. Two were sitting up, looking much better after a bottle of isotonic saline and anti-diarrhea medicine.

"In about twenty minutes, but if the three still getting intravenous don't improve they can't go. We'll take them to Great Lakes Hospital," I told him matter-of-factly, watching his concerned look turn to agitation.

"No. You can't do that," he said in an authoritative voice.

"What do you mean I can't do that?" I put on my most professional airs and kept my eyes locked on his.

"I am in charge of this plane load of men. My orders are to deliver 172 men to Langley Airbase. If I show up with 172 bags and only 169 bodies, there'll be hell to pay."

Coolly, I explained that one, the drugged one, possibly could stop breathing, and the other had a systemic infection with unstable blood pressure and needed hospital care now, not in six or seven hours.

He was unrelenting, so after fifteen minutes I called Sergeant Vega over. I had noticed that he had taken in much of this dialogue. "Sergeant Vega, draw up a paper stating that this sergeant has agreed to assume all responsibility for the lives of the three men, against medical advice from Captain Humphrey; that it is his medical advice that travel for six more hours without hospital care might result in great harm to them. In fact the sickest will certainly die within four hours without intensive care." I studied the sergeant, his mouth hanging open, eyes flickering from the men to my face. "Have him sign the paper and you witness it."

"Damn, Captain," he sputtered.

"After he signs it, pull the I-Vs and take the men onto the plane." I prayed he would sign, because the knot in my stomach begged for relief. While Vega drew up the paper, I visited my decision. I considered calling Colonel Ward but realized that I was responsible for the health and life of these soldiers. No other options existed in my opinion. My guys would go with them to Great Lakes, north of Chicago, I-Vs and emergency meds running the entire way. Besides, I outranked the man claiming ultimate responsibility.

Vega pushed the paper in front of me. I scrutinized it and handed it to the sergeant, his medals swaying from his gyrations. "No," he said. "You want to pull three of my men off the plane against my orders, go ahead and may God help you." He ordered the rest of his men back on the plane, while I reviewed with Vega the likely changes in the three soldiers he might encounter in the hour drive to Great Lakes. I had little concern, for he had years of experience.

Over the roar of the engines from the plane racing down the runway, he said, "Tough call, Captain." He broke into a smile and added, "But the right one."

"Thanks, Tom," I replied and realized that was the first time I called him by his first name. He liked that.

Back at headquarters building, I flopped on the call bed. I don't believe I was really asleep when the phone shrieked at me. Picking up the receiver, I noted 2:42 A.M. glaring at me from the bedside clock. The dialogue was professional. The admitting officer at Great Lakes needed to confirm the details given to him by Sergeant Vega. He asked about the other sick soldiers, and I asked how the three were doing. Reasonably well except the one with pneumonia still had unstable blood pressure, might not make it.

I reported to Colonel Ward before I left for the day. He seemed dour and let me know he already knew about it. Langley had called. He told me to remain the morning and give my account to his adjutant. I did that with great apprehension. He reveled in my plight, letting me know that a general at Langley had asked just who it was that jerked his men off a plane. He smiled and said I should expect a visit from IG, the Inspector General's office. They never paid me a visit and other than creeping, recurring feelings of paranoia, I never heard another word.

During the remainder of my time at the dispensary I heard, maybe sought out stories of medical officers clashing with other officers over medical problems. I guess I never felt at ease, although later I inquired and found out all three of my patients survived. I think I fretted because Colonel Ward remained silent, most unusual for him. All of us greenhorns had episodes, although none seemed so severe as mine. What a night to remember.

ON THE LAST DAY of my active duty, with great glee I roamed the aisles of the PX searching for essentials in my coming days as a civilian, a surgery resident, making 35 dollars a month. My tranquility was dashed by a familiar voice. I turned and faced Colonel. Vogel, post commander of the IG. Shortly after I had arrived in 1957, he had appeared in the clinic. He had a suspicious mole in front of his left ear. I told him it should be removed, could be a malignant melanoma and I would make an appointment for him in the plastic surgery department at Great Lakes.

"I don't have time to go up there for something so minor. You do it, Captain," he said, more a command than a suggestion.

He was about fifty and good looking and would have a scar for the world to see, so I timidly replied, "I just finished internship. You deserve the skills of a surgeon, sir."

"Crap, Captain. I've seen what you and Roberts do. Schedule me here for next week. You'll do it."

That conversation rattled in my brain. The mole turned out to be benign and at time of suture removal the incision looked great.

I had managed to close the hole by making the scar fall on his whisker line in front of the ear. But his mischievous look betrayed that memory. He stepped close, turned the right side of his face to me and said, "See? No scar, doctor."

I stammered, recalling with some doubt that I cut the left side.

He laughed and turned the left side to me. "This is the side. And no scar. I owe you." He loved the game but I was still wary even though it was difficult to recognize the thread-thin white scar along his whisker line.

"Sir, you do not owe me. I am happy it turned out benign."

"After I go back to my office and remove all the papers under my blotter, ones directed at a Captain Humphrey, and I destroy them, I will not owe you." His eyebrows twittered, his devilish smile spreading from ear to ear.

I really wanted to know which papers he referred to. Had Colonel Ward checked out my revolver? Who ran interference for me over the three I sent to Great Lakes? I knew of some minor disagreements, but no other countermanding of orders as far as I could recall. I decided the revolver could have a few sleeping partners. I had completed my military obligation and had learned lessons not taught in books.

AUTHOR'S NOTE: MY MILITARY tour dispelled several misconceptions about the military. First, discipline is crucial to an organization whose mission is so vital to the security of a nation, especially under fire and severe duress. We independent-minded physicians entered service with doubts about strict discipline and the ability to deliver first class care to our patients, the soldiers. Military medicine our troops receive is first class, delivered by junior officers, many not on a career path, but supervised by career senior officers who are committed to seeing that the health and safety of troops is paramount.

After two years active duty we were required to spend four years in the reserve, attending two evening meetings and a weekend meeting each month. In addition, two weeks of active duty each summer was mandatory. One of those summers I spent in the Burn Center at Brook Army Medical Center in San Antonio, and another summer I spent the two weeks at Fitzsimmons Army Hospital in Denver. Both facilities were impressive in the quality of care rendered. In fact, lessons learned by the military physicians in the Burn Center have become standards of care for civilian physicians. Treatment of burns, triage of trauma patients, debridement of penetrating wounds of extremities and appropriate use of helicopters are but a few of the military innovations that have improved the survival of our citizens.

The second misconception was that military discipline does not allow for individuality, in personal beliefs and behavior or medical practice. Quite to the contrary, the military, through the maturity of its career officers, accommodates the individual. Religious beliefs are diverse, even pacifism, and are not challenged as long as the practice does not hamper the mission. Indeed, in our group of seven were catholic, Jew, protestant, black, white and a lot of very different personality types.

Let us all give thanks for the superb men and women who practice medicine in the military. They save many lives of the young who defend our country, and they advance the quality of care we citizens receive.

By Captain Loren Humphrey
U.S. Army Medical Corps
Fifth Army Headquarters
Chicago, Illinois

Tiger on the Prowl

QUINN FULLER HAD AN itch to fly from the time he was old enough to reach the pedals of his tricycle, and that itch never subsided as he made his way through elementary school, high school and then college. When the Korean War broke out, he saw his chance to realize his lifelong ambition. He enlisted in the Air Force and applied for aviation cadets.

In March of 1952 he was called up and posted to Greenville AFB in Greenville, Mississippi, where his instructor was a retired WW II fighter pilot. Greenville was a civilian contract school and most of the instructor pilots were crop dusters who could not get aviation fuel out of their blood.

Quinn was a natural pilot. He was among the first in his class to solo in the AT-6 aircraft. He loved tearing holes in the sky and putting his plane through every conceivable maneuver. After basic, he completed his advanced training and then moved on to gunnery school. He was given his lieutenant bars and his silver wings. Soon, he received orders to report to K-2 in Taegu, Korea where he was checked out in the F-84, a straight-wing, single-seat jet designed for low-level interdiction missions. Quinn was one proud young pilot. On the morning of his first combat mission he was given an F-84 named *El Tigre,* which was the plane normally assigned to a good friend. As this was Quinn's first combat mission, he did not have his own plane yet. Quinn had his picture taken by *El Tigre* with the bombs slung below the belly of the plane clearly visible. His smile stretched forever.

He climbed into his aircraft, taxied to the runway, closed the canopy and shoved the coal to the engine. At the end of the runway was a rising landform aptly named "bust-your-ass-hill" because it had claimed the lives of a couple of pilots who were unable to reach altitude in time. Quinn's take off was normal. His target was on the Haeju Peninsula, some fifteen to twenty minutes from his base.

THE F-84 FLEW TWO different types of missions: A dive-bombing maneuver that began when the pilot performed a "Split-S" — the pilot
turned his craft on its back, pointed the nose to earth in a steep dive;
and when he reached his desired altitude, pulled up and righted
the aircraft. The flight path resembles the top of an "S". It was a
hairy maneuver, but a favorite among the jet set. It starts at some
25,000 feet and the bomb is released about 5000 feet. The napalm
run was something different. The pilot went in at tree top level and
released his bomb as he began a climbing turn.

QUINN WAS SCHEDULED TO make a napalm drop. He began his run
at 40 feet — lower than most of the trees in the area. He released
his napalm and watched the flame spread below him. Just then, he
felt a bump and then a second and a third. His right wing was on
fire and he was far too low to bail out. Every warning light in the
cockpit went on — fuel warning, engine over heating, and fire warning. He had to gain altitude. He pulled back on the stick and while
he was climbing, remembered that he had been told in jet training
that when the fire-warning light came on the pilot had about seven
seconds before the aircraft blew up.
How the hell did they know that, he wondered.
When he reached 1100 feet, he was hit by ground fire and the
wing blew off. Obviously, it was time to get out. Quinn blew the
canopy and ejected. His chute opened and he was in for an amuse-
ment park ride to the ground . . . or so he thought. But the enemy
had formed a circle below him and began shooting as he descend-
ed. He was hit in the forehead and blood began dripping through
his eyes and down his face.
His squadron called in F-80s and P-51s for support. They formed
a cap and strafed the enemy, and kept them pinned down.
Quinn landed in a rice paddy being tended by Korean farmers.
He was completely exposed so he stripped off his chute and took
off for the tall grass. Two enemy soldiers ran toward Quinn, firing
their rifles. Bullets sprayed over his shoulders and past his head.
Quinn tried to return fire with his .45 pistol but he was so scared
he forgot to inject a cartridge into the chamber — and never fired a
shot.

Another F-84 pilot, George Clapman who, according to Quinn was the worst shot in gunnery school, caught one of the Koreans in his sights, and fired a short burst. According to Quinn, the soldier absolutely disintegrated. The other soldier decided he'd had enough of war, threw his rifle away and ran for the tall grass, which was on the other side of Quinn. He almost ran over Quinn on his way to the reeds.

"He came within two feet of me," Quinn said. "I don't know how he missed bumping into me. But he was on a mission, a mission to get the hell out of there."

Both men reached the tall grass. Both hid from the other.

Quinn watched as the 84s, 80s and 51s kept making passes, firing at anything that moved. This went on for about an hour until the cap began to run low on fuel. The 84s had to return to base. The others did their best to protect Quinn until a chopper could pick him up.

Quinn's URC-4 radio crackled. A helicopter was on the way. Owen Clark and his medical attendant, Elmer Davis, had volunteered to fly the mission. An eternal few minutes later, the copter arrived and dropped a sling. Quinn slipped into the sling but he had no training in a sling pick-up and did not get it on correctly. Nonetheless, the copter took off with Quinn dangling at the end of a very long rope. The F-80s and the P-51s retired. The enemy stood up and started shooting at Quinn again as he swung back and forth a few hundred feet above them. A winch pulled Quinn inexorably toward the cockpit.

Finally, Quinn reached the copter but failed to follow the instructions. Instead of holding the rope, he reached up and grabbed the floor of the helicopter . . . and slipped out of the sling. . . .

Inside the copter, Elmer Davis held on to Quinn's B-15 flight jacket, which was ripping up the back. Quinn was holding on with hands that were freezing, and Davis began losing his grip. The copter couldn't land because of the enemy below. Ground fire hit the copter but did no real damage. Owen flew back to the friendly side of the line where Quinn fell fifteen feet, spraining an ankle.

Within two hours, he was taken to nearby base K-16 for medical treatment and finally after a few more hours returned to his base at K-2 where he was met by his friend whose plane he had flown that day.

"What in hell did you do to my plane?" The pilot asked.

"I broke it!" Quinn replied.

QUINN FULLER WAS NOT required to complete his tour of 100 combat missions because he had successfully escaped from behind enemy lines. Nonetheless, he was given a new plane that he named *Rice Paddy Ranger* in which he flew ninety- nine more missions without further incidents; none anywhere near as exciting as his first.

Quinn returned to the States with a Distinguished Flying Cross, a Bronze Star, three air medals, a Purple Heart and a Presidential citation. Owen Clark, who had volunteered to pick up Quinn, was awarded with the Distinguished Flying Cross. However, Elmer Davis, the man who held onto Quinn's flight jacket received only a thank you from Quinn, and nothing from the air force.

QUINN FULLER SPENT THE next twenty years in the service, flying everything that had wings, after which he retired to Pell, Alabama. He and Owen Clark became good friends and attended Air Force reunions together. The two men spent the next fifty years writing their Congressmen, petitioning anyone who would listen, making every effort to get Elmer Davis the recognition he deserved. Finally after fifty years, on February 11, 2005, a four star General, John Handy, presented Elmer Davis with the Distinguished Flying Cross in an emotional presentation in Washington DC attended by both Owen Clark and Quinn Fuller.

By Ted Gushee,
relating the story of
Lieutenant Quinn Fuller and friends
of the 8th Fighter Bomber Squadron
49th Fighter Bomber Group
U.S. Air Force, K-2, Taegu, Korea

Doing His Share

"LET ME GET THIS straight," Orlan said. "You were a clerk in Norfolk, Virginia, serving your country, and you had a fear of flying, and yet you volunteered to become an air gunner?"

"Yes," Uncle Fred replied, "I didn't feel like I was doing my share. So when a memo from headquarters came around citing a shortage of aerial gunners and requesting volunteers, I signed up."

UNCLE FRED'S COMMENTS TO my cousin Orlan were hardly surprising. As a volunteer at Tucson's Pima Air & Space Museum, I've talked to hundreds of WWII veterans, and scores of aircrew members—many of them gunners—and noted the characteristic modesty and sense of duty that surface when they recount wartime experiences.

My uncle, Frederick Wichman, grew up a farm boy in northwestern Ohio. He was named after his father but to avoid confusion at mealtimes, little Fred acquired the nickname "Fritz." For a growing boy, farm life soon proved demanding. Chores began before sunup and ended after sundown. But it was a healthy, nourishing environment and Fritz, like his siblings, grew up straight and strong. He volunteered for the draft on his eighteenth birthday. The local draft board gave him a brief deferment so that he could graduate from Ayersville High School, Class of 1943.

Uncle Fred dropped the nickname, Fritz, the moment he walked into the U.S. Army reception center in November 1943 at Ft. Hayes, Columbus, Ohio. America was at war with Germany, and the moniker "Fritz" was synonymous with the enemy. His grandparents were *Plattdeutsch,* lowland German farmers from the agricultural region near Hamburg. They had immigrated to America late in the 19th Century. Even though Fred's Uncle George, a first generation American, had been an Army "doughboy" and served in France in World War I, young Fred and his older brothers and sisters had been discouraged from speaking German outside the home following The Great War.

ENDING HIS BRIEF STINT as an Army Air Force clerk in Norfolk, Fred transferred to Tyndall Field in Panama City, Florida for gunnery training. The principal ground-training weapon was the 12-gauge shotgun. It was fixed to a swivel base and mounted on a light truck; trainees raced around a mile-long track using it to shoot at clay pigeons launched without warning from more than a half-dozen traps. Learning to lead a moving target proved no great challenge for a farm boy experienced at bird hunting, but actual gunnery practice from an open window in a B-17 Flying Fortress was a different matter—the chief concern was to avoid shooting holes in the tow plane pulling the target sleeve. While at Tyndall, Fred learned that he would be assigned to a B-24 Liberator bomber training base. This worried him; he'd heard that the B-24 was an unforgiving, dangerous airplane to fly.

After graduating from gunnery school, he was given a 10-day furlough to visit his family in Ohio. From there he traveled by rail to Gowan Field in Boise, Idaho, for aircrew training. On the train he met the enlisted men who would become his crewmates. Fred's crew soon became familiar with the four-engine B-24. They flew the "J" model. It was easily distinguished from the earlier "D" model by its pugnacious, twin-gun, powered nose turret. The B-24D had several manually operated .50-caliber machine guns in the nose, but they were only usable one at a time, inadequate defense for frontal attack by enemy fighters.

Most of the enlisted men in Fred's crew were qualified gunners, and some did double duty, like the top-turret gunner, who also served as flight engineer. Fred manned the right-waist gun position, probably because he was a strapping six-footer and could swing, aim and fire the heavy .50-cal. Browning machine gun while bundled up in motion-limiting high-altitude flying gear.

When their stateside training was completed, Fred and his nine crewmates, along with dozens of other aircrews and support personnel, journeyed by rail to New York City. There they boarded the ocean liner *Queen Mary*. Fred, along with 14,000 other soldiers, spent Christmas Eve and Day, 1944, in New York harbor aboard ship. They sailed before New Year's Day.

The Atlantic crossing took five days at high speed. The *Queen Mary* was fast enough to make successful attack by U-boats nearly impossible. She was painted in wartime camouflage—a dull-gray—but that didn't conceal pockets of her interior elegance, if you could see around the thousands of soldiers packed in the salons or congregating in the passageways.

Topside, standing on the afterdeck and leaning over the railing, Fred liked to watch the tumultuous wake generated by the *Queen Mary's* huge marine propellers. He felt a little lonely, and at times, nostalgic. He wondered what a civilian passenger might have paid in peacetime for passage to England on such a magnificent ship. Unknown to him, a former neighbor was also aboard. Don Glick, who grew up just across the river from the Wichman farm, was on his way to France. Trained as an M4 Sherman tank crewmember, Don—by a quirk of fate—would join an anti-aircraft unit guarding the captured Remagen Bridge over the Rhine River. Fifty years would pass before they learned of their joint Atlantic Ocean crossing.

To FRED, THE TRAIN ride he and his crewmates made from the Clyde in Scotland to their designated airfield in England seemed endless. Their base was Seething, in East Anglia near Norwich, home of the 448th Bomb Group, 8th Air Force. They were assigned to the 713th Squadron, one of four that clustered about the airfield. Aircrews and ground personnel alike lived in Nissen or Quonset huts and fueled their stoves with coke, a distilled coal, to fight the chilling damp and cold.

On February 26, Fred became the first member of the Wichman family to visit his ancestral homeland. Greeted with anti-aircraft fire at 22,000 feet, Fred and his crewmates' first combat experience proved to be spectacular. The target was Berlin and Fred's plane flew in a formation of 1200 heavy bombers, B-17s and B-24s, stretched over 300 miles. It was the biggest attack mounted against Berlin by the 8th Air Force to that date. Fred saw no enemy fighters that day, and had no opportunity to test his gunnery skills. The anti-aircraft fire over the target was described as "moderate"—little consolation to the aircrews of the 16 bombers lost on the mission. On the homeward flight Fred's crew did see the exhaust trail of a V-2 rocket climbing vertically from the Baltic coast on a trajectory to its target, either London or the Channel port of Antwerp.

Fred flew his second mission the very next day. The target was the vast marshalling yards at Halle, 20 miles northwest of Leipzig. It was an all B-24 mission; 350 Liberators participated. Flak was light but a series of small problems plagued Fred's airplane. Their radio compass failed in flight and they didn't rendezvous with their own bomb group. Instead they flew formation with the 389th Bomb Group. On the bomb run with 9/10ths cloud cover, their bombs failed to release by toggle switch so they were dropped *en masse* by salvo.

There were risks flying at high altitude. Temperature decreases with height; on a standard day the temperature at 25,000 feet was 30 degrees (F) below zero. In winter—the winter of 1944-45 was one of the coldest on record—readings of 40 to 50 degrees below were not uncommon. Frostbite became the most frequently treated aircrew injury during the war. Called "dry gangrene," it could result in the loss of fingers or even hands.

As one of two waist gunners, Uncle Fred was especially at risk for frostbite. He soon learned to dress for the occasion. His first layer of clothing consisted of GI shorts and an undershirt, or more often, long johns. Next came a flight suit—lightweight coveralls—followed by the "blue bunny" electrically heated suit. On top of all this he wore a sheepskin-lined jacket and pants. He put on heavy socks and soft, heated shoes beneath his fleece-lined flying boots. Like the rest of the crew, he wore snug-fitting nylon gloves under his bulky, five-fingered flying gloves. To perform work at altitude requiring dexterity, crewmen had to remove their flying gloves, also electrically heated, but they dared not touch any interior metal of the B-24 with their bare hands—the slightest moisture in their skin could bond them to the frigid metalwork, then strip them of their own flesh.

Aircrews didn't just dress for high-altitude flight; they also dressed for combat. Fred always strapped on a parachute harness (but not a parachute) as well as a Mae West life preserver. He donned a leather flight helmet containing a radio headset. To this were added an oxygen mask and goggles. He did have a few flight gear options: he could choose to wear a steel helmet, much like those used by ground troops, and a protective flak jacket. But at 20 pounds, the jacket was heavy and further limited mobility. Waist gunners were obliged to stand on their feet in combat and manhandle a heavy .50-caliber machine gun, so many of them chose not to wear body armor.

MARCH 1945 TURNED OUT to be the month in which Fred's crew flew the majority of their missions and faced the greatest challenges in their combat tour. Targets included Paderborn, Kiel, Hanover, and Berlin, among others. The weather was frequently dismal. Cloud cover over parts of the continent, or the primary target, was often 10/10ths—meaning the ground was blanketed by total overcast. That made accurate bombing difficult, if not impossible, even when they used radar. At times on the return flight they had trouble locating their own airfield in the thick haze or ground fog, obliging them to request that flares be shot up to help them find the runway.

Fred's planes—they often didn't fly the same ship—suffered a variety of in-flight mechanical problems, including an occasional engine failure, but they always made it home. On many missions they had to use their oxygen masks for up to six hours, an uncomfortable, abrasive necessity.

Fred and his crewmates soon developed a healthy respect for German anti-aircraft defenses. Long-barreled, radar-directed 88mm. and 105mm. anti-aircraft batteries could lob explosive shells higher than any American bomber could fly. On their second mission to Berlin, flak was intense and accurate. Fred's plane took 12 combined hits, including an 18-inch gash in the waist of the Liberator. Part of their elevator, the hinged device attached to the stabilizer that controls climb and descent, was shot away. They were flying the war-weary B-24 "Egress Queen," which, paradoxically, was on its 100th consecutive mission without once having aborted. Their pilot, Neil McCluhan, considered this an honor, and was determined to bring the ship home. He planned to buzz Seething airfield in celebration of the event but thought better upon arrival at their base; the elevator was barely operable.

My cousin Orlan and I had purposely avoided asking Uncle Fred questions about fear—other than his lifetime fear of flying—when we collaborated on an interview with him six years ago. I sensed that those of us who hadn't experienced combat in a war zone could never understand how terrifying and gut-wrenching it could be, even if a veteran tried to describe it. We did, however, ask Fred about the risks of injury or death in the skies over Europe.

"I always felt bad for the men that had to fly early in the war," Uncle Fred said. "They had it a lot worse. The odds that they would survive were less than 50-50. I consider myself fortunate in getting over there as late as I did. We did fly one mission I'll never forget." Uncle Fred was referring to Operation Varsity. On March 24, 1945, more than 21,000 Allied paratroopers and glidermen were airlifted to drop zones and landing sites six miles behind German defenses on the Rhine River. It was the largest daylight air assault in history.

The low-flying B-24s, lumbering along at 150 m.p.h., made big, easy targets for the Germans manning 20mm cannons, machine guns and small weapons. Twenty Liberators and their crews were lost. Fred's B-24 was badly shot up and two of their engines could no longer provide full power. Their plane struggled up to 5,000 feet. When they passed over the enemy coast, they decided to attempt to cross the English Channel. Just as they made landfall in England, their No.1 and No.4 engines failed. Within sight of their airfield, the No.3 engine quit. Reduced to one engine, they purposely approached for a landing at airspeed faster than normal—having lost their hydraulics, they couldn't lower the landing flaps. They had virtually no brakes.

Shortly after touching down, they collided with a taxiing B-24, clipping its right wing and vertical stabilizer. They had narrowly missed hitting it broadside. Miraculously, no one was hurt.

APRIL 1945 PROVED TO be the final month in which 8th Air Force bombers flew combat missions in Europe. Uncle Fred's first mission after Varsity was on April 4. The target was an Me-262 airfield in northern Germany. Because cloud cover was 9/10ths, and they had been instructed not to drop their bombs unless the target was visual, the 448th Group's B-24s began turning away from the target still carrying their bomb loads. As they did so, they were jumped by a dozen Messerschmitt Me-262s.

"They came through the formation so fast we couldn't train our guns on them," Uncle Fred said. "Three B-24s went down on their first pass." The Me-262, a swept-wing, twin-engine jet, was a hundred miles per hour faster than our best piston-engine fighters, but were too few in number and appeared too late to turn the tide against the Allied bomber offensive.

On his last combat mission, Uncle Fred flew in the top turret gunner's position for the first and only time. It was also the last time his entire crew made any flight intact. The target was again the marshalling yards at Halle; escort fighter support was excellent and flak was meager—a fitting end to their combat tour. The 448th Bomb Group flew 262 missions in World War II, dropped 15,272 tons of bombs and lost 135 aircraft, 102 of which were destroyed in combat.

Fred and his crew, along with a half-dozen soldiers hitchhiking a ride home, flew a B-24 back to America in four legs, beginning June 13 and ending June 28—spending eleven pleasant days en route at Gander Field, Newfoundland. They landed stateside at 5:50 P.M. at Bradley Field, Connecticut.

Fred's military service, however, wasn't quite finished. He was scheduled for training in B-29s and deployment to the Pacific. He was stationed near Las Vegas when word came in August that the Japanese had surrendered.

Although he felt close to his crewmates while serving in Europe, Fred never saw them again. Uncle Fred wasn't a war hero.

He received no major personal decorations and was fortunate not to have earned a Purple Heart. He is one of hundreds of thousands of uncelebrated veterans, mostly citizen soldiers, who willingly served their country in time of need.

By Dennis Hull
The story of Sergeant Frederick W. Wichman,
B-24 Liberator aerial gunner
713ᵗʰ Squadron, 448th Bomb Group, 8th Air Force.

As We Say in French

SAMUEL NOTKIN HAD TRIED to enlist in the Air Force during 1943 but was turned down because he didn't have perfect vision. A year later he enlisted in a specialized officer-training course and spent four months at Louisiana State University learning electronics. That program was abruptly cancelled, as more ground troops were urgently needed. Sam found himself a private in the 99th Infantry Division. After combat training in Texas he sailed out of Brooklyn in a converted passenger liner, bound for Europe. He found out later that he'd been part of one of the war's largest convoys. It was Sam's first time away from America.

The 99th landed in Liverpool, and was assigned to the British Army base at Blandford Forum in the county of Dorset. With allied troops pouring into Normandy following the D-Day landings, nobody knew when they'd ship out, so no 24-hour passes were given. Sam paced the barracks, frustrated because the great city of London was only hours away, but entirely out of reach.

In time, B company crossed the stormy English channel in an oversize LSI (Landing Ship Infantry), big enough to carry jeeps and other light vehicles. The voyage produced large-scale seasickness, but once the ship's ramp crashed onto the beach, and the men were greeted by a cool, salty breeze, everyone felt better.

SAM'S PARENTS WERE RUSSIAN Jews who landed at Ellis Island in the 1920s. Relatives had been left behind in Russia, France, and Germany. Letters arrived frequently and the news worried everyone. By the late 1930s, Jews were forbidden to work in certain professions, and barred from desirable neighborhoods. The deportations and concentration camps came later.

Sam's fellow soldiers were mostly southerners, the sons of poor tenant farmers. They had grown up in the Great Depression, with little high school and no knowledge of the outside world.

"Tell us again Sam, what are we doing here?" It was something his buddies often asked.

At first it was one or two young privates, lonely and disoriented in a foreign country, asking Sam what the war was about. There was a morale officer to handle that kind of thing, but he never seemed to be around. Sam started giving impromptu talks to his homesick buddies, and there was one point that always impressed his audience:

"These Nazis are bloodthirsty killers. We either beat them over here or they'll be in our own backyards. Would you rather stop them in Europe or have to fight them in the States?"

Sam appreciated the irony: here was a lowly private lecturing on the world situation. Every once in a while some of the older men—sergeants and the like—would drift over. They'd pretend not to be listening, but everyone was interested. Sam gave some of the men a little insight and a sense of purpose. That went a long way in their new and dangerous world.

Word got around that Private Sam Notkin was a good person to know. He spoke some French. At first, Sam was puzzled by visits from a number of soldiers he didn't really know. The men who were suddenly interested in French didn't seem the type to sign up for voluntary language classes. Then he realized the phrases they wanted to learn were for one particular intelligence operation: picking up girls from the nearby Normandy farms.

Sam made a deal with his would-be students: he'd teach the men what they wanted to know, as long as they promised to memorize one other thing: "*Est-ce qu'il y a des Allemandes pres d'ici?*" (Are there any Germans nearby?).

Sam was nineteen years old and the company radioman. He traveled everywhere with his FM-300 field unit which was a heavy beast but it had good range and a strong clear tone. He sometimes rode in the jeep with the radio and Captain Miller, the company commander. He often hefted the FM-300 around on his back and that, together with the standard M1 Garand rifle, was a lot of weight for one person. Sam requested a pistol but was told they were for officers only. For a while he used an automatic carbine that was much lighter, but after it jammed during a firefight he went back to the M1. The M1 weighed a ton, but it would fire under any conditions: mud, rain, hail, or lightning.

Sam, and the radio, had to be within easy reach of Captain Miller at all times. As a result, Sam got called to the command post at odd hours, and he was glad when it happened. The captain always had a decent tent set up and that meant a break from the rain and cold.

When one of Miller's staff found Sam cleaning his rifle and ordered him to report to company HQ immediately, he assumed it was time to check in with Division again. Sam moved through the misty camp on the double, and found Captain Miller and his Executive Officer alone in the command tent, bent over a folding table covered with maps. They looked up, and Miller motioned Sam over.

"Notkin, we're moving into a combat area and I understand you've been instructing the men in French. You're now the company interpreter."

"Sir?"

"That'll be all, Notkin."

"Sir, I do have some high school French but it's mostly reading and writing . . . very little conversation. I might make a mistake that could get someone killed."

The Captain clamped a big hand on Sam's shoulder and said, "Son, any mistakes you make will be nothing compared to what we'd do. You're the only guy in this outfit who speaks French, and I'm telling you that you're now the company interpreter."

Sam thought back to his high school in Roselle Park, New Jersey and his French teacher, Valerie Smith. She was a gentle, refined lady with a slight English accent who was fond of saying, "Now pay attention boys. You might need your French one day."

AT FIRST SAM JUST gathered intelligence. One of the company's two drivers would take him out in a jeep and visit the ancient Norman farms that slumbered in the gray landscape. The drivers weren't pleased about it. They'd been in dangerous situations before, and preferred being in a tent back at company HQ. But Captain

Miller said it would look more authoritative if his new interpreter showed up in a jeep, instead of on foot.

Unlike most of their fellow countrymen, the old Norman patriarchs were not happy to see the American army. They weren't exactly collaborators, but they'd gotten on just fine with the occupying German troops. There was a clear understanding that if the farmers didn't engage in resistance in any way, the Germans would leave them alone.

At each farm Sam began the same way. *"Bonjour monsieur. Je suis Americain."* (Good day sir. I am American.)

He went on to apologize for American troops who might have trampled over crops, and explained it was a necessary part of the war effort. He promised compensation for any damage "we may have caused." He emphasized the "we," because retreating German troops had been through the area, taking whatever they wanted.

The Norman farmers were a surly bunch and it wasn't easy to get them to cooperate. Sam asked to be introduced to every family member, and looked for sympathetic faces. Sometimes he noticed a smiling farmhand, or overheard someone saying, *"Regardez! Un Americain, bienvenu!"* (Look! an American. Welcome!), and he'd start there. Sam was working with his own simple high school French, and their heavy Norman dialect didn't make his task any easier. He learned quickly, asked the locals to speak slowly, and had them repeat anything that sounded important.

The farmers were interested in acquiring army rations and kept asking if Sam had any to spare. American soldiers didn't carry "spare rations," he replied, but had plenty of "trading rations." Some of those rations were readily available if B Company could stay on the farm for a couple of days.

"En passant, vous avez vu des formations Allemandes?" (By the way, have you seen any German units?).

One farmer might shrug and reply, *"Je ne sais pas,"* ("I don't know"), but another would tell him that two German companies had recently been through, and a friend in a nearby town had seen an armored column. Miller was right. Sam's rapidly improving French skills were going to help the company.

At one remote stone farmhouse miles from HQ, a man offered to trade *calvados* for some C-rations. When Sam said he didn't know what that was, the farmer handed him a stone jug. Sam took a long swig and was pleasantly jarred by a sharp, fiery liquor, carrying with it a bouquet of lush summer orchards. *Calvados* is a strong apple brandy. Sam felt warm for the first time in weeks, and he quickly arranged a substantial trade.

Sam knew that exchanging U.S. Army supplies for locally-distilled booze was more than a little against regulations, so he told Captain Miller that he'd secured some valuable calvados in return for ordinary rations. At first the captain was angry, but Sam reminded him that the potent brandy would be useful "for medicinal purposes" in the relentless cold and damp. Everyone agreed not to mention anything to Battalion HQ, and the calvados traveled with the captain's personal stores well into Belgium.

THE FIRST STINGING WINDS of winter arrived. B Company, still in their summer gear, was nipping at the heels of the German army that was in full, but orderly, retreat into Belgium. In time, the Germans halted and dug in. The 99th and the 106th Infantry Divisions were ordered to hold the front and avoid major confrontations. B Company probed the enemy lines for weak points, engaged in firefights, gathered intelligence, and picked up an occasional prisoner. The FM-300 was always close by; Sam doubled as radioman and interpreter.

As the weather worsened, a strange routine began. Just after daybreak, each morning, two or three men would appear from the other side, unarmed, and with both hands clasped over their heads—Austrians, conscripted into the German army. They brought sad rations of hard black bread with them, and were suffering from serious malnutrition. The Austrians were finished with the war, and the Nazis.

Prisoners were supposed to go directly to Division HQ, but Captain Miller wasn't going to miss out on any local intelligence that might protect his company. Sam had picked up some German, and the Austrians spoke a little French, so prisoners unofficially went to him for field debriefing, before being escorted to Division.

At first the Austrians went by the book, giving only their name and rank. Sam asked if they'd like to eat and they'd nod enthusiastically. He'd say, "Let's talk about German units and then we'll get you some hot food." He didn't like exerting pressure on prisoners, but it was light pressure, and the valuable daily intelligence he gathered saved American lives.

One afternoon the frost-covered landscape seemed to hum, and the air became heavy under the heartbeat of massed engines. Dark shapes roared across gray skies, first one at a time, and then dozens more—squadrons of B-17 Flying Fortresses on their way to pummel Germany's war effort. It was a comforting sight, watching the heavy bombers thunder into enemy territory, knowing that every mission was helping to shorten the war.

As the Germans resumed their retreat and fell back further into Belgium, encounters with the French Resistance, the *Maquis*, became commonplace. The tough bands of freedom fighters had been defying the German occupation since 1940. Sam served as the sole point of communication between them and his company. Sometimes requests came in from other companies too; they'd captured some Germans and needed to borrow the resourceful, multi-lingual interpreter from B Company.

On Thanksgiving Day, 1944, Sam was hunkered down in a snowy foxhole somewhere in the forests of the Belgian Ardennes. He was trying to keep warm and alert during lookout duty, when a soldier appeared with a hot mess kit full of turkey, stuffing, mashed potatoes and cranberry sauce, right up there at the front line. It was the happiest moment he'd experienced in weeks: real food, and happy thoughts of what Thanksgiving Day might be like back home. At that instant, the heavens opened and his luxurious meal was swimming in rainwater. Somehow, it didn't bother him. Sam was too impressed that the quartermaster had managed to get such a wonderful meal up into the combat zone in the middle of a winter war.

Eisenhower had concentrated his troops in preparation for a narrow offensive, and that left the 99th and the 106th dispersed over an extended and thinly held front. The Germans knew exactly where to attack: the junction of those two units. On December 16, they launched a massive surprise attack with 24 divisions. It was known as The Battle of the Bulge, and was Hitler's last desperate gamble of the war. The Nazis intended to punch through to Antwerp, divide the British and American forces and negotiate a truce.

A tank assault, supported by ground troops, exploded upon Sam's sector. When the infantry line was breached, the 99th received a general order to fall back. Instead of a disorganized retreat, the infantrymen condensed into small groups of two, three, six, and fought on against superior forces through terrible weather and dense, snow-covered woodland. The fighting was fluid; nobody knew quite where the lines were.

On December 17, Sam was part of a combat patrol, gathering information and trying to take prisoners. Quietly, they slipped across the Belgian border and advanced two miles into Germany itself. From the forest's edge, they stared in wonder at scores of giant concrete hemispheres. Half buried in the ground, the ominous line of bunkers squatted only 500 yards away. Sam had reached the Nazi's great defensive perimeter, the Siegfried Line.

"That was as far as they'd let me get," he later said.

The explosion must have temporarily deafened him, because he heard nothing in the snow-covered no-man's-land between the patrol and the Siegfried fortifications. A German artillery shell had detonated in a tree above him, and a shell fragment ripped through his boot, lodging in his left foot. There was only silence, and searing pain. Sam fell to the ground. He had the FM-300 with him; Company HQ was expecting an intelligence report. Other shells exploded and more men went down. He wriggled out of the radio harness, but held on to his rifle. Henry Bragdon, a fellow private, saw Sam get hit. Henry crouched down low and ran over. Another shell exploded high up in the treetops and shattered branches rained down around them. Sam couldn't walk. There was no way Henry could get him back to safety and carry the radio. Despite the overwhelming pain in his foot, Sam turned back to the FM-300 lying twenty feet away, abandoned in the snow. The radio was an old friend that he'd carried through five countries. It had, more than once, been the company's only lifeline, but he couldn't let a working radio fall into enemy hands. He crawled back, still under fire, aimed his M1 and fired four rounds into its casing.

Sam was carried on a stretcher to a mobile army surgical unit, and then went by road to a French hospital. He awoke in a rickety ambulance, propped himself up on one elbow and gazed through a tiny window as the bewitching streets of Paris flashed by. It was his only view of the city he'd longed to visit all his life. He swore an oath that after the war he would, somehow, get back there.

A C-47 transport plane ferried Sam back to England. And then he crossed the Atlantic again, westbound this time, and on a hospital ship. He made it home to New Jersey during the spring of 1945. Some weeks later, on May 8, he happened to be in Manhattan visiting friends. He was walking slowly, with a cane, through Times Square when he heard an unexpected commotion. People began cheering and crying and then general pandemonium broke out. Sam was one the few men in uniform among the crowds, and every one of them were being picked up, hugged and kissed.

The words, "Germany has surrendered. The war in Europe is over!" were rolling around Times Square in giant illuminated letters.

SAM RECEIVED A PURPLE Heart, and a Bronze Star for "Meritorious action against the enemy." After the war, he looked up his old French teacher, Valerie Smith. She had retired and, although pleased to see him, was curious about the purpose of his visit.

"Mrs. Smith," he began. "Do you remember how you used to tell us to pay attention in class, because one day we'd be glad we knew some French?"

She nodded.

"I have a story to tell you about an army interpreter in France."

By Geoffrey Notkin
The story of Sam Notkin,
Private First Class, B Company,
393rd Regiment, 99th Infantry Division

AUTHORS AND CONTRIBUTORS

Dale A. Adams is a retired mechanical engineer but has been a lot of things including a cowboy, pilot, bandleader, WWII vet, and a deputy marshal of Tombstone, Arizona. In 1949 and with a brand new pilot's license, he and a friend flew a small aircraft into Mexico—a hair-raising adventure recounted in Dale's book, *Hole in the Sky!*

Indeed, he wears many hats, but mostly he is a storyteller. This is reflected in the casual way he writes, his stories carrying an old-fashioned stubbornness as he remembers when a firm handshake could be trusted and tipping your hat to a lady was expected.

"When I write, I visit a wonderful world," he says, "and sometimes I live a little of my life over again." He has published articles in *Arizona Highways* and *CQ Magazine*, and has other books and short stories in progress.

Dale served as a Director of The Society of Southwestern Authors.

Shirley Chaska Baird earned her way through college at North Dakota State University, graduating in 1943 with a B.S. Degree in Foods and Nutrition. In 1952 she was commissioned 2nd Lieutenant in the Medical Specialist Corps of USAF. For the following 20 years, she performed as Medical Food Service Manager in the larger USAF hospitals and as Consultant to Regional Medical Commanders. She retired as Lieutenant Colonel, USAF, from her final assignment as Staff Advisor to the USAF Surgeon General, Washington, D.C.

She earned an M.S./Institution Management, University of Wisconsin, Madison, under sponsorship of USAF. Upon retirement, she earned an MEd in Allied Health Leadership from University of Houston/Baylor College of Medicine. In 1977 she earned an EdD in Administrative Management from University of Houston. She headed the Nutrition Department Branch, Texas Woman's University, Houston, and after 10 years retired in 1986 as Associate Professor Emerita.

Faye Brown was graduated from Kansas State Agricultural College with a degree in Home Economics and Industrial Journalism. She was employed with Capper Publications in Topeka, Kansas, working on *Household* and *Capper's Farmer* magazines. In Marysville, Kansas, she was a staff reporter, photographer and feature writer for *The Marysville Advocate*, a weekly newspaper.

She moved to Tucson, Arizona, in January 1984. She is a regular contributor to *Lovin' Life After 50*, formerly *Arizona Senior World*. In 1998 she published the book, *Letters Home. The True Story of Lt. Harry Frank Hunt, Veterinary Reserve Corps, American Expeditionary Forces, WWI.*

Marylyn Chapman had stories and articles published in *Lovin' Life After 50* (formerly *Arizona Senior World*) and the *Oelwein* (Iowa) *Daily Register*. She continued to write about her family's experiences while living in Europe. She has completed a personal memoir.

She is a graduate of Northern Iowa University. She previously taught preschools and currently is active in volunteer organizations in Tucson, Arizona. She teaches Creative Writing and Memoir courses for seniors in Stillwater, Minnesota

She and her husband enjoy traveling by car, ship, and airplane around the world filling journals with their adventures

---

Norma Connor started out her writing career in Journalism but ventured more into fiction in her later years. Several of her stories won awards and were published in *Story Teller* magazine of the Society of Southwestern Authors.

Norma was a Navy wife during her husband Jim's service, and by association she learned a great deal about diving, explosives and the incredible courage and ingenuity that men like Jim in Explosive Ordnance Disposal Units had in solving difficult underwater problems. In an effort to keep some of Jim's adventures alive for their family, Norma has recorded his storytelling and put the accounts of his experiences on paper.

Carol Costa is the author of four novels; the most recent being *A Deadly Hand* (Avalon Books). Previous novels include: *Labor of Love* (Avalon Books); *Love Steals the Scene* (Avalon Books); and *My Bargain with God* (Xlibris). She also is co-author, with Jim Woods, of a collection of short fiction, *Olla Podrida* (Publish America); and author of three nonfiction books: *Video Poker: Play Longer with Less Risk* (ECW Press); *Teach Yourself Accounting in 24 Hours* (Penguin); and *The Complete Idiot's Guide to Surviving Bankruptcy* (Penguin).

She is an award-winning playwright and a member of The Dramatists Guild. Her plays have been produced in New York, Los Angeles, and in regional theaters across the country. Her short stories have been published in magazines and in the *Woman Sleuth Anthology* series published by Crossing Press. Her nonfiction articles have appeared in *Family Circle* and other major magazines and newspapers. She has also worked as an editor, theater critic, business correspondent, and literary advisor.

Carol served as a Director and the Treasurer for The Society of Southwestern Authors

James S. Craig is a graduate of the Pingree School in South Hamilton, Massachu-setts, and holds a B.S. from the Rochester Institute of Technology. He received his Navy commission through the Aviation Officer Candidate School in Pensacola Florida in 1989, and earned his wings of gold as a Naval Aviator in 1990. He flew from the carrier *U.S.S. Theodore Roosevelt* in the first Gulf War and later from the deck of the *U.S.S. Saratoga*.

His decorations include the Air Medal, Joint Meritorious Unit Award, Navy Unit Commendation, Battle Efficiency Award, National Defense Service Medal, Southwest Asia Service Medal, Armed Forces Service Medal, Sea Service Ribbon, Kuwaiti Liberation Medals (Saudi Arabia and Kuwait), Navy Expert Rifle and Pistol Shot Medals.

He lives on Martha's Vineyard with his wife Gail, son Riley and daughter Amelia, where he now works as a police officer.

Bill Critch was born in California and currently is a resident of Oro Valley, Ari-zona. His parents, both Australians, and Bill, returned to Sydney before World War II. His father, a veteran of World War I, died soon after that relocation. Sub-sequently, at age 13, Bill was orphaned, and at age 22 returned to the United States.

In 1957, he became a USAF aviation cadet in Class 58H. After graduation, he was commissioned a 2nd Lieutenant, and was assigned to the Military Air Trans-port Service. After being "grounded' for heart disease at age 35, he went to work for the Boeing Company in Seattle in their Flight Crew Training Department as a technical analyst writing procedures for airline pilots, and eventually to writing audio visual and television scripts and instructing in flight simulators.

At the time of this publication, he is writing his memoirs about growing up in Australia, and also is working on a children's book—on aviation naturally— *Larry Goes To Oshkosh*, the story of a little airplane that could.

Duval Edwards, born near Olla, Louisiana, calls himself a Texas short horn as his father was a Texas longhorn born in Brownsboro, Texas. Duval hoboed to Texas in 1932, and graduated in 1933 from San Antonio's Thomas Jefferson High and is an honorary graduate from Bolton High, Alexandria, Louisiana.

In WWII—1941-December 1945—he was a CIC Special Agent two years in southern States, and two years overseas in MacArthur's Theater from Australia into Japan.

Retiring to San Antonio, he wrote a manual for claim adjusters and subroga-tion attorneys in Texas. Moving to Seattle, he wrote *The Great Depression* about his struggles as a hobo in 1932. Moving to Tucson, he completed a history book titled *Spy Catchers of the US Army in the War with Japan*. In 1999 he wrote, *The*

Senator and the Runaway Teenager in the Great Depression, sequel to his first Great Depression book.

Duval is a Past Statutory Agent and legal advisor for The Society of Southwestern Authors

---

Jane Eppinga is a graduate of the University of Arizona. Her writing credentials include more than 200 articles for both popular and professional publications covering a broad spectrum of children's fiction, travel, personal profiles, biology, construction, food, and public relation pieces.

She won the C. Leland Sonnichsen 1995 award for the best paper in *The Journal of Arizona History.* Her book, *Henry Ossian Flipper: West Point's First Black Graduate,* won a Spur finalist award from the Western Writers of America.

Her books, in addition to the above named biography of Henry Ossian Flipper, include *Arizona Twilight Tales,* and books in Arcadia Publishing's *Images of America* series focusing on Tucson, Nogales, and Tombstone, Arizona. Subsequent works include a history of the Arizona sites, Apache Junction and the Superstition Mountains; and the history of the Society of Woman Geographers.

Helen Gallant, an English teacher for more than fifteen years, has been involved for much of her life in writing and teaching young people to write. She was a prize-winning poet as a child in Newport, Rhode Island, and was elected class poet when she later attended high school in Newport. While attending New York State College for Teachers in Albany, she served as Student Editor for the *Alumni News.*

She won first prize for a memoir, " The White Ensemble," published in *The Story Teller,* a publication of the Society of Southwestern Authors, and she contributed articles to the Society's newsletter, *The Write Word.*

Her memoir was accepted by the *Elderhostel o.d.y.s.s.e.y.* 2005. She proudly proclaims to also be her family-designated historian.

Stephen Gladish teaches writing part time at Pima Community College in Arizona. Prior to that, for twenty years, he worked as a writing instructor in the Ohio and Arizona Departments of Corrections. Following retirement from full-time teaching in college, university, and prison systems, Stephen devoted his time to completing four adventure and romance novels.

His novel *Moonlight, Missiles, and Moana,* was released in 2005; his second novel, *Mustang Fever: Run Free with Wild Mustangs,* in June of 2006, both by Publish America. Subsequent titles include *Tornado Alley,* and *Never Trouble Trouble.*

Stephen served from 1959 to 1963 in the USAF, predominantly with the 6th Weather Squadron (Mobile), Fourth Weather Group, Tinker AFB, Oklahoma.

His two sons, both First Lieutenants, are on active duty in the Army National Guard.

Jeanne Pafford Glasgow was born in Cottonwood, Arizona. She attended Roskruge elementary and junior high schools through the ninth grade, in Tucson, Arizona, then three years at Tucson High School, graduating when she was 16 years old. During World War II, she attended the University of Arizona, majoring in Business Administration.

She is a soprano soloist and has sung in churches, local singing groups, and for weddings, funerals, and luncheons. She was a member of the Arizona Opera Chorus.

She enrolled in her first writing class in 1997. A gift to her children for Christmas, 2005, was a book of memoirs titled, *Jeanne's Journey*. She has been published in *Reminisce* magazine, and in *Good Old Days*.

Willma Willis Simpson Gore, a lifelong writer, lives in Sedona, Arizona. She leads writer workshops and writes a humor column in *The Villager*, a Sedona monthly journal.

She is the author of two published adult books: A how-to, *Just Pencil Me In — Your Guide to Moving & Getting Settled*, Quill Driver Books/Word Dancer Press (2002); and a humorous novel, *Something's Leaking Upstairs*, Publish America, (2005). She also has nineteen children's books, published variously with Children's Press and Enslow Press (1975 through 1993).

She is listed in the 2006 edition *Who's Who Of American Women*.

Ted Gushee is a retired advertising executive, having served with the J. Walter Thompson Agency, supervising the company's Ford Europe branch in London; and subsequently advancing to Chief Operating officer and General Manager of the firm's Detroit office. He graduated from Williams College, Williamstown, Massachusetts, where he majored in English and minored in theatre.

His life was not always so secure. He served as a combat pilot in Korea, flying the B-29 Superfortress, and was awarded the Air Medal.

Ted's current books include *Someone's Picking the Daisies; Guardian Devil;* and *Kira's Diary*. His story in this collection is derived from his soon-to-be-published book, collected accounts of Korean War airmen, titled *52 Charlie*.

J.R. (Jim) Holbrook began his Army career as a private and retired as a Lieutenant Colonel in 1989. Along the way he taught Russian at West Point and the National Security Agency, served as an Army Intelligence officer in Washington DC, Vietnam, both East and West Germany, and at the American embassy in

211

Moscow. He was a staff officer and detachment commander in Vietnam in 1967-68.

His experiences in East Germany are the focus of his self-published *Potsdam Mission: Memoir of a U.S. Army Intelligence Officer in Communist East Germany*. His follow-on second book is *Moscow Memoir*.

Jim holds a BA and MA from The American University and a Ph.D from Georgetown University.

Doug Huestis grew up in Montreal, Quebec, went to high school in Port Hope, Ontario, and eventually medical school at McGill University in Montreal, graduating in 1948. He and his wife, Rosemary, a Montreal girl, lived in Pittsburgh, then Chicago, and finally Tucson, Arizona. They raised five kids, and now have five grandchildren.

Doug is a retired medical school professor who has written 100 scientific articles, plus four editions of a textbook, numerous book chapters and shorter pieces. He also has written medical history, essays, book reviews, and fiction.

He writes for the joy of it in his home/office at Tucson, Arizona.

Dennis Hull, a native of Ohio, spent his early childhood in Detroit, Michigan, during the 1940s. He is writing a memoir of that experience. He moved west in 1963 and obtained a B.A. in history at UCLA where he has also done graduate work.

A lifetime student of military and aviation history, Mr. Hull, a former glider pilot, is a longtime volunteer docent at the Pima Air & Space Museum in Tucson, his home. His special interest is the Wright brothers and their aircraft.

He spent 30 years working at credit unions in Los Angeles serving aerospace industry employees. He retired as Senior Vice-President, Hughes Aircraft Credit Union, Manhattan Beach, California. He is a biker and enjoys travel.

Dr. Loren Humphrey received his medical education at the University of Illinois Medical School in Chicago. He served his internship at the Illinois Research and Educational Hospitals in Chicago from 1956 to 1957 and general surgery residency from 1959 to 1963 with military service in between those periods. He studied immunology at the State University of New York in Buffalo from 1963 to 1966, receiving a Ph.D in 1967.

During his academic career he wrote more than160 scientific articles. He retired from medicine in 1995 to devote full time to writing and speaking. He has published five books

---

George Isenberg is a decorated combat infantryman. He entered the army in the spring of 1942 and spent three years in the South Pacific with the Americal Division during World War II.

He went to Korea with the 2nd Infantry (Indianhead) Division in the summer of 1950 as a mortar platoon leader and later a Heavy Weapons Company Commander in "H" Company, 38th Infantry Regiment. He has a total of 48 months in combat in both wars.

A graduate of San Jose State University, he divides his time between Oregon in the summer and Arizona in the winter. He is a member of the Rincon Writers Group and the Society of Southwestern Authors in Tucson. Several of his WWII memoirs have been published in the *Tales from Tin Boxes* anthology series.

Richard M. Kerr graduated The Ohio State University with a B.S. in Wildlife Management 1950 and attended Graduate School Colorado A and M University, 1950 and 1951. He was called into service as a reserve officer, field artillery and spent 10 months fighting in the Korean War, 1951 into 1953.

Afterward, he worked as Game Warden and Conservation Officer for Colorado Game and Fish Dept, 1953 into 1954. Working with the Bureau of Land Management in 1956, he served as Range Manager, Acting District Manager, Assistant District Manager, District Manager, State Wildlife Biologist, Assistant to the Chief of Wildlife (Washington D. C.), Wildlife Staff Leader, Big Game Ecologist, Wildlife Cooperative Education Director and Assistant Professor of Fisheries and Wildlife Science, New Mexico State University.

His previously published books include: *28 Sonoran Birds; Justice at Timberline;* and *A Ride to Devil's Lake.*

Francis Scott Key (August 1, 1779 - January 11, 1843) was an American lawyer and amateur poet who witnessed the bombarding of Ft. McHenry during the Battle of Baltimore, September 13, 1814, and was inspired to write the poem, "The Defense of Ft. McHenry." Subsequently, the poem was put to music and named "The Star-Spangled Banner." In 1931 the Congress of The United States of America enacted legislation that made "The Star-Spangled Banner" the official national anthem.

Francis Scott Key is an alumnus of St. John's College, Annapolis, Maryland.

Robert McCartan was born and raised in Douglas, Arizona. He earned a Bachelor's Degree from Arizona State University in 1952 where he was commissioned a 2nd Lieutenant, through ROTC, in the United States Air Force.

He amassed more than 3000 hours in SAC's B-47, and after teaching four years at the Air Force Academy, he flew 165 combat missions in Vietnam in the

EB-66, 35 over Hanoi. He then served four years in the Flying Training Division at Air Force Headquarters in the Pentagon. His last assignment was as Wing Commander of the 3400 Technical Training Wing, Lowery AFB, Colorado. He was awarded the Legion of Merit with two Oak Leaf Clusters, the Distinguished Flying Cross, the Bronze Star, the Air Medal with 11 Oak Leaf Clusters among others. He retired from the Air Force in 1980.

Robert McCartan published *My Journey, More Than I Ever Imagined*, a memoir, in 2004. He also has published many short articles for Air Force publications, most related to combat flying.

Dr. Hughlett L. Morris is Professor Emeritus of Speech Pathology, the University of Iowa. Before professional retirement he had clinical, teaching, research, and administrative duties in the College of Medicine, Department of Otolaryngology-Head and Neck Surgery, and the College of Liberal Arts, Department of Speech Pathology and Audiology.

His earlier publications, numbering 126 papers and books, are technical and scientific, in topics about diseases and disorders of the head and neck. His books are *Luther's War* and *Luther's Women* (2005); and *Missouri Chooses* (2006).

He is a native of Tennessee and now lives in Tucson, Arizona

Robert Anthony Natiello, after spending more than two years in the Marine Corps, spent his career as a Madison Avenue advertising and marketing executive. While creating national marketing campaigns for America's corporate business leaders, he won the coveted EFFIE award for the marketing effectiveness of General Electric appliances.

In addition to planning dozens of Dupont TV Specials and GE commercials, Natiello created and produced New York's first weekly TV program on the subject of real estate, "All About Real Estate." His personally written program, "Real Estate Made Easy," won Cable TV's Best Business TV Program Award. He also created and produced New York's first weekly radio program on the subject of mutual funds. "All About Mutual Funds."

He holds a Bachelor's degree from Villanova University where he was awarded the Villanova Medal for outstanding contributions to the university. Natiello earned an MBA from the University of Pennsylvania's Wharton School.

Geoffrey Notkin was born in New York City and raised in London, England. He studied fine arts and creative writing in London, Boston and New York, and received a BFA from Manhattan's School of Visual Arts. He is a widely published science author and photographer, specializing in paleontology, meteorite studies, and adventure travel. He is active in field research and has participated in expeditions to Chile, Siberia, Iceland, and all across the U.S. and Europe.

He owns a graphics firm, Stanegate Studios, which focuses on book design, website development, and working with clients in the natural history field. He has also worked as a geologist, meteorite hunter, and professional musician, and has appeared on numerous records and radio and TV shows. He lives in Tucson, Arizona.

Marilyn Pate is a native Arizonan—born in Phoenix; raised in Arizona and New Mexico. She's graduate of Tucson High and Sophia University, Tokyo. She taught elementary school in the DOD (Department of Defense) school, Yokohama, and with the San Diego Unified Schools. She worked with adults at Tokai Aluminum, Kanagawa, Japan, ESL (English as Second Language), and Northland Pioneer College, Show Low, Arizona, and taught memoir writing to groups of senior citizens.

She's been published in numerous newspapers, magazines, including *Arizona Highways* and in *Chicken Soup for the Military Wife's Soul*. Her historical fiction saga, *Mary George, Her Book,* is based on her grandmother's life; *Everyday Evil,* is a nonfiction book about her father.

Marilyn lives with her husband, a retired naval officer, Clyde T. Jr., called Terry, in Green Valley, Arizona. They have three children, four grandchildren and one great grandson.

Penny Porter has published stories in a wide range of national-circulation magazines, including *Reader's Digest, Arizona Highways, American Heritage, Catholic Digest, Guideposts, Woman's Day, Honda,* et al., and her work appeared in numerous international anthologies, world wide text books, and eleven *Chicken Soup for the Soul* books. A mother of six, grandmother of eight, great-grandmother of one, former teacher and school administrator, she is a frequent speaker at writers' workshops.

The recipient of *Arizona Highway's* 2001 Silver Award for Excellence in Writing, Penny is the author of five books, most recently a collection of short stories for all ages, *Heartstrings and Tail-Tuggers,* (Ravenhawk Books). Previous young-adult and children's books include *The Keymaker* (Harbinger House) and *Green Eggs and Sam* (Singing Valley Press).

Penny served as a Director and is a Past President of The Society of Southwestern Authors.

Janet Sabina first saw her words in print as a high school news reporter for her small town paper, *The Maumee Valley News* (Maumee, Ohio), in the 1950s. Thirty years later this pleasure was repeated when she turned from hands-on youth work at various churches in Denver, Colorado to writing curriculum for United Church Press of New York City, Living the Good News of Denver, and The Society of Friends of Philadelphia, Pennsylvania.

Her young adult novella of a Navajo brother and sister caught in events of 1864-1868, *I Will Not Weep*, won first prize in its category at a Pikes Peak Writers' Conference.

Can't We Do Something? is a *book*-length narrative of the band of citizens whose grassroots campaign moved the Arizona Department of Transportation away from plans to expand a two-lane scenic road into a four-lane highway through Sedona, Arizona.

Dr. Linda Bloomberg Simon is a practicing chiropractic physician in Scottsdale, Arizona, and author of *Avatar*, her debut novel written under the pen name, Leah Bloom.

Born in 1960 in Brooklyn, New York, she is an only child, first generation collegiate, and proud mother to two teenage boys. Married to Dr. Ira Simon following her graduation 1985, they have owned Simon Chiropractic, a multiple disciplinary clinic since their marriage.

Dr. Simon began her writing career after arriving in Arizona as the Health Editor of *Today's Arizona Woman* and contributing author to *Arizona Living Magazine*. Other contributions have been as faculty member to Bridgeport Chiropractic College authoring online continuing education classes for colleagues.

Connie Spittler's writing life unfolds from a mixed bag, as writer, teacher and facilitator on storytelling and aging.

Her award winning short stories, essays, memoir and poetry appeared in anthologies, journals, magazines and newsletters: *Chicken Soup; Sowing the Seeds; Healthy Aging; Letters from Americans; Cowboy Poetry at the Bar-D Ranch; Land of Many Stories; Holding Up the Sky; Sisters of Mountain Flowers;* and *Our Spirit, Our Reality.*

As writer/producer, her *Wise Women* video series was selected for the Library on the History of Women

---

Harvey Stanbrough is a former United States Marine, retired after 21 years. Once a southwesterner, he now lives on a farm in Indiana with his wife. Harvey also is a poet, writer, freelance editor and speaker who has addressed the Society of Southwestern Authors' Wrangling with Writing Conference several times.

His latest poetry collection, *Beyond the Masks* (Central Ave Press, 2005), was nominated for the National Book Award and was submitted for nomination for a Pulitzer Prize, the William Carlos Williams Award, the National Book Critics Circle Award and others. Of his two nonfiction titles, *Punctuation for Writers* (Central Ave Press, 2004) is entering a second edition, and *Writing Realistic Dialogue & Flash Fiction* (Central Ave Press, 2005) is in its second printing.

Dr. Nomi Sweetfire started writing in the 1950s at Unity School of Christianity in Lee's Summit, Missouri. Later, at the USAFA in Colorado Springs, Colorado, she created articles in which the officers shared their stories about the Korean War and World War II with the new cadets.

She worked at several newspapers in Phoenix, Arizona. After moving to California, she began writing a personal column, "Food for Thought" which ran weekly in the *Newhall Signal*. Later, in the Orange County area, she wrote a column introducing new businesses to the beach communities. Most recently, after returning from living on the Hawaiian Islands for almost a decade, she self-published a collection of short stories called *Auntie Nomi...Talks Story.*

Dr. Sweetfire has a degree in Spiritual Psychotherapy and has raised a family of seven sons and one daughter.

Sam Turner is a freelance writer regularly contributing to *Arizona Highways* and a variety of other publications. He teaches memoir writing and beginning astronomy through Pima Community College, Tucson, Arizona.

He and his wife, Phyllis, published *This Might Help: A Three-Year Walk Through The Valley With The Compassionate Friends.* The book is a compilation of their monthly columns published in *Walking This Valley,* newsletter of the Tucson Chapter of The Compassionate Friends, an organization that offers guidance, comfort and hope to parents who have suffered the death of a child.

Sam served on the Society of Southwestern Authors Board of Directors.

Lon Wolff was born in Casper, Wyoming. After graduating from high school he joined the U.S. Army and eventually was assigned to an aviation company composed of UH-1B and D-model helicopters, stationed at Bien Hoa, South Vietnam.

After he returned from the war, he attended the University of Wyoming. In 1974 he married Mary Ann, the woman who shared his dream of homesteading in Alaska. They spent nearly two decades in "The Last Frontier" before returning to the lower forty-eight. Today he and his wife live in Sedona, Arizona, where he volunteers as a Curator of Exhibits for the Fort Tuthill Museum of Military History in Flagstaff, prospects for gold, and hones his writing skills.

His work has appeared in *Alaska Magazine, The Arizona Daily Sun, Threshold, Gold Prospector Magazine, Legions of Light* and *The Story Teller*, the latter a volume of writing-contest winners, published by The Society of Southwestern Authors.

Jim Woods has published more than 400 articles in *Outdoor Life, Popular Mechanics, Petersen's Hunting, Guns & Ammo, Shooting Times, Guns, Southern Outdoors, Western Outdoors, Gun Digest,* and other national periodicals; and has contributed to several anthologies including *Hunting in Zimbabwe,* (Safari Press, 1992).

He is co-author, with Carol Costa, of the short-fiction collection, *Olla Podrida,* (Publish America 2006). His other books include an adventure novel, *The Lion Killer* (Publish America 2005); collected accounts of his world hunting adventures, *Honk if You Love Geese and Other Hunting Stories* (Publish America, 2004); a collection of short fiction, *Journeys,* and a writing tutorial, *Two Dozen Lessons From an Editor,* both by the McKenna Publishing Group (2002).

He worked as Editor, Editorial Director and Managing Editor for Petersen Publishing Company, Los Angeles; and Field Editor with Publishers Development Corporation, San Diego.

Jim served as a Director of The Society of Southwestern Authors.

Charlotte J. Rickett Wykoff is a retired Addictions Counselor and Founder/Facilitator of the Desert Crones of Tucson (Midtown Branch). She was born and raised in New York, New York and moved to Arizona in 1984.

After retiring, she began to write and has been published in *Lovin' Life after 50, OASIS Journal, Crone Chronicles, Sage Woman, Buffalo Woman's Vision,* and various newsletters and local papers. Her prize-winning memoir, "Little Daddy," was published in *The Story, Teller,* 2002, a publication of Society of Southwestern Authors.

She is the mother of four adult sons, has three grandchildren and resides in Tucson, Arizona, with her husband.

Printed in the United States
59445LVS00005B/133-510